Signals Comments

James Galbraith, Chair in Government/Business, University of Texas "better than Piketty".

Rohan Bedi, 16 year old student "absolutely loved reading it."

Dr. Tun Mahathir Mohamad, former Prime Minister of Malaysia for 22 years "Dr. Pippa Malmgren's book is essential reading".

Sir Stuart Rose, former CEO and Chairman Marks and Spencer, says the ideas are "a Tour de Force".

John Bruton, Former Prime Minister of Ireland "an interesting topic and a great book".

Dr. Liam Fox, former British Defence Minister "Pippa's work is impressive and groundbreaking.

Toshio Fukui, Former Governor Bank of Japan "fascinating, stimulating book! First-class quality."

Peter van Manen, Mclaren (F1) "opens our eyes".

Peter Pereira Gray, Wellcome Trust "a delightfully easy read, a precious gift indeed".

Leslie Sheppard, MIT Forum for Supply Chain Innovation "gives us great optimism".

Art Laffer, former US Presidential Economic Advisor "Making economics colorful, intelligible, cool and accessible to the general public, Pippa has written a winner for one and all."

SIGNALS

The Breakdown of the Social Contract
and the Rise of Geopolitics

by

Dr. Philippa Malmgren

Grosvenor House
Publishing Limited

This book is published by
Grosvenor House Publishing Ltd
28-30 High Street, Guildford, Surrey, GU1 3EL.
www.grosvenorhousepublishing.co.uk

A CIP record for this book
is available from the British Library

ISBN 978-1-78148-740-2

Table of Contents

Dedication

This book is dedicated to my Dad who taught me that there is always a difference between the story being reported in the news and what actually happened. He showed me that the world economy, from textiles, to steel, to agriculture and auto parts, is absolutely fascinating. I am ever so grateful for many many things he has done for me (including going beyond the bounds of duty when it came to my education). He gave me so much encouragement to tell this story.

As you say, Dad, "a state that is defaulting on its citizens will obviously seek to obfuscate this, so it is the duty of good citizens to illuminate". This book aims to throw light upon this matter. To that end, I have tried to follow the advice of your mentor Sir John Hicks, who won the Nobel Prize in 1974, and his wife. Sir John's wife, Ursula, was one of the leading experts on public finance in the 1940s and 50s. She always said to her highly mathematical husband, "that's all very nice dear (referring to the extraordinary ability he had with math and numbers) but if you can't explain it in plain English, you will never affect public policy".

How lucky I am that my mother studied with JRR Tolkien and CS Lewis and WH Auden and that she passed on to me a command of language that permits me to "tell the story" of the world economy in plain English. She would have been delighted that I managed to show that the evil Gollum from Tolkien's tales lives above the doorway in the Oval Office, which he certainly does. I saw him there myself. He may have found a new perch over at The Federal Reserve Bank as well.

I will give thanks at the end to the many people who supported and advised me as I pursued this book and it relentlessly pursued me.

My book is also dedicated to my daughter, Penny. The economy of tomorrow is already being built today and she will be part of something very new and dynamic. The trick is to follow the advice of the Queen in Alice in Wonderland and try to imagine at least six impossible things before breakfast every day because the impossible is what inevitably actually happens. And, if you do what you love and work pretty had at it, everything else will follow.

Acknowledgements

Let me begin by saying that this book would never have happened but for the many opportunities I have had to stand in front of a live audience and test out these ideas. I am extremely grateful for the "real time" and repeated feedback that has come from all countless meetings I have spoken at or participated in over the years. It was from these conversations and experiences that it became clear to me that I suffered from the problem a funny New Yorker cartoon captured years ago where the doctor says to the patient, "There's a book in there and its got to come out".

There are a couple of authors whose work influenced me greatly in telling this tale. Peter Drucker's very first and very best book, *The End of Economic Man*, was a great inspiration. He finally published it in 1939, having hesitated, fearful of ridicule, knowing he could not prove what he was saying. He argued that the storm clouds of conflict were gathering. I was also moved by *The Dying of Money*, which was written by Jens O Parsson (aka Ronald Marcks) in 1974. He spoke about the rise of inflation and its social consequences well before the inflation itself was an accepted fact. The task at hand, as they showed, is to take a risk and argue the case before the proof is available. By the time you can prove it, it's already thrown people's lives into disarray. EH Carr's The Twenty Years' Crisis: 1919-1939 and Karl Polanyi's The Great Transformation were sweeping, epic stories that shaped the intellectual foundation for several generations. Their success in taking an eagle eye view of the world also helped encouraged me to try and describe the big picture.

I also sought the advice of a few specific people who were kind and patient enough to give me the intellectual support that allowed the book to progress. I owe a special thanks to Dr. Tom Hoenig for his generosity with his time and his gracious invitations to the annual Kansas City Federal Reserve meeting in Jackson

Hole where I built many friendships and gained many insights. He encouraged me to keep the humour in the book and to not to worry about the high priests of economics, of which he is one, who might attack or dismiss it because it is written in accessible English. I am glad to have found the courage to tell a tale of the world economy which uses no data or models, but includes stories and the image of a supermodel. He served at the Federal Reserve Bank longer than just about anyone alive today and I think his views ought to get more air-time. The whole point of having regional Federal Reserve Banks is to ensure the interests of the real economy and the interior can balance against the interests of Wall Street and the big financial institutions.

I would also like to thank Dr. Liam Fox who is a longstanding Member of Parliament and who has served his country in various cabinet and shadow cabinet positions. During his time as the Defense Minister in the UK, he encouraged me to connect the dots and weave a holistic picture that shows how economics, politics and defense are all interrelated, if not inseparable. I wish policy makers and politicians everywhere understood the world as comprehensively as he describes in his extraordinary book, *Rising Tides: Facing the Challenges of a New Era*, Midas 2013.

Larry Lindsey, who served at the Federal Reserve and as the President's Economic Advisor, played a critical part by opening the door to my experience in the White House. I could never have written this without having worked for the President. I am ever so grateful I had the chance to serve when so many things went awry from Enron to 911. It was the Ph.D. in public policy that money cannot buy.

Many famous and anonymous traders, money managers and financial experts around the world gave me their insights over the years and specifically helped me with my thought process for this book. I can't name them all. But I would like to mention a few who were especially supportive. All kept the conversation imbued with the dark humour and the technical nuances that are inherent in such a serious subject. These include Craig Thorburn from the Future Fund in Australia, who is the source of the comment by Goldfinger from the James Bond novel, Karl Massey in London,

Christopher Selth in Australia and Rich Carty in New York who have all been an intellectual allies for many years. These people were the first I knew to realize the debt burden was so great that it would change the course of history and leave us with extremely challenging social consequences. Greg Williamson at BP always gave the benefit of his time and insights during the writing process while still managing to be the best performing pension fund manager in the United States and for which I am endlessly grateful. Stephano Quadrizio managed to combine a wave of enthusiasm and sharp business acumen in his review of the content. Peter Pereira Gray runs one of the world's largest investment institutions and yet he took the time to read the draft and to help me drive it to a finish.

Many business people also offered me their thoughts. Peter van Manen took time out from his busy life building the sensors and applied technology at Mclaren to read the manuscript not just once but twice. Thank you for advising me to sort out Chapter Two! Leslie Shepperd, who runs the Forum for Supply Chain Innovation at MIT, was wonderful in introducing me to the MIT Media Lab, which is the epicentre of all that is cool about innovation. Hugh Morgan has been unfailing in his enthusiasm for my work. I have benefitted enormously from conversations with him given the great expanse of his professional experience from mining to central banking.

There are too many current and former policymakers and economists who assisted me to name as well. But, I especially thank Ambassador Richard McCormack for the insights gleaned from serving almost every President, officially or unofficially, since the 1960s. Martin Donnelly kindly let me test drive the manuscript on him and his enthusiasm was hugely helpful. Jacob Frenkel encouraged me to focus on the notion of the social contract and supported the idea that this underpins all of economics. Board members from the Federal Reserve including Esther George and Jeffrey Lacker and Bob Jenkins from the Bank of England and many others all offered important guidance along the way. I had several absolutely delightful conversations about all this with Alan Meltzer, the Federal Reserve's official historian, over the years. He is one of the few people around who has a sense of history and a sense of the personal character of the players in the realm of economic policy. He encouraged me to reveal that Gollum, JRR Tolkien's character, plays an important part in the making of monetary and economic policy. I am also grateful to the Bank of England, some of the regional Federal Reserve banks and a number of central banks in Europe, South Africa, the Middle East and Asia for giving me a platform to talk to their staff about the gap between the actual rate of inflation versus the official rate. Their skepticism and insightful questions helped me further refine my arguments.

James Galbraith deserves special thanks for taking the time to take a fine-tooth comb to the text. It takes an exceptional character to tell someone how they can make their argument more strongly even though you might disagree with some of it.

The Ditchley Foundation in Oxford England played an important role in the formation of the book as well. That wonderful country house has provided a place for people who work in these areas to come together and talk about tricky issues ever since Winston Churchill conducted the Lend Lease negotiations there. The conferences I have both held (usually with my great insightful friend Devon Cross) and attended there very much strengthened my resolve to "connect the dots". Nowhere else am I able to assemble or find so many diverse experts from around the globe who are in the fields of economic policy, foreign policy, defense, intelligence, politics and business. The board at MIT run by Iqbal Qadir and at Indiana University's School for Public and Environmental Policy board also provided countless opportunities to learn and to test my ideas out.

The Defense community in the US, the UK and elsewhere, have opened their doors to me and my ideas on many occasions. This has provided me with the substantive knowledge to be able to explain the links between economic forces and strategic security outcomes. Policymakers in China and Russia including Ambassador Yakovenko, the Russian Ambassador to the United Kingdom, and others in the US, Europe and across emerging markets that might prefer not to be named, have also been remarkably willing to explain how the world looks from their point of view. We have entered another difficult period in history where the superpowers are finding it increasingly difficult to talk to each other. The official dialogue is constrained by fear, suspicion, spying and strategic concerns. So, it is with a special debt of thanks that so many people were relatively open with me about the events that have occurred and how they are interpreted (rightly or wrongly). I hope we can avert anything like the Cold War environment that I grew up in if everyone understands the economic and security drivers better.

I tested out the ideas in the book on quite a few "civilians" or rather, people who are not experts on economics and who are not working in the world I occupy. No doubt I tested the bounds of friendship by doing this. I am indebted to Elizabeth Dempsey, Elizabeth Robinson, Nikki Shehadeh, Kate Lalley Giles, Jesme Fox, Rohan Bedi and Lady Moody Stuart. The latter, Judy, missed her calling to serve as the Editor in Chief of some serious publishing house. Her attention to detail and ability to help me explain myself better was a welcome surprise.

I started collecting the ideas for this book a long time ago. So, I am very sure that there are others who played a part in the conversations that led to this book. A fascinating psychologist mentioned John Bertrand's book about the America's Cup. A fabulous physicist mentioned Wittgenstein's Poker. A brain surgeon mentioned Sid Watkins book on safety in car racing. A military historian brought Admiral Lord "Jacky" Fisher to my attention. The bartender at the Peninsula in New York who was keen to discuss the economic forces that produced Al Capone played his part too, as did all the taxi drivers I have chatted with over the years and the audio visual guys who mike me up before conferences. My greatest disagreement with the publishing world is this: economics is not a boring subject. People of all incomes and all education levels want to know what is going on and how to make sense of the world economy. Yes, it zaps us all now and again but the subject can be cool and sexy too. Please be assured that even if I have not named someone here, I am ever grateful for the contributions made by all the fascinating people who are trying to make sense of things.

I must thank Katia Haddian who served as my professional editor during the writing process. She worked quickly and relentlessly and always found the nicest possible way to tell me something did not make sense. The tone of the book owes a good deal to her keen ear and her polishing efforts.

Philip Blackwell's encouragement was particularly valuable because nobody knows books better than a Blackwell. Every book I inherited or stole from my parents has a Blackwell's seal on the binding and, appropriately, Blackwell's published JRR Tolkien. Philip provided invaluable advice and contacts regarding the book publishing business, which helped me make the decision to "hack" the book publishing business model (not that he necessarily approved of my conclusion). Heidi Roizen is a Silicon Valley investor whose suggestion that I look at crowd funding culminated in the decision to write about and make use of such a platform myself.

Wayne Harburn, my business partner and friend, also deserves special thanks for supporting my decision to take an unconventional path, which has required resources, sweat and time to execute. He has given me the infrastructure and true friendship I needed to be able to tell my story in my own voice. The generous Robinson family in Middlebury Vermont must also be thanked for allowing "the crazy lady in the attic" to keep typing and thinking without interruption while keeping me fed and in good humour as I finished core of the book during a holiday there.

My Dad, Harald, the Hon. Ambassador Professor Doctor, also brought his long experience and tough editing skills to bear on the manuscript. Thank you for doing so with such incisive skill and raucous laughter!

The World Economy is Signalling

This book presents one view of the world economy. It is not necessarily the only view, and there is no "correct" view, for the world economy is a marketplace of many, often conflicting ideas. It is offered in the hope that you can become more skilled at arriving at a view of your own, so that you can better manage the continuous waves of change that the world economy sets in motion instead of being tossed about or even nearly drowned over and again in the sea of economic surprises and uncertainty.

Whoever you are, wherever you are and whatever you do, you are being bombarded by many powerful signals. The world is a high frequency place. Signals are rich with information, with messages if you like, which can tell us something about the future. Interest rates, the price of oil, the unemployment index, the price of a house or of milk, are all signals that tell us something about what is going on in the world economy. These signals offer clues as to what we should be preparing for. No one can predict the future, but it is also true that events are usually preceded by signals. Magazine covers, innovative artworks and fashion all send signals that tell us something about what is going on in the world economy. The challenge is whether we have the capacity to receive these signals and properly interpret what they mean for us, knowing that every person has a different set of skills, circumstances and aspirations and therefore different people can act on the same signal in very different ways with very different outcomes. Some awareness of the signals around us will help us realise the future we want to secure instead of being rendered speechless victims of economic forces we never saw coming. For this to happen, we need to be attuned to signals.

I am grateful to British Vogue and Condé
Nast for permission to use this image.

In May 2007 I tried with all my heart to convince one of my best friends to sell her house in Ireland. She trusts me. She knows what I do for a living. Nonetheless, even though I sold my own home to prove my conviction, she trusted the bank manager and the real estate agent who both assured her that her house would be worth "another half a million in six months". When we come to believe that a house can be worth that much more in such a short period without even a new coat of paint, it's a signal.

Signals are everywhere. I could not help staring at the cover of British *Vogue* in April 2008 because it also sent out an important signal.

It took me a while to figure out what it was. Of course it's easy to stare at Natalia Vodianova, one of the world's leading supermodels, especially when she is completely nude and remarkably curvy for a model. But something unsettled me. "What's wrong with this picture?" I asked myself. One of the world's leading fashion magazines had a cover with absolutely no fashion. In fact, it showed no clothes at all. It showed a mother of three who, while enviably slender, was certainly not the sort of underweight waif that had dominated magazines for so many years. Yes, that cover was an important signal. It signalled the simple fact that the fashion industry had lost its old customer base – the young who were receiving unsolicited credit cards with large borrowing balances in the mail. Once the financial crisis hit, the fashion industry became aware that it had no idea who its new customer would be. Who had money to spend on fashion? Maybe now it would be the somewhat older woman, a mother, who was a very different customer. In short, the whole industry was suddenly engaged in a massive rethink. It went back to scratch, as it were. It went back to the human form, unclothed, and started to design for a customer who could be anyone from a beautiful young supermodel to a mother of three, knowing full well that both ends of the spectrum were still cash constrained.

Years later, in 2012, I spoke about that cover with the lead fashion director at British *Vogue*, Lucinda Chambers. My sense was that she and the fashion team absolutely did not think in this way, nor did they intend to send any "signal". No doubt this is true, but that is the point. Often it is artists and creative people who feel and project the zeitgeist without realising they are doing so, which is one reason we should pay attention to them instead of relying so heavily on the opinions of those who dominate the business press alone. In retrospect, a *Vogue* cover with no clothes was clearly reflecting some kind of change or feeling of uncertainty.

By 2013, when the financial crisis had evolved into something much more profound, slowing economies worldwide and forcing the reinvention of business models, a traditional signal was emanating from the fashion world: the hemline. Some say hemlines go up in the good times and down in the bad. Usually, everyone knows exactly where the hemline is supposed to be. Yet as I write, there is no agreement whatsoever. Hemlines are all over the place. For that matter, nobody knows what the silhouette or cool shape ought to be either. Why? Perhaps it is because the fashion industry still cannot figure out who its customer really is. Fashion can send signals about the condition of the economy.

Fashion signals

I was inspired by a conversation I had with Tony Colman in May 2007, before the financial crisis began. In 1969, Colman and his two partners, Sir Philip Green and Richard Caring, founded Topshop together with Sir Ralph Halpern. It has been one of London's most iconic clothing stores ever since. He went on to found many other successful British fashion brands. Few men know clothes better than Tony Colman.

As I listened to his stories, I translated his fashion sense into economic signals. Coming away from the conversation, I realised that there was a powerful signal in the loud patterns and bling that had come to dominate fashion just before the financial crisis. Something was very, very wrong when every woman was wearing (and every shop was selling) very loud Pucci-inspired prints. Pucci is an elegant Italian fashion label that rose to prominence in the 1950s and 1960s when Grace Kelly, Marilyn Monroe, Sophia Loren and Jackie Onassis (who had been John F Kennedy's wife) wore its vibrant patterned scarves and stretch-knit clothes on the Riviera. The clothing is bright and attractive, mainly on petite women. It looks pretty ridiculous on everybody else. So, why was every shop selling such bold patterns? The answer was obvious: Chinese factories were churning out clothes evermore cheaply and in higher volume. This forced designers to take more risks with their patterns in order to differentiate and attract buyers away from other suppliers and make shoppers content to own something that would not last long just because it was new and different.

By 2007 every shop was filled to the brim with poorly made, garish and eccentric copies of the Pucci look. Young women were receiving unsolicited credit cards in the mail and were delighted that Chinese factories could produce less and less expensive clothes. You could buy a blouse for a handful of loose change. In retrospect it seems clear that women were spending more than they could afford even though each item cost very little, especially since most items would only ever be worn once or twice before their fabric made them out of fashion.

They were cheap and disposable. But, these customers were becoming increasingly indebted and therefore, at some point, their consumption would have to slow down. When that happened the stores would feel it.

Retailers themselves had so much access to cheap bank lending and public capital markets (IPOs) that they had lost all their cash-flow management and inventory skills. Shops were buying too much stock and would be caught short when the economy weakened, which it was bound to do as customers hit their credit limits. After all, almost everyone was spending beyond their means. The famous singer-songwriters Eric Clapton and JJ Cale picked up on the signal in their song "It's Easy" from the *Road to Escondido* album, released on the 7th of November 2006. His lyrics were a signal:

> If cash is your problem, you might regret
> Use that old plastic, slide two third in debt
> It's easy, easy you see
> If tomorrow never comes, everything is free

But, tomorrow *always* comes. The music stopped in August 2007, when the financial crisis began. Suddenly, fear replaced optimism. Initially, the crisis seemed to be contained, exclusive to the financial markets and seemingly applicable only to the United States. The Federal Reserve announced interest-rate cuts and other policy actions, which are usually powerful signals. But, most players in the world economy did not take much notice of what was happening. It was only when Lehman Brothers failed one year later, in September 2008, that the markets and the public alike registered what was going on and a sudden collapse of confidence and economic activity ensued.

Many retailers went bust, became unable to borrow and unable to sell their overabundance of cheap fashion to customers who had quite a few items of clothing already, no money for any more and frankly no need for them. After all, with the economy now shedding jobs fast, suddenly what was needed to keep a job or get a new one was a plain white shirt and a black skirt, or a good old-fashioned conservative suit. When the economy is that bad, you do not take the risk of loud clothing getting in the way of a pay cheque.

Around the same time, a clothing chain called Zara started to take off just as all the other retailers were going bust. Zara's success was a signal. What is different about Zara? To start with, this Spanish fashion firm never manufactured much in Asia. Around three-quarters of its stock was made in Europe. It buys fabrics from around the world, brings them back to Spain and keeps them in massive refrigerated warehouses to protect the fabric until Zara's designers need them. When the financial crisis struck they did not have the shipping time or cost that weighed down their competitors. They could get new stock into the shops three or four times a week instead of waiting every three or four months for a shipment from Asia like everybody else.

It struck me that Zara has several other reasons for its success. You can always find a good black or navy skirt and a great white shirt there, which are office staples. Anyone looking for a job is going to dive into Zara and know they can find good quality classics. Zara does produce good "fashion" items that are trendier, but it usually has plenty of classic items and very few fashion items. As a result, the stock turns over very fast. People go in to check out Zara anytime they pass by because they know the stock will be new and something they like will be gone if they wait. This is because the goods don't come from Asia, where shipping time alone is six to eight weeks. Some 50% comes from Spain and about 25% from elsewhere in the EU, so the stock in a European shop can be updated almost overnight. This speed of turnover guarantees a steady stream of returning customers who are already drawn in by the "value for money" proposition.

Once the slowdown hit and unemployment started to rise, Zara's classic value-for-money staples combined with continuous fresh, new, trendy designs assured the company did well in spite of an otherwise collapsing market for retail. Zara is also a private family-owned company. In a world where all its competitors found their share price diving and the bank calling to take back

6

the overdraft, line of credit or say the IPO had been cancelled, Zara had sufficient self-generated cash flow to keep going.

So, the naked model on the cover of *Vogue* signalled that the whole business model for retail clothing needed a rethink. Zara's success at that particular time was a signal of a significant change in the world economy. Disposable fashion, where you buy a new item a day and toss it in the bin, died when the financial crisis stalled the economy. Zara's success, compared to so many failed companies, revealed the flaws in the traditional women's retail model, which depended heavily on a high volume of cheap, highly differentiated clothes (crazy designs) with long delivery times coming from Chinese and Bangladeshi factories, and unlimited funding coming from banks, private investors or the capital markets.

Glamazon and Gatsby

Looking back at that *Vogue* cover, the fact that Vodianova is a mother was also an important signal. After the athletic, "glamazon" look of the original 1980s supermodels (Christy Turlington, Linda Evangelista and Naomi Campbell), fashion photographers favoured very skinny, very young models that looked fragile – a look epitomised by Kate Moss. It is interesting to note that "skinniness" in women seems to be associated with periods of great wealth creation. One thinks of the skinny, *Great Gatsby*-style flappers of the 1920s or the Twiggy lookalikes of the 1960s. It makes sense. After all, it is very hard for most women to be thin. It takes time, effort and money to be a skinny adult woman unless you are one of the few with the DNA programming for that.

When things get rough, comfort matters more. Perhaps this is another signal in the world economy. For example, when times are hard, women will give up fashion but they won't give up make-up, especially lipstick. Estée Lauder survived the financial crisis better than anyone expected as a result of this human tendency: lipstick and lip gloss sales went up as these are affordable and indispensable items, even in a slowdown. For me, the rising sales of lipstick and lip gloss soon after the financial crisis was a signal that the

7

world economy would carry on and not cease to exist as many then feared.

The fashion team at *Vogue* thus signalled something important by choosing to photograph Vodianova without any fashion (but with lipstick and lip gloss). They signalled the fact that fashion could no longer survive simply by appealing to people's hopes and aspirations for the future, when we would be flush with cash and skinny again. Instead, fashion would have to appeal to real women with real cash right now, regardless of their body size or shape or age. The trend to put "plus size" models on magazine covers and in fashion advertising has only accelerated since the beginning of the most recent economic downturn. That is a signal too.

Today, governments in the most important economies in the world – the US, the UK, Europe, Japan and China – are all sending extremely forceful signals in the world economy. Perhaps the most important signal in any economy is the price of money. Most of the industrialised countries are suppressing interest rates, which is the price of money, to historic lows. This signal has already pushed up hard asset prices like property and food and stock markets around the world. So, it is important to understand what the economic signals are and then to consider how they might impact on our daily lives.

But, most people are afraid of economics. It seems to be very complex; all math and algorithms. So, I decided to write a book that will help a person with no background in economics to better understand the world economy. The journey I am taking you on weaves across wide territory. We will begin with an alternative explanation of wealth creation and the source of GDP. Rather than being a fixed formula, it really arises from our personal efforts to balance our fears and our hopes. It is the accumulation of our personal choices that creates wealth and GDP, so it makes sense to begin with our personal efforts to engage in calculated risk taking. This chapter, chapter two, is called "Hubris and Nemesis".

Queen Elizabeth II famously asked the simple question, which I would paraphrase this way, "How is it possible that everyone missed the signals that led to the last crisis?" I try to answer this question in chapter three: "A Letter to the Queen". It has everything to do with failing to see, discuss and properly interpret the many signals that are always there. No one can predict the future but we can be better prepared by having a robust debate about economic signals and by better balancing our own personal risk-taking choices in light of those signals.

When I worked in the White House I learned that most people believe that a few smart people in the West Wing (or its equivalent elsewhere in the world) can sort out the world economy. When I worked on the trading floors of the world's largest investment banks, people assumed that the wealth of skill and technology would allow those "smart" people to see things the rest of us can't. Sadly, having been one of the "smart" people in these rooms, I fear that we expect too much. They are smart but not *that* smart. They are not smarter than the collective decisions made by everyone in the economy. And, by the way, there is no crystal ball in the White House or on a trading floor or anywhere else (I looked for it quite hard during my time in the West Wing and can confirm it is not there). So, it makes sense to try to understand the motivations of those officials, and other players in the world economy, so that we can better understand the meaning and purpose of the signals they send. This chapter, chapter four, is called "The Algorithm Made Me Do It".

There is a tendency to think that we can fix economic problems by tweaking a few things, by lowering the price of money or by raising the tax rate in order to generate more revenue. But, something more profound is occurring. Worldwide, we are witnessing the breakdown and renegotiation of the social contract that exists between citizens and their states. This has already generated historic events, from the Arab Spring to the return of a "Cold War" environment between the US and other superpowers. I explain this in chapter five, "The Social Contract". In chapter six I hope to explain why it is that we used to have a quite wonderful world economy that seemed to be constantly generating wealth and meeting everybody's needs and then why this stopped. This chapter explains "The Perfect Circle" of capital and interests. But this has all been disrupted by what I call "The Vice", which is the title of chapter seven. This refers to the "pincer" movement in which every single person, family, company and nation is now caught. They are trapped. On one side the forces of deflation and debt bear down, which together damage growth and kill hope. On the other side, they now feel the force of a rising cost of living or even inflation. In fact, there is a strong perception that the US and other industrial nations are doing their level best to create inflation... and it is working. Protein prices push to record highs. Energy prices remained very high in the aftermath of the financial crisis.[1] Asset prices have risen to record highs since Quantitative Easing began, including the price of property and stock markets. The value of an asset is its ability to produce goods and services in the future, so clearly the rising prices reflect a re-pricing of the future value.[2] So, some argue that inflation *is* occurring, it is just working in emerging markets first and more forcefully. Quantitative Easing is leading to Qualitative Squeezing of the general public in various ways. This chapter helps explain the impasse that now exists on this topic both between the Federal Reserve and its emerging market counterparts. It is an impasse that is also dividing the Federal Reserve internally.[3]

As Christine Lagarde, the Head of the IMF, noted, the "ogre" of deflation and the "genie" of inflation have now both come to life. Each has a different form and power in different locations but the end result is a "vice" of pressure as we are stuck between these

---

1 When the price of oil began falling in late 2014, emerging markets like Russia were quick to blame US policy as well. The collapse of the oil price and the ruble leaves Russia even more susceptible to inflation than before. China, in contrast, seeks to take advantage of the lower oil price but remains vigilant that it could go up at any time.

2 Central banks, generally speaking, do not like to include asset prices in their inflation calculations because they are so volatile. Many also like to leave out food and energy for the same reason.

3 Many will argue that there is no inflation in the industrialised world. Instead the cost of living is "higher" because incomes have fallen. That may be true in some places, but even where there is an "internal devaluation" where incomes have fallen, any price rise is felt even more than before.

two demons. The resulting pain bearing down on us causes people to ask a simple question: "Why is the wealth in my society being distributed to someone else and not to me?"

Once this question arises, government leaders know they must supply the population's needs, they must ease the pain, or else they will be removed from office – whether by a ballot box or by public demonstrations in the streets. So, governments start to do whatever is necessary. This is what causes geopolitics to re-enter the landscape of the world economy. Chapter eight explains why the "Perfect Circle" I explain in chapter six is breaking down. In this part of the book, I go into greater detail about the central idea of the book: economic signals are provoking more than technical, economic policy responses. They are also provoking social unrest and military events. Chapter nine is called, "Enter Geopolitics: Commodity Conflicts". What we face now is not so much a "Cold War" as an era of commodity conflict. Chapter ten carries on the argument and explains the return of geopolitics in terms of Russia, the Middle East and other parts of the world.

In these chapters, I explain why China is reaching for energy and food assets in the South China Sea and across the globe and why Russia is doing its best to hang on to increasingly valuable assets such as the food production of Ukraine. Most emerging markets now feel they are being defaulted upon. In their view the decision, in the US and across the industrialised world, to deal with the debt by inflating it away leaves many emerging markets believing they will pay the price in terms of food and energy costs. This leads to social pressure. As a result, they feel justified in their reach for assets and their desire to forge a new set of rules in which the US does not dominate the world as much as in the past. I don't condone the military events that are unfolding but I do think the economic dimension is both overlooked and used as a reason or excuse. Therefore, it is worth understanding this important driver. To paraphrase the 18th-century military theorist Carl von Clausewitz, military action has become a continuation of monetary policy by other means in many parts of the world.

There is no doubt that this is tough stuff. But, happily, there is a solution: innovation. Chapter ten explains how people are innovating and already building the economy of tomorrow because of these pressures. I am not writing about gadgets here. Innovation covers everything from the creation of the new social contracts that are being put into place from Tunisia to California and also includes the personal acts of reinvention that allow people to forge a new and different economic future. The state is innovating too. States are voracious in their appetite for cash, because they are "broke", having overpromised and having less revenue to meet the needs of the public. The balance of power between the state and the citizen (including the corporate citizen) is changing. Chapter eleven explains the many ways in which this is occurring.

Chapter twelve explains that there is a way out of the economic pressures we face. It involves "Cutting Through the Gordian Knot", which, happily, is already occurring. People are already building tomorrow's economy today. I try to illuminate the many signals that this is so. The few examples I cite are so dazzling and far reaching and I hope these will inspire the reader to become better attuned to the many signals that the world economy is sending. Awareness can only enhance a person's ability to manage their way through whatever pressures and possibilities the world economy presents.

Signals I have seen

Perhaps the concept of "signals" needs further clarifying before we begin. Here are some more of the signals I saw that caused me to duck hard (sell everything, including my own home, by May 2007) in preparation for the financial crisis. Perhaps this background will help explain why I want people to notice the many signals that the world economy is sending today.

Scary china dinner sets, cabaret and mortgages

I saw many signals that the world economy was in trouble throughout 2006 and 2007, before the crisis began. For example, I accidentally wandered onto the top floor of Bloomingdale's in New York and was overwhelmed by stacks of china plates painted with gaudy Halloween designs. "Who can afford to spend money on a china set that will only be used once a year?" I asked myself. "Where would they keep it for the other 364 days of the year?" I wondered, "Have houses become too large if they can accommodate a rarely used Halloween dinner service?" How much would it cost to heat such a house? Were people spending more than they were earning? If people are spending tomorrow's income today, instead of saving some of today's income to pay for what might come, it's a bad signal. If they are willing to spend such unearned income on Halloween china plates, it's a signal.

Another signal was the sense of "affluenza" that permeated the atmosphere at that time.[4] The rich felt increasingly angry that they could not generate "enough" money. Somehow, everyone felt that everybody else was even richer. Even the rich began to feel left out or left behind. My editor, Katia Hadidian, remembers going to an Eartha Kitt concert at the time, and Kitt changed the lyrics of her hit, "Just an Old-Fashioned Girl",[5] from wanting to marry "an old-fashioned millionaire" to "an old-fashioned billionaire", winking at the audience and purring, "inflation..." The funny thing is, she was right! You have to be a millionaire to own a nothing-special, two-bedroom flat in town in many cities these days. So, only a billionaire will do.

Another signal came in September 2007 when the Hong Kong Shanghai Bank (HSBC) announced it was setting aside nearly one billion US dollars to cover losses associated with its purchase of Household Finance, a company that provided mortgages.[6] It struck me that this announcement of loan provisioning was a signal that the whole mortgage market must be in trouble. Ultimately HSBC would write off nearly $20 billion-worth of

---

4 See *Affluenza* by Oliver James, Vermillion Press, 2007
5 "Just an Old Fashioned Girl", lyrics by Marve Fisher (1958): "I'm just an old fashioned girl with an old fashioned mind/ Not sophisticated, I'm the sweet and simple kind/ I want an old fashioned house, with an old fashioned fence/ And an old fashioned millionaire
6 See *The Telegraph*, 22 September 2007: "HSBC hit by sub-prime crisis" by James Quinn

mortgages. If a big bank has made such a huge loss, what are the chances every other bank also made the same mistake? It turns out that the banks collectively lost so much money the losses have had to be shifted onto the taxpayers (which means you, the reader, as we shall see). The announcement was a big signal, though few registered it at the time.

A further signal appeared around that time. I found that everything I bought that had been made in China kept breaking. This worried me, but I could not quite figure out what the problem was. In retrospect, China had moved so far down the value chain that even inexpensive goods were not worth the unbelievably cheap price.

Then, I detected a signal that seemed really important. Every financial trader I knew talked about the "inevitable financial crisis" but refused to sell anything on the grounds that he was smarter than all the other traders and therefore he would get out (of stocks or property) first. This was an extraordinary manifestation of hubris. After all, each one was declaring themselves smarter than the market and also suggesting that they could do something nobody has ever managed to do consistently, which is to pick the exact right time to sell the market. That signal alone made me sell my house and move my family into rental accommodation at the time.

Handbags at dawn

Finally, and perhaps oddly, I noticed that women were spending a fortune on handbags. I have never met a straight man that was turned on by a handbag (though I concede they must exist). Men, it seems to me, often get real pleasure from looking at women's shoes. But in a booming economy, women had enough cash to indulge in something that had no meaning to men. Could it be that handbags are designed for women to compete against other women? I think this may be true. Rather than duelling with sabres at dawn, I was witnessing duels with oversize handbags at cocktail parties. After the financial crisis, when women became more aware of the need to look after their financial and personal future, they stopped buying so many bags and instead turned to shoes. Shoes began to outsell bags as a fashion accessory, but both the handbag duels and the shift to shoes struck me as a significant signal.

Such signals about the world economy are interesting and important, but also easy to miss. Most people can quickly figure out the meaning of a flirtatious glance or that the smell of something burning on the stove requires our attention. Some signals are simple to receive, interpret and act upon. The child cries and we react to its distress. The traffic light turns red and we stop. The office gossip tells us colleagues are being fired so we neaten our ties and skirts to avoid the same outcome. The price of our currency versus the Euro goes up or down so we schedule or cancel the trip to Paris.

But, just as the smell of burning toast is a signal that makes us stand up and pay attention, so should the many signals that emanate from the world economy, which, in general, have a profound impact on our lives. Prices change and our life changes too, whether we know it or not. This is true for every price we hold dear, including the price of our mortgage, our wages and our healthcare as well as the price of bread, meat and chocolate. It is also true of the prices we may never think about but which can impact on our life, like the price of bread in Egypt (which I will argue helped catalyse the Arab Spring) or credit default swaps on Wall Street. There is also a price the market will pay for our time and our skills. This changes too.

Numbers versus humans

Nonetheless, we are sometimes not very attuned to signals from the global financial markets and the world economy, in spite of their tremendous importance. The word "economics" conjures images of complex mathematical equations and dry concepts such as "marginal additional demand". It is not surprising that we sometimes shy away from thinking about such things. I know from long experience that people think "economics" is incredibly boring and mathematically challenging.

Typically, economic signals are all described in the language of maths: numbers, statistics, probabilities, measurements, graphs, charts, and percentages, all adjusted for things that are not easily understood, such as inflation and seasonality. This is just convention, however. Economics is not actually about numbers. Economics is about human behaviour too. Numbers are merely a way of expressing human behaviour, though they are perhaps the least engaging way to observe economic signals. Simple events and the things we can easily observe are much more compelling.

Miami airport and the siren

Mr. Damon Emery and his family were probably not thinking about the wider economy in the early autumn of 2008.[7] Of course, the newspapers were full of headlines about the "Global Financial Crisis", but he did not work for a bank, so he no doubt assumed it would have little to do with him. He proceeded to take his family on vacation from England to Disney World in Florida. He decided to keep his costs down by flying with a recently launched cut-price airline called XL. He and his family were shocked by the signal the world economy sent them: the wail of sirens when police cars surrounded the aircraft at Miami airport because the airline had gone bust. The company's creditors were seizing the plane.

Did it occur to Mr. Emery that he might be taking a big risk by flying with a company that had massive debt that could not be serviced from the firm's cash flow alone? Probably not. Did he understand that the only thing keeping XL in the air were bank loans? Probably not. It must have been bewildering. The credit crunch was the culprit that caused XL to go bust. The signal that a credit crunch was underway was the sound of the wailing siren.

The dog that did not bark

My neighbours got the same signal from silence. Their dog simply did not bark. They had hired a building company to construct a garage on the side of their house. One morning, the dog did not bark because the builders did not come. They never came again because the firm went bankrupt. It did not occur to my neighbours

---

7 See *The Daily Mail*, 13 September 2008: "Another 30 airlines will go bust before Christmas, warns BA chief" by Michael Seamark

16

that they were at the heart of the 2007 financial crisis, which, after all, had been driven by over-investment in property, mortgages and building. Nor did they understand that many building companies would go bust. So, they hired another firm to finish the job. The new firm asked for payment up-front because it was suffering from a lack of cash flow caused by the universally bad circumstances. The family paid because they really needed that garage. Once again, the dog did not bark because the new builders did not show up. Yes, the family lost their money twice.

These may seem to be small examples. But, the history of wars, nation states and families are all driven by economic events. Economics usually underpins great events in history that create and destroy businesses and push and pull on private lives.

Nations and their cash woes

It is always an important signal when a nation runs out of cash. The Soviet Union collapsed in 1991 partly because it ran out of money. Its tax receipts were insufficient to finance the government's expenditure. The Suez Canal ended up in British hands in 1936 when Egypt had an economic crisis and needed the cash. One of the reasons Saddam Hussein invaded Kuwait was because he ran out of cash and decided to take the oil fields next door as a means of replenishing his coffers.

Scotland ceased being an independent state and was forced into the Act of Union with England in 1707 due to a financial crisis. In the late 1600's the Scots became jealous of England's East India Company, which was generating untold wealth for England from the colonies, leaving Scotland behind. The Scots decided to create their own version of the East India Company, called the Company of Scotland. After a few failed attempts to establish Scottish colonies in New Jersey and South Carolina, an entrepreneur called William Paterson came up with an idea that the Company of Scotland decided to back: The Darien Scheme. Paterson's idea was to establish a Scottish colony in Panama called "New Edinburgh", in order to tap local riches and create a base for trading with the Far East. The goal was to make the citizens of Scotland wealthy. Unfortunately, it turned out that Darien,

Panama, was a swamp. The first, second and third wave of settlers all died from various waterborne diseases including malaria and cholera. The Spanish, who wanted it for the same reason that Scotland wanted it, ultimately turfed out those who survived. Only a handful of settlers made it back home.

More than half the Scottish population had invested one-fifth of Scotland's total wealth in the scheme. Scottish losses amounted to roughly one-third of the nation's savings (bigger than the losses in the recent sub-prime crisis). A bailout was required to save the population from living the rest of their lives in poverty. England was the obvious saviour. The price of the bailout from the Bank of England for Scotland was the loss of Scottish independence. In exchange for the bailout, Scotland signed the Act of Union. The gain for England was that this financial accident allowed the Kingdom to join forces after many years of war and strife. Thus the United Kingdom was born.

In 2007, nearly three centuries to the day later, the Royal Bank of Scotland and several other of Britain's largest banks had to be bailed out by the government with the taxpayer's money following massive losses incurred in the financial crisis. As a result, the public had to endure not only losses on their investments but also discovered that their taxes would rise and the level of services delivered by the government would fall. By 2010, British voters were so angry about these losses that they elected a hung Parliament. (This means that the public elected two Prime Ministers, David Cameron and Nick Clegg, who would share power and run the nation together.) The minority members of the Coalition, the Liberal Democrats, who had strong Scottish roots, immediately requested lower taxes and greater autonomy for Scotland as part of the price for their participation in the new government. Scottish secession remains a major political discussion in the United Kingdom. It is ironic that the 2007 financial crisis has provided Scotland with an opportunity for greater independence even though its largest bank was one of the principal sources of the catastrophe.

The fact is that borders are becoming more fluid everywhere. In the Middle East the borders of Iraq and Syria are being redrawn by the tide of refugees and the will of political leaders. In the South China Sea, China's neighbours are ever more forcefully challenging where the territorial borders lie, sometimes in courts of law and sometimes through military conflict. In Eastern Europe, the borders of nations have been redefined in countries such as Ukraine, sometimes by military force. In the US, the mass migration of Latin Americans who want to be a part of what America has to offer have caused the border of the US and Mexico to weaken as well. Perhaps this is not a coincidence but a signal that economic pressures are pushing up the cost and value of many assets. Iraq had become expensive to the US but it is valuable territory for Iran, China, Russia and local political powers. Eastern Europe is a large food producer and the site of Russia's only real warm water port, which takes on more value when food prices are high. It is not surprising that many pick up on the signals that Texas has become a booming economy where energy, innovation and property are growing apace, and want to move there.

Money signals

Similarly, family histories are entwined with economic events. My grandmother came from Sweden to the US in 1927. She found work as a seamstress, which allowed her to make a living right through the Great Depression. She was very focused on ensuring her children would be sufficiently educated that they would not have to do manual labour. She made my father understand that he had two choices: win scholarships or get stuck in a menial job for the rest of his life. He became very attuned to a simple price signal – follow the money. He had to win scholarships anyway he could. He won them for running and golf (which he learned only because caddying paid better than anything else for a 14 year old) and for math, engineering and academic excellence. He ended up at Yale on a full scholarship and later at Oxford as a Henry Fellow in the late 1950s. He took the Henry Fellowship over the more famous Rhodes Scholarship in part because it paid more. He went on to be mentored by six Nobel Prize-winners, including Tom Schelling and Sir John Hicks. By following the money, he became an

19

economic advisor to many heads of government around the world and a successful entrepreneur because he learned about prices as signals early on.

My mother dreamed of studying Middle English and Medieval French poetry. Why someone would want to do this, who knows, but it is part of the miracle of the world economy that someone can pursue this kind of dream, or indeed any kind of dream. The economy accommodates the wishes of the many. In her case, the signal that permitted her to pursue that dream, in spite of the fact that her parents had modest incomes in Los Angeles, was the exchange rate.

There was only one way the child of a public school teacher in the California state system and an electrical engineer in the city of Los Angeles could afford to go to Oxford in the late 1950s and study with JRR Tolkien, author of *The Hobbit* and *The Lord of the Rings*, and CS Lewis, the author of *The Chronicles of Narnia*: the exchange rate. At the time, the exchange rate between the American Dollar and British Pound meant Americans were downright rich once they arrived in England. Exchange rates are powerful signals.

My mother never understood how much the favourable exchange rate helped propel her onto that path. I only realised years later, after becoming the Chief Currency Strategist at Bankers Trust and hearing her complain bitterly about how expensive Europe had become. I looked at a chart and saw that in 1956 the US Dollar-Sterling exchange rate (or "Cable", as it is known in professional circles because it was initially traded across Trans-Atlantic under-ocean cables) was most advantageous to Americans. Mom wasn't rich in America, but she was rich in England, which had seen its currency value collapse in the aftermath of World War II. So, it is not only signals of trouble that require attention. Some signals are positive and lure you toward hope, growth and opportunity.

Monks throwing bricks

Some people are overwhelmingly excited by economic signals such as price changes. Others may find their eyes glaze over at the very thought. You may say, "I don't do economics", and I myself don't want to speculate. The problem is, you cannot "check out" of the world economy, not even if you are a Tibetan monk who one would imagine to be above such things. Yet, in March 2008 Tibetan monks came out of their temples and started throwing bricks, rocks and any other hard objects that were easy to hand. Why? No doubt the Tibetans have long-standing frustrations about their relationship with China. No doubt there are many Tibetans who would prefer a different form of government than the one they have. But monks don't typically wake up in the middle of the night and declare: "I have to have self-rule tomorrow." However, they might well wake up hungry and angry that they can no longer afford rice because its price has risen so much. Global rice prices rose by 50% in 2008. Once there is no rice in hand, it makes sense to pick up a brick and throw it, even for a monk. So, monks throwing bricks turned out to be a signal that the price of food was escalating and causing suffering.[8]

Why did the price of rice rise? Now we enter the world of economics, where supply and demand define such things. We will argue about what causes prices to move throughout this book. But the first thing is to notice that price movements are occurring and to think about what they mean for you.

No specialist equipment required

The world economy and the financial markets will influence, if not define, the direction of your life and the choices you make. Prices define how much you will pay for rice and everything else that matters. How do you know when to borrow and when to buy? When to invest in skills and when to get paid for them? You form a view and act. But on what basis do you form your view? Which signals do you observe? Which signals do you miss?

The signals are always there, but the question is how to recognise and interpret them. I have spent my career working in the financial markets; for the President of the United States

---

8 See my article, "The China-Tibet inflation Black Swan and Global Implications", 19 March, 2008

advising on economic policy; and advising traders, investors and government officials around the world. From my seat on various trading floors to my seat in the White House, I have been paid to identify, interpret and act on these signals. At times it has been my job to send signals as well.

The world of markets and economics may seem the preserve of the privileged, those insiders who are well supplied with high-tech equipment such as Bloomberg and Reuters machines, expensive trading floors and access to specialist information from trade publications to meetings with policymakers and CEOs. And yes, trading floors in banks and fund management firms are brimming with cutting-edge technology, in-depth news and research, and expensive talented people, all of which seems to be essential to receiving economic and financial signals (though it isn't).

When I sat on such trading floors, I had access to all the right people and all the right equipment and I learned a good deal. But, I also discovered that there are many people in that privileged position who miss the signals and get it wrong. In fact, throughout history it is typically the privileged financial market experts who get it wrong enough to trigger crises, recessions and put the taxpayer's personal future at risk. I also learned that many people who have no such privileges, such as artists and clothing retailers and editors at *Vogue*, are perfectly capable of discerning, interpreting, creating and acting upon signals. Lots of people build real businesses, create jobs, innovate and make a lot of money out of catching and interpreting signals. Why not you, too?

The same questions

I have discovered over the years that whether I am talking to professional fund managers or friends who have no clue about money or heads of government (who also often have no clue about finance and markets either, even though they are expert in politics), I am repeatedly asked the same questions. "Will interest rates go up (or down)?"; "When?"; "Will unemployment get better (or worse)?"; "Will my mortgage become more or less expensive to service?"; "What will happen to the value of my house, my savings, my investments, my skills, my business?";

"Will the economy grow faster (or more slowly) in future?"; "Will the price of (oil, gold, stocks, bonds, iron ore, milk) go up or down?"; "Should I expand or contract my business?"; "Should I borrow and invest or sell and take my profits?"; "Should I study more or work now?"; "Should I change jobs or stay put?"

We all want to know how to prepare for the future, how to see events coming before they occur and act well before these events are priced into the market and on the front page of the newspaper. No one can divine the future, but there are an awful lot of people who manage to make fortunes, or better protect themselves, by preparing for possibilities and probable events. We can all be more alert to possible and probable outcomes.

There may not be a crystal ball, but there is a conversation that goes on about what the future holds, which may be useful to know about. It is a conversation that involves traders, fund managers, pension fund trustees and sovereign wealth funds as well as entrepreneurs and people who run local businesses. Policymakers, economists and the media are constantly engaged in this conversation and there is every reason to become a part of it. After all, your future depends on the actions you take, which in turn depend on your views and your thoughts – or lack of – about signals.

Today, for example, the world is divided between those who think deflation is the greatest threat bearing down on our future and those who think inflation is the greatest threat. There are signals for both cases. The debt burden keeps growing larger even though interest rates remain at historic lows, thus signalling that the debt problem will leave us with deflation or falling prices and low employment for years to come. On the other hand, there are many examples of inflation signals as the price of beef and milk, diamonds and property rise to record highs. The outcome will impact on every one of us either way. The political consequences of the pain they both cause will be felt whichever one is contributing more to the malaise.

This book offers a version of the many various conversations that I have personally been involved in during my career and, in particular, before and after each economic or financial crisis. It is not the definitive explanation; it is simply one of many possible explanations. But it is a place to start thinking about how the world economy works and how it will affect you. It is a daunting and endless task. Signals often conflict. Some are important and others are just noise. Signals can be overwhelming, once you start to look for them. Oscar Wilde got it right when he said, "It is a very sad thing that nowadays there is so little useless information."

Hokum

There is a large and prominent group of people who may say all this is hokum and nonsense – many of them are economists. Most of them argue that the markets have perfect information at any given time so it is useless trying to anticipate how prices are going to move. This view has moments of prominence (usually when markets are working smoothly) and moments when it is discredited (usually when markets have experienced a crisis). I will address this view throughout the book, but for now let's just say that there is another large group of people who have made a fine living from trying to judge what is going to happen next and how prices, risk and the economy will move in response. Some of them are the people who manage your savings. Others build and grow businesses that provide goods and services and employment.

Developing a view and conviction

The first step is to understand the meaning of signals. *The Wall Street Journal*, *The Financial Times*, Bloomberg and others have no monopoly on these signals. In fact, anyone can pick up signals that the financial media miss, just from their own observations. The key is to know which signals are important to you. Which ones make sense to you? Only from this can you form a view that will be the foundation for action. Having a view creates the possibility to anticipate and prepare. Signals either change your view or reinforce it, thus creating the conviction that is necessary to successfully pursue your goals. Without conviction, a person can never be brave enough to stand against the markets and say "My idea will work" or "The prices are wrong" or "I am going to do something different from everyone else because that is what will make money or protect me from economic uncertainty and turmoil". Not having a view is actually a choice with profound implications.

It's hard to navigate successfully if we are ignorant of signals or don't have a view, however. Luck can only carry us so far. So, as the observant author Henry James put it, we will now "Try to be one of the people on whom nothing is lost."[9]

---

9 In "The Art of Fiction", essay by Henry James in *Longman's Magazine*, 4 September 1884 and reprinted in *Partial Portraits* (Macmillan, 1888)

Hubris and Nemesis

For many people, the word "economics" is accompanied by a wave of fear and a sense of exhaustion. "Economics" conjures images of numbers, algorithms, mathematical models and a highly technical quantitative subject. If this sounds familiar, consider a different possibility: the economy begins inside the human soul, driven by the never-ending battle between the Greek goddesses Hubris and Nemesis for possession of our psyche. The ancient Greeks described Hubris as the spirit who lights the fire of desire or greed and compels us to take risks to achieve what the ego desires. The ego wants more: more status, more money, more success, more material possessions, more recognition, more knowledge, more confidence, more money. Hubris is a powerful force in the world economy, because it propels individuals and societies to innovate – which is always risky – and thereby generate growth, wealth and GDP.[10]

Nemesis is the goddess of retribution for those who indulge in too much hubris. Nemesis douses the fire of hubris with doubt and punishes hubris with loss. Nemesis lurks at the edge of every business and every balance sheet and every job. She peers over the shoulder of every risk taker, threatening to undermine the hope

---

10 There are many arguments about how to measure and weigh wealth versus growth versus GDP. Wealth is not the same as GDP because a government can generate GDP by taking more and more of the wealth in the economy and redistributing it. Wealth creation is really the key to success. GDP is an arguably flawed way in which to measure wealth creation. If anything, governments are now taking more and more private wealth in the belief that they can use it to create GDP. Wealth creation is what drives an economy forward, not its redistribution by governments.

and aspiration of the endeavour. Hubris gives rise to hope and nemesis give rise to fear, but both are critical to the proper functioning of the world economy. It is the balancing of the two that permits people to successfully achieve their goals and contribute to a flourishing economy. Too much hubris or too much nemesis is likely to end in economic catastrophe.

This balancing act within each one of us is what underpins the economic cycle. Each time we (individually, or collectively as a society), reach for something we want, something that is just a little beyond our immediate grasp, something that involves risk, growth occurs. That's where "value added" is created. When we reach and succeed, confidence grows as well as GDP and wealth. Conviction in our abilities increases alongside productivity.

When we reach and fail, loss occurs – sometimes financial, but also loss of confidence, loss of pride, loss of dignity. Yet, even in failure, lessons are learned that serve us well when we are ready to take a risk again. Failure is also a critical component of GDP and wealth creation. Only through failure do we become more skilled at risk-taking and therefore more likely to be successful in the future, as the *Harvard Business Review* noted in April 2011 in an issue that celebrated failure.[11]

What is learned from mistakes can be more important than what is learned from success. The 19th-century American essayist and poet Ralph Waldo Emerson wrote that, "All life is an experiment. The more experiments you make, the better." This idea that experience is, in itself, valuable, was personified by the inventor Thomas Edison's repeated experience: "I have not failed 1,000 times. I have successfully discovered 1,000 ways to not make a light bulb."

This is why the economist Joseph Schumpeter (1883-1950) concluded that the economic cycle is fundamentally driven by innovation and "creative destruction". He did not say innovation and destruction. He said *creative destruction* because people learn from their mistakes. Creative destruction means the enterprise

---

11 See *The Harvard Business Review*, April 2011: "Strategies for Learning from Failure" by Amy C Edmondson

may be lost but the desire to have a successful enterprise, and the skill needed to build it, is usually not lost.

Through upturns and downturns, success and failure in the economy serve a purpose. The downturn teaches lessons and makes us more skilled at balancing and preparing for the adversity and opportunity that the future is bound to bring. Upturns and downturns alike reward those who have taken calculated, forward-looking risks and entice others to do so as well. Every time the economy changes, it emits new signals that allow us to navigate our way forward, if only we catch and interpret those signals.

Have a view

The purpose of paying attention to signals is to better inform one's view of the world. Without a view, we are adrift at sea without a North Star and without a life raft. Without a view, navigation becomes impossible. Instead, those who have no view about the economy or its possible future direction are simply floating around in a sea of uncertainty.

When I worked for Bankers Trust, Charlie Sanford, the CEO at the time, used to wander around the trading floor, randomly chatting with his employees. His first question was always the same: "What is your view?" You could not *not* have a view. He would say that "not having a view" is the most dangerous position to be in, because "not acting is sometimes the biggest risk of all".

To have a view, it becomes necessary to stand against the crowd. After all, if prices are "correct", then there is no bet to be made. It is only the belief that the current price of your wages is wrong that encourages you to seek a higher paying job elsewhere. It is the belief that the market is not supplying something, or supplying it at the wrong price, that motivates a person to build a new business. It is the conviction that the stock market or bond market is at the wrong price that causes a person to bet that the price is going to change.

So, how can a person learn how to have a view on the world economy? Luckily, this does not require a degree in economics. It does require an alert power of observation, common sense and character, however. Signals are everywhere and can be observed.

28

Common sense is not always universally present (it was notably absent in financial market circles in the run up to the financial crisis) but it can be cultivated. The tricky piece of the puzzle is character.

Character

Without risk there is no reward. Alan Greenspan put it nicely when he said, "Risk-taking is indeed a necessary condition for the creation of wealth", or, to put it another way: "The ultimate value of all assets rests on their ability to produce goods and services in the future. And the future, as we all know, is uncertain and hence all investments are risky."[12] Although he was talking about financial investments, what he said applies to all the investments we make, including the investments made in ideas, aspirations, education and dreams. Risk-taking is the key to economic growth, and calculated, well thought-through, well-directed, well-managed risk is the key to *sustained* economic growth.

Calculated risk-taking in the world economy is a character test. To succeed in the world economy we need to be comfortable with our view. It may be that our view is the same as everyone else's, but this leaves us in danger of that all-too-human inclination to buy high and sell low. It feels comfortable going with the crowd. But, by the time something is "obvious", everyone has already done the same thing and there is usually little or no more value left in the investment. So, calculated risk-taking usually means having a different view to everybody else.

This is true of all investing, including investment we make in ourselves. When I went to college, it felt like everybody in the United States wanted to become a lawyer. Harvard Law School had legendary status, perhaps due to the lingering appeal of iconic films such as *Love Story* (1970) and *The Paper Chase* (1973), not to mention TV shows such as the classic *Perry Mason* (1957-1966) and *LA Law* (1986-1994). The next generation came to realise that there were too many lawyers. It was clear that the pay was no longer so great now that the competition was more

---

12 In a presentation at the annual Economic Symposium sponsored by the Federal Reserve Bank of Kansas City in Jackson Hole, Wyoming, 29 August 1997

intense, and outperforming everybody else required serious skill and dedication. By the early 1990s Wall Street began to visibly prosper and suddenly everybody's sights turned to financial markets. Stanley Weiser and Oliver Stone's film, *Wall Street* (1987), and Michael Lewis's book, *Liar's Poker* (1989), drew a young generation to a field for which these writers had nothing but criticism. Demand for MBAs started to outstrip demand for legal degrees. In the aftermath of the recent financial crisis the value of an MBA has now collapsed. Too many people have them now and there is little conviction that those armed with MBAs have any ability to actually make money. In both cases, the glut of lawyers and then the oversupply of financial market MBAs made these degrees lose their value. People were increasingly forced to differentiate themselves in some other way.

Investing in the market follows the same principle. If you believe that the current price of shares in Heinz – or copper, government bonds, or breakfast cereals for that matter – is right, then there is no point buying or selling them because you can't make a profit. In order to make a profit, you have to believe the current price is wrong and that it is going to move in the direction you expect. Risk taking therefore requires sufficient character, self-confidence and conviction to believe that your view is right and the view of the millions who make up the market and determine the price at any given moment is wrong. If the price is "right" then there is no point taking any risk. There won't be any reward.

This is one reason the lessons of traditional "free market" economics are not that useful when trying to judge the future. Too many economists assume the markets are "perfect". They think markets have "priced in" or accounted for all the information about the price. In real life, however, it is fairly obvious that prices are signals that change all the time. If you want to have a view, a view that you are prepared to take a risk on, it becomes important to look for signals that support or detract from your view.

A skyline in Wuhan

Consider Hugh Hendry's videos of the Wuhan skyline, which he took from the window of his hotel one day in 2009. Hendry is a legendary hedge fund manager based in London. He has described the critical character qualities that define success in investing: "First and foremost, an ability to establish a contentious premise outside the existing belief system, and have it go on and be adopted by the rest of the financial community."[13] *Barron's* magazine asked Hendry in 2012, "Where do you find yourself outside the existing belief system today?"[14] Hendry then described the simple signal that he saw that day in Wuhan, which told him to avoid what everyone else was doing – investing in China. He saw the signal from his window in the form of a skyline. He simply observed the outline of the city buildings against the sky and realised something was very wrong.

> "I made a YouTube video of the empty skyscrapers… Goldman Sachs and others articulate a very reasonable and compelling argument of being invested in China. With the evidence of my own eyes, I concluded that China had a very robust system of creating gross domestic-product growth, but forsaking the creation of wealth."

That skyline was covered in new but unfinished buildings with huge metal cranes perching on top. The property developers had run out of cash once China's economy began to suffer from the financial crisis in the West. The building work stopped before the roofs were put on. At the time, most people thought China would grow even though the West was in trouble. It turned out that Hendry was right. Americans stopped buying goods from China and, as a result, unemployment in China began to accelerate.

China's building boom had been driven in part by the belief that every farm worker would move to a major city in search of a new and better life. Property developers went crazy building for a population that was arriving in urban areas in huge numbers.

---

13 See *Zero Hedge*, 29 April 2012: "Hugh Hendry is Back: Full Eclectica Letter" by Tyler Durden

14 See *Market Montage*, 22 February 2012: "Hugh Hendry's Interview with Barron's" by Mark Hanna

They also bet that China would be exporting manufactured goods to the rest of the world for years to come. The fact that foreigners continued to invest more and more capital in China further fuelled optimism. When the financial crisis happened, the Chinese property market started to crash. The Chinese government attempted to prevent the haemorrhage by throwing more money into the property market, thus encouraging a further wave of construction of buildings and infrastructure for which there was no need and no market.

Hendry's "sell China" call took character. He was prepared to be laughed at and considered a crazy outlier. This is precisely what is required to navigate the world economy successfully – the character to come to a view of your own and the ability to know whether your particular skills and circumstances permit you to profit from your view.

Credit, *credere* and character

Character is itself a signal. Investors often lend on the basis of the borrower's character. The word "credit" is derived from the Latin word *credere*, which means "to believe". This is what led to J.P. Morgan's famous maxim of the 19th of December 1912, when he was testifying before a House Committee on the nation's finances. The Committee's counsel was trying to make Morgan explain the basis on which he made loans. Morgan said, "The first thing is character, before money or property or anything else. A man I do not trust could not get money from me on all the bonds in Christendom."[15]

Similarly David Swenson, who has managed some $20 billion for the Yale University Endowment since 1985, says allocating capital is all about character assessment. When asked, "What are the most important qualities in choosing a fund manager and giving capital to him or her?" he replied, "There are three: character, character and character." This aligns with Warren Buffett's view. He has said, "In evaluating people you look for

---

15 See "The Money Trust Investigation" of The Committee on Banking and Currency, House of Representatives, 19 December 1912

three qualities: integrity, intelligence and energy. And if you don't have the first the other two will kill you." Even scientists who push beyond traditional ways of thinking and thereby invent needed solutions, or philosophers who open up new ways of thinking, are engaging in the same creative, productive act of balancing between hubris and nemesis as they reach beyond the known. Albert Einstein also believed in the fundamental drive of character. "Most people say that it is the intellect that makes a great scientist," he said. "They are wrong: it is character."

In sum, the world economy produces an overwhelming number of signals. The question is, which signals lead to a view and the conviction to pursue that view? Who not only has a view but the ability to properly balance hubris against the risk of nemesis in pursuing it? The recognition and interpretation of signals is in part a question of character. The world economy demands that one's views are put to the test rather often.

Living on the edge

It is the business of pushing the boundary of the known that drives the world economy and creates wealth, growth and GDP. Invention, innovation and profitability all stem from this drive. The English Victorian poet Robert Browning put it simply: "A man's reach should exceed his grasp, or what's a heaven for?"[16] Edgework is the business of pushing against the boundaries of the unknown. It is argued by psychologists that this is essential to life.

The American novelist Ernest Hemingway believed that, "There are only three real sports, motor racing, mountain climbing and bullfighting. All the rest," he disdained, "are mere games." By his measure, the others didn't sufficiently push a man to the edge. Perhaps it is the simple fact that a person has to risk his life in these sports that attracts edgeworkers. Stirling Moss, the legendary British Formula One racing driver, has said, "To achieve anything in this game, you must be prepared to dabble

---

16 From the poem "Andrea del Sarto (Called the 'Faultless Painter')" by Robert Browning (1855)

on the boundary of disaster." The world economy may be the same. Having a view and then the character to pursue it requires the same sort of "edgework" that is pursued by racing drivers, astronauts, experimental aircraft pilots and extreme sailors. They may all be throwing themselves at the boundary of physics, but the world economy compels us to confront the borders between the current state of affairs and the possible. Think of it this way – just as sex involves pushing physical and psychological boundaries, crime challenges the boundary of the law, and music and drugs allow people to push the boundary of time and imagination, so innovation challenges the boundary of the world economy.

Boundary pushing is not simply a matter of curiosity. It is a means of both discovering and meeting the basic needs of the human psyche. In his 1943 paper, "A Theory of Human Motivation", the American psychologist Abraham Maslow identified boundary pushing as an essential component of life.

> What a man *can* be, he must be... This need we may call self-actualisation. It refers to the desire for self-fulfillment, namely, to the tendency for him to become actualised in what he is potentially. This tendency might be phrased as the desire to become more and more what one is, to become everything that one is capable of becoming.[17]

Survival and success in the world economy depend on boundary-pushing edgework. Jazz artists like Miles Davis, Charlie Parker and Dizzie Gillespie all realised they would never be anything more than one-hit wonders, mere players paid for time on stage and easily replaced by other skilled musicians, unless they engaged

---

17 In *Man For Himself* (1947), the German social psychologist Erich Fromm wrote in agreement: "Man's main task in life is to give birth to himself, to become what he potentially is." A century earlier, the Irish poet Thomas Moore (1779-1852) felt something similar when he wrote, "Nothing is more important in a person's life than to gain soul by expanding the limits of what defines him. This is transcendence, and it is an essential part of religion."

in edgework.[18] By changing their style and pushing their music beyond the accepted definition of their day, they gained control of their future. They wrote their own material instead of playing the work of others: that is how they became legends. Miles Davis in particular changed his musical style quite radically every four years or so. Innovation, the single most important event that occurs in the economy, the thing that creates sustainable GDP, is edgework. Clearly it required a lot of conviction and character to move away from popular music and to keep introducing new and unfamiliar music. But, this is exactly what caused Parker and Gillespie to emerge as icons.

It is not only individuals who are inventive and innovate, however. Companies, countries, and brands do edgework as well. In their book, *Luxury Brand Management*, Michel Chevalier and Gerald Mazzalovo write:

> In order for brands to become a factor of progress... they must be able to activate... the qualities that are necessary for progress: innovation, curiosity, a sense of action and of risk, a desire for conquest, the will to surpass oneself, solidarity, a love of hard work, confidence in one's own abilities and so on.[19]

The luxury brands they describe engage in edgework "with talent and taste, to promote values like seduction, sensuality, eroticism, and sensual pleasures without crossing the line into the vulgar or the shocking".[20]

Countries that excel at edgework affirm their place in history: Persia and India in the Middle Ages both preserved and advanced science and technology while the "Dark Ages" in Western Europe saw literary and scientific traditions banned and burned. Britain's role in driving the Industrial Revolution still affords it a stronger

---

18 See *The 50th Law* by 50 Cent and Robert Greene (G-Unit Books, 2009)
19 See *Luxury Brand Management: A World of Privilege* by Michel Chevalier and Gerald Mazzalovo (John Wiley, 2008), page 228
20 As above, page 229

entrepreneurial quality than is apparent in many other nations. Japan's role in creating modern, high value-added manufacturing of cars, machines and technology remains its core competitive advantage. China's role in broadening manufacturing processes over the last twenty years is also a good example of a nation's successful edgework.

Stop the world economy, I want to get off!

There are some for whom this all sounds too exhausting. Many don't want to go over the edge. They want to stay cosseted inside their cozy comfort zone. The risk-averse would rather not participate in any edgework, let alone press up against the unknown border of possibility.

After all, where is the edge? Where is the boundary beyond which real growth is created? The poet TS Elliot noted, "Only those who risk going too far can possibly find out how far one can go." The journalist and novelist Hunter S Thompson made a living out of being on the edge all the time. He wrote: "The Edge... there is no honest way to explain it because the only people who really know where it is are the ones who have gone over."[21] Edgework is undeniably frightening, especially when it involves our personal future.

For some, simply getting the rubbish into the right colour container and out the door in time for the binmen to pick it up is an act of edgework. But, no matter where our personal edge lies, the act of reaching beyond it increases economic productivity, growth and contributes to the creation of value added and thereby wealth.

Still, there are always those who long to "check out" of the world economy. They don't want to have a view or pay attention to signals. This instinct underpins all those who rail against globalisation and the market economy. This is impossible. Standing still is not an option because, as the now legendary management consultant Peter Drucker noted, "All economic

---

21 From *Hell's Angels: The Strange and Terrible Saga of the Outlaw Motorcycle Gangs* by Hunter S Thompson (1966)

activity is by definition 'high risk'. And defending yesterday – that is, not innovating – is far more risky than making tomorrow."[22]

After all, we will always have competition. Someone else is always innovating, even if we are not. As somebody else resets the bar higher and higher, we get left behind unless we get focused. The only constant in life is change. Change alone can throw us off balance, more so if we have no means of anticipating change.

We could take our chances and let the world economy push our lives along willy nilly, but what are the consequences of such an approach? As the American President Calvin Coolidge observed, "Those who trust to chance must abide by the results of chance." This, in the end, subjects us to even more risky outcomes than a controlled approach to managing risk, which is why the riskiest thing is often doing nothing or being unaware. Jack Welch, the former CEO of GE, put it more sharply: "Control your destiny or someone else will!"[23]

"It's beyond my control"

Balancing and edgework, indeed day to day living, require paying attention to signals. A pilot would not dream of flying from London to New York without checking the temperature, the wind speed and whether ice was forming on the wings, even if he was flying a plane that was nearly always on autopilot. Nor would he take the exact same flight path as everyone else at the same time. A sailor would never proceed without looking to see if the clouds were indicating a storm or fair weather. Yet how many of us live life and make important decisions without taking any account of the condition of world economy, usually because it feels "beyond our control"? My central purpose in writing this book is to give people the ability to notice signals and thereby proceed into the future with a greater sense of the context that will influence any individual choices that we might make.

---

22 From *Innovation and Entrepreneurship* by Peter Drucker (Elsevier, 1985)
23 Quoted in *Control Your Destiny or Someone Else Will* by Noel M Tichy and Stratford Sherman (Harper Collins, 1993)

It's hard to blame anyone for being passive. Consider the fact that many pension funds do exactly this. Their managers fly from one destination to another without considering any signals along the way. Does it really make sense to choose a financial destination of, for example, a return of 8%? Can we really pluck a performance target out of thin air and then choose the assets we think will perform to that result, set the course and effectively forget about it? This "set and forget" approach helps explain why many pension funds lost nearly ten times as much money as the banks did during the financial crisis of 2007/8 and why most pension funds around the world remain hugely underfunded today. When the signals changed, the pension plans did not adjust their strategies. Pensioners around the world are now angry that they have to retire later than they expected or live on less than they expected.

Individuals do the same thing. We love to do what everyone else is doing. We want to follow the crowd and pursue the same path as everyone else, often wilfully ignoring the signals being broadcast from the world economy. My mother was determined to buy a house in 2006 in Northern Virginia because, she believed, "house prices would only rise" and "everyone else is doing it". She and I interpreted the housing market signals very differently. When prices began to rise at a faster pace than the historical average, it gave her comfort that she had made the right decision. That same signal gave me indigestion. When house prices collapsed, she ended up with negative equity. She was glad that luck was on her side, though: I willingly paid the bills in the aftermath. For me this was not luck, however. I anticipated this outcome and set aside a portion of my income to manage her expected loss from the moment she bought that house. And so we see one signal, two interpretations, two very different views about the future and a better set of consequences than if we had both been completely surprised.

Similarly, the vast majority of business and law school graduates decided that they wanted to have a career in financial services during the boom years. The financial sector drained much of the mathematical and quantitative talent away from other sectors in the economy. Then when the financial markets imploded in 2007, many found they had lost their jobs and their careers as well. Those who took a different path and became engineers, even though the wages were low and the glamour factor for the job was zero, now enjoy demand. The current global shortage of skilled oil engineers is so great that drilling firms are prepared to pay experienced 60- and 70-year-olds pretty much anything they want for a few weeks of work every year. Financial markets drained all the mathematical and engineering talent out of world economy for a long time. Now the real economy, which includes things like mining and energy extraction and agriculture, can compete again and outbid financial services for that human capital.

Perhaps this is all just supply and demand? Indeed. But, if you know that everyone else is pursuing a particular path, it might make sense to consider that a signal and step away toward a different path. Choosing a different path from the crowd is hard, however. Many of us feel like shouting, "I hate the world economy and want to get off!" There is no way to get off. Economic change, loss and gain, occur whether we like it or not. The size of the loss or gain the economic cycle brings to individuals and societies matters. Large gains (that usually require large calculated risks) allow permanent increases in income and wealth but also risk great losses. Japan discovered this in the 1950s when it moved from manufacturing plastic flowers to manufacturing luxury automobiles. Large losses can destabilise societies for prolonged periods, and profound loss can bring down a government and even a nation. The Soviet Union was once the greatest and most commodity-rich land in the world, forged from revolution and war, yet it ceased to exist simply because it ran out of the cash required to run the economy.

Hurt versus injury

The normal ebb and flow of the world economy can wreak havoc with private lives. Economic storms can be severe and cause hurt and injury, thereby slowing down economic growth even more than circumstances warrant. When confronted by such economic events, we experience fear, and we are right to feel afraid.

Sportsmen know the difference between being hurt and being injured.[24] We can still play if we are hurt, while injuries preclude playing in the game. In the world economy we are hurt when we lose our job to a competitor. But we are still in the game and can go for another similar job or change professions or strategies. In contrast, we can be injured by the world economy when we find, as many did during the last few years, that at the age of fifty, our pension fund value is cut in half by losses, thus forcing us to work for years longer for a lower standard of living than we anticipated. Given our age, we cannot, must not, take big financial risks because now we cannot afford to lose any more capital. Our capacity to recover and re-enter the world economy is limited. That's an injury. If we have no skills and society has left us without the means to acquire them, then whole generations can be left permanently sidelined.

Today this problem plagues the young generation in the Eurozone, in less advantaged communities in America, and the large poor and uneducated populations of emerging markets. This is worse than an injury. This constitutes a break in the fundamental contract between citizen and state: the social contract. To one degree or another, citizens are entitled to expect that their government will not leave them in such a perilous condition for very long. Naturally, hurt and injury give rise to a sense of hopelessness against the unknown forces of nature. This feeling of helplessness against our times remind me of what Peter Drucker wrote in 1939 in his very first book, *The End of Economic Man*. On the subject of the Great Depression, he said it proved that:

> ... irrational and incalculable forces also rule peacetime society: the threat of sudden permanent unemployment, of being thrown on the industrial scrap heap in one's prime or even before one has started to work. Against these forces the individual finds himself as helpless, isolated, and atomised as against the forces of machine war.

---

24 See *The New Yorker*, 19 October 2009: "Is football any better than dogfighting?" by Malcolm Gladwell in the "Annals of Medicine"

He cannot determine when unemployment is going to hit and why; he cannot fight it, he cannot even dodge it. Like the forces of war, depression shows man as a senseless cog in a senselessly whirling machine which is beyond human understanding and has ceased to serve any purpose but its own.

The German social psychologist Eric Fromm, writing in 1942, explained how the psychology of being a "senseless cog", proved fertile soil for the rise of Fascism in Germany, Italy and elsewhere in Europe after the population endured searing losses from multiple causes including war, hyperinflation, the rapid decline in savings and the destruction of normal price signals in the economy. In the US at the same time (1933-1938), the state came to the rescue of perplexed and overwhelmed citizens in the form of the "New Deal", whereby the government started providing support for the public through job programmes, Social Security, mortgage assistance and deposit insurance. As in the 1930s, today there is an inclination to believe, to hope, that someone in the corridors of power in the nation's capital can fix the problem.

Most of us can cope with a stock market that goes up and down, even one that moves violently. What most of us cannot tolerate is a world in which our faith and belief in the market mechanism is broken, and where prices no longer reflect normal market forces. Those who would normally oppose the expansion of the state become quiescent, conceding that only the state has the power to address economic problems that are far beyond the comprehension or abilities of an individual member of the public.

Without tools to understand or manage the process of economic change, Fromm says, "freedom itself becomes an unbearable burden". "It then becomes identical with doubt" and "a kind of life that lacks meaning and direction". The tendency is to run from such freedom, preferring to give up the rewards of calculated risk-taking for the security of known outcomes, even if such certainty requires handing power over to Fascists and dictators or the friendlier faces of central bankers. Anyone will do as long as they can restore order.

I am not suggesting that central bankers and Fascists have much in common; I am suggesting that the public wants somebody to sort out the problem. If it needs to be the state, so be it. Indeed, when casually observing the world economy today, we find that the state has emerged as the most important participant in the market. It is a profoundly serious signal that central banks have become the most important price makers in the market (now that they are the biggest buyers of their own governments' debt). If they buy, everyone must buy. If they sell, everyone must sell. Some people feel better knowing the state has "control" when we feel we have lost control, until we realise that government is not usually supposed to be controlling prices.

The balance of power

The balance of power has now shifted from the market to the state. This raises an important question for modern democracies. Do we want a world where the state controls the distribution of wealth, power and prices, or where the market is in control? This is not just an economic question. It is a political question. It is a question that forces us to consider the nature of a proper balance of power between the state and the market. It seems ironic that the West fought long and hard to "win" the contest between Capitalism and Communism. It was only in 1992 that the economist Francis Fukuyama proclaimed that Capitalism had decisively and permanently "won" in his book, *The End of History and the Last Man*. Today, it is less and less tenable to say that we know that Communism does not work and yet approve of a world where the state controls asset prices – or at least governments have become the principle driver of asset prices – and the state increasingly controls distribution of wealth through monetary, fiscal and regulatory intervention.

It is hard to accept that risk is inherent to the creation of GDP and wealth. No one wants to believe there is no reward without risk. If it is true, then many of us would like the state to protect us from risk. We want to believe the Security and Exchange Commission in the United States, the Financial Services Authority in Britain and their counterparts around the world can simply

42

outlaw or prevent fraud and bad judgement and plain old management mistakes. We want to believe that the world's central banks can make all the losses go away by engaging in "Quantitative Easing" (QE, which is the policy of flooding the markets with free money). But, in the end, managing the risks in the markets cannot be devolved to some third party, like the state, who can make the future safe. Risk and opportunity are our own responsibility. This is an uncomfortable thought and a lot of people won't like it.

Adapting to change

Happily, human beings are pretty good at adapting to change even if they don't like it. We do it, even if we are unaware we are adapting in response to signals. Charles Darwin is interminably misquoted on this point. He did not actually say, "only the strong survive". He argued, "only the *adaptable* survive".[25] In general, we manage the small changes in the world economy very effectively. We can adjust to a life with higher or lower oil prices, and higher or lower growth rates or interest rates. We often adapt without even realising it. In fact, the purpose of prices in the world economy is primarily to provide a signalling mechanism that permits us to adapt to economic change.

Consider the Australian schoolteacher, who, by her own admission, has no idea about the economy or its signals. She is a friend of my daughter Laura and lived in Western Australia. In 2005, well before the financial crisis, she was vaguely aware that the bulk of the economy in that part of the world evolved around mining iron ore. By 2007, she knew that the miners were doing well and spending their money pretty freely. This made for great parties come Friday night, because everybody was flush with cash (a signal), but it also drove up house prices (another signal). At

---

25 From a conversation with Charles Darwin's great-great-granddaughter, Sarah Darwin, and her husband, the German botanist Dr Johannes Vogel, an authority on Darwin, who at the time was Keeper of Botany at the Natural History Museum in London (2004-2012). They were producing a film on Charles Darwin that makes exactly this point (a recreation of Darwin's voyage on the Beagle, *Beagle: In Darwin's Wake*, on board the sailing ship *Stad Amsterdam*).

that time, her fellow school teachers started joking about the fact that the truck drivers, not to mention the men who do the dangerous underground work, were in such short supply that they were now paid a multiple of a teacher's salary (a signal) just to get the iron ore to the coastline where it could be shipped to foreign buyers. Soon, she realised that she would never be able to afford a house on her salary and resigned herself to renting. She then discovered that the Australian dollar was now so strong that she could afford a jaunt to Paris (a signal) with her girlfriends. The currency had strengthened to reflect the growth being generated by Australia's resources boom.

Rents started rising as more people showed up looking for high-paying jobs in the mining boom. Eventually the landlord wanted to raise her rent, which she could not afford, so she considered moving back to the East Coast where things were less expensive. Soon she was forced to share a house with friends, though she enjoyed vacationing in Paris.

Around this time, the property market in that part of Australia suddenly collapsed in the wake of the global financial crisis. Mining firms started to fire their employees. The local schools started firing teachers because they had run out of money, now that the miners were no longer paying big tax bills. The really good teachers were told to hang tight. The weaker, less committed ones went on to do something else for a living. Soon rents fell and now the teacher, my friend, who was diligent and focused and able to survive the "cull" as a result, found that she could afford to rent a whole house all by herself and still afford to vacation in Europe with her friends.

As they sat in Paris enjoying a lovely bottle of Burgundy, they felt pretty pleased with themselves that they managed to organise and pay for the trip. The schoolteacher had no idea what the price of iron ore was. For her it was not a signal of any importance. She did not "know" that a powerful reason she was in Paris was because the Australian dollar had become very strong, reflecting the fact that commodity prices, like iron ore, had risen so much. She did not think, "Gosh, my prosperity, my being here in Paris, depends on whether China keeps growing and therefore continues buying commodities like iron ore from Australia." Nor did she really appreciate that the many small decisions she made to improve her teaching skills now acted as a cushion against economic uncertainty. She did not fully realise that sharing a flat with friends or living in her own home was not a choice of her own but a function of economic circumstances. When economic forces touched her life, she did not "get" what happened, at least until we discussed it together one afternoon. But, she adapted nonetheless.

Now that she "gets it", she asks more questions about what's going on in the world economy. She now makes an effort to understand how the news will impact on her life. She now keeps an eye on the price of iron ore and the price of the Australian dollar and has come to appreciate the importance of interest rates to her life. Australia has no long-term fixed-rate mortgages, so she can only protect herself from higher interest rates by saving more now to pay for higher interest costs later, which she now does. She cannot predict the economic cycle but she can prepare for it by paying attention to signals. She now invests much more time in improving her skills. She saves more than before to cushion herself against the inevitable shocks. She is better able to balance hubris and the risk of nemesis.

Being a part of the world economy is a lot like surfing. It involves being constantly alert and responding to ever-changing conditions. The choice is simple. We can be buffeted about by the storms and lulls on the high seas of the global market, constantly taken by surprise and treating life as a process of fate over which we have no control. Or, we can try to be the captain of our own ship and respond to signals that warn us of the future.

Fight, drift or navigate. That's the choice. To navigate, we need to have a reference point. Leonardo Da Vinci said, "If you fix your course upon a star, you will be able to navigate any storm." We have to have a view. We have to learn to live with being wrong. We have to learn to make different choices than others. This means strengthening awareness of signals and sharpening our character enough to act on those signals in a way that is appropriate for each person.

45

The cutting edge is a bloody place

There is substance to the old cliché that business is the cutting edge of the world economy. Edgework requires care and attention because sometimes the cutting edge is clearing the path before us and speeding us on our way, and sometimes it is mowing us down, leaving us flailing helplessly in its wake. As the computer scientist Zalman Stern observed, "The problem with the cutting edge is that someone has to bleed." Given a choice, I have to believe that most of us would choose to bleed a little rather than to bleed a lot. We could choose to have the world economy work with us instead of against us. That requires reading signals, balancing hubris and nemesis, and taking calculated risks.

No one is arguing for recklessness, though this often describes how we manage our careers and investments, from property decisions to education decisions. Before jumping headlong into a risky decision, one should consider US General Patton's admonition: "Take calculated risks. That is quite different from being rash." Warren Buffett admonishes, "Risk comes from not knowing what you're doing, so figure out what you need to know before taking risks."

Even careful, thoughtful risk-taking involves failure and loss, however. These are important events in life because, as Woody Allen once said, "If you don't fail now and again, it's a sign you're playing it safe." One thing is for sure – Wayne Gretzky, the famed Canadian ice-hockey player, was right when he said, "You miss 100% of the shots you never take."

Luckily, changes in the world economy are always preceded by signals. The problem is that we often see these signals clearly only in retrospect. The 19th-century novelist Mark Twain complained, "I was seldom able to see an opportunity until it had ceased to be one." The reality is that anybody can learn how to pick up on economic signals. The rest of this book will address that. Interpreting and acting on signals is another matter. That takes character. You have to assess not only the signals out there, but your own ability to make use of them.

A Letter to the Queen

3

It is hard to challenge conventional wisdom. It is hard to set up a business that is different. What can account for the fact that Colonel Sanders kept trying to finance his fried chicken recipe even after 1,009 people turned him down? The one thousand and tenth person said yes and Kentucky Fried Chicken is the result. Could persistence be a function of character? It requires a good deal of character to stand up to the crowd of public opinion and follow another path, or to walk away from your goal because the conditions are not right for the moment.

Consider the story of the chef Daniel Rose, a young man from Chicago who spoke no French but loved cooking. He moved to Paris to study at university, instead turned to fine cuisine and in 2006 opened a restaurant called Spring, at the height of the booming economy. He is now one of the highest ranked chef-restaurateurs in France in spite of having to close, move, re-open, close, re-open and re-invent his restaurant several times due to the whims of the world economy. It now takes one year to get a reservation there.

This balancing between hubris and nemesis, hope and fear, and taking risks that involve the possibility of real failure and real success has always been a popular theme for writers, poets, psychologists and other observers of the human condition. After all, it reveals and reinforces character. Shakespeare's enduring appeal largely rests on his ability to understand and portray the true nature of man. Macbeth cannot find a good balance between his ambition and his fear of failure: "I have no spur/ To prick the sides of my intent, but only/ Vaulting ambition, which o'erleaps itself/ And falls on th'other."[26]

Character drives all good stories, including economic ones. But what does character have to do with the world economy? Put simply, character underpins all investment decisions. After all, the consensus is already priced into the market. By definition, this means it is difficult to make any money out of the view that just about everyone shares. The chances that such an asset will rise in value are small because everyone already owns it. There aren't that many new buyers left to push the price up. The investment decisions that pay the best are the ones with the less than best odds, where there is an element of risk. The risk is what you get paid for. Character defines the economy.

The word "character" might imply that some people have good character and others not. Recently the *New York Times* argued that there is no such thing as character at all because people change their behaviour depending on the circumstances and whom they are with. What I mean by character is this: the ability to arrive at a view of the world based on our own reasoning rather than that of the crowd; the capacity to execute and stick with that view; and the willingness to change it fluidly with circumstance in order to achieve a committed goal that is beyond our normal reach. Not everyone is an edgeworker or an entrepreneur, but everyday life requires us to make decisions about buying and selling. Even these decisions both test and reveal our character.

Most people ask me, "What should I buy?" They rarely ask, "What and when should I sell?" They forget that there is no such thing as a profit until you take the cash off the table and put it in your pocket. Before that it may look like a profit, but it's just hope. One of the truest tests of character is when we buy something like a house or stock and the price just keeps going up. Most people become afraid to sell, afraid to give up the potential gains. Instead of having a clear goal, we hesitate. This illustrates the old adage: Bulls make money, bears make money, pigs get

---

26 *Macbeth*, Act 1, scene 7, lines 25-28

slaughtered. Selling something that is still rising in value will be met with endless derision. It takes character to stand up to that and take the cash home while it's still on offer. Failure to sell at the right time (before everyone else is selling) leads to "coulda, woulda, shoulda" stories about how a person "used to have a profit" when in fact they had nothing but a possibility.

Those who invested in Google and Microsoft in 1995 made a fortune – if they sold before 1999. Why would anyone sell such a successful story when the Internet has clearly transformed the way the world works. The simple reason is this: by 1999 many new Internet businesses had been founded by those who were chasing the consensus view. These new businesses typically had no profits, however. In some cases the share price went up even though firms had no revenue, let alone profit. It took a good deal of character to choose which firms had a viable sustainable business with genuine cash flow and which were just part of a popular mania. Those who sold out, or even only sold out before the Internet bubble burst in 2000, made a fortune. Sadly, there are only a few of these success stories because it was very hard to make such a decision. It involved being ridiculed at dinner parties – "What kind of idiot would sell the Internet story?" – and it takes character to survive that.

Peter Drucker noted that companies face the same problem. The market starts to value companies based on the possibility of profits well before the profits actually appear. This tends to cause companies to misjudge their own success. Unless a firm earns more than the value of its resources, he says, it does not create wealth; it destroys it.

Success comes from long periods of thinking and rethinking and challenging your own thought process and comparing it to reality. These long periods of thinking but not necessarily doing are followed by sudden, intense periods where action is required. Then everybody figures out what is going on and they all jump on the bandwagon. Being ready to recognise an opportunity and take a leap before the confirmation of the crowd requires character.

We like to think the economic cycle is unpredictable. We like the idea that no one could have anticipated the boom or the bust because that absolves us of the responsibility of preparing for and managing the economic cycle. The economists Ken Rogoff and Carmen Reinhart capture this imbalance between human nature and character in their book, *This Time is Different: Eight Centuries of Financial Folly* (2009) in which they systematically outline the extraordinary similarities of the many over- and under-investment cycles that have hit the world economy throughout history.

For the Love of God

If we ignore or fail to register the importance of signals, it is in part because we don't want to. Think about the signal, *For the Love of God*, the artwork produced by Damien Hirst and presented to the world on the 1st of June 2007, just two months before the financial market crisis hit on the 13th of August. This artwork is comprised of the skull of an 18th-century man, quite literally encrusted with diamonds, which allegedly cost £14 million to produce. *The Daily Mail* headline screamed: "Damien Hirst unveils his jewels in the crown, a £50m diamond-studded skull!" Hirst had become one of the most renowned, avant-garde, edgeworking artists of his generation. He had first shocked the world by pickling a shark in a vat of formaldehyde – *The Physical Impossibility of Death in the Mind of Someone Living* (1991). He went on to paint the horns and hooves of a dead calf in 18-carat gold and then suspend its body in a golden tank of formaldehyde (*The Golden Calf*, 2008). His ability to judge the public mood and capture the zeitgeist was well proven and well rewarded by the time he revealed *For the Love of God*.

I confess that I missed this powerful signal at the time. With hindsight, it is so obvious that he was signalling the end of an era; that the rich had accumulated so much wealth that upon their death they could encrust their own skulls with diamonds, should they choose to do so. Hirst was reminding us that you can't take it with you. In an era of extraordinary wealth, what did you really have to show for your life? There was a biting irony to an artwork that confirmed there are limits to wealth while selling for more than any artwork ever known: $100 million. In retrospect, I now realise that the skull was hissing, "For the love of God, how much money do you need?" Many of those who could afford to buy *For the Love of God* found their financial circumstances change for the worse only a few months after the sale took place. Indeed there were rumours that the market had already turned when the artwork was presented to the public and Hirst or his supporters had to lend money to the buyers to purchase it.

Maybe the wealthy buyers at the time could not recognise the signal for what it was, because acknowledging it would have meant many changes. They would have had to sell assets, draw down risk, sell their businesses, acknowledge that their net worth was a smaller number than they had believed. It is hard to give up a life that defines us just because times have changed. It is so much easier to believe that our circumstances were not the result of luck. No, we tell ourselves. We are skilled. We are smart. Therefore, we can manage any economic storm. This is why so many smart, successful people lose everything in a crisis. Confusing luck with skill is deadly.

My point is that observing signals is not enough. Action is required, and action demands having a view. To have a view of the future is to reveal our character, as Ralph Waldo Emerson observed: "People do not seem to realise that their opinion of the world is also a confession of character." Our view of the landscape and our perception of risk reveals our character. Our choice of what to reach for and when to reach for it, requires and reveals character.

The Girl and the Goat

It also takes character to recognise that gifts are sometimes wrapped in sandpaper. A serious fall in the market is the opportunity for many. When can we acquire property and a talented workforce cheaply? Only during the "bust". Consider the hubris of the American chef Stephanie Izzard who, in 2008 at the height of the financial and economic crisis, decided to open a new high-end restaurant, The Girl and the Goat. No one would lend her any money other than friends and family in spite of the fact that she had recently won a reality TV-show cooking contest. Circumstances forced her into a cheap location. She chose a part of the West Loop in Chicago that no one would ever have imagined as the home of what has now become one of the best-ranked restaurants in America. She not only created an extraordinary venue that employs more than 150 people and where the waiting list is full nine months in advance; there is a secondary market in the rights to the private dining room. The entire neighbourhood has now transformed into one of the hippest parts of Chicago.

Character versus capital

Character is the linchpin of the economic cycle. When the economy hits the worst of the downturn, when confidence is shattered, this is the moment that we find capital pits itself against character. During the boom times, capital is usually easy to access. As a result, we begin to think, "My business or my idea would work if only I had more capital." President John F Kennedy wisely noted that, "When money is seen as a solution for every problem, money itself becomes the problem." Usually the best deals are done in the worst times and the worst deals are done in the best times precisely because easy access to capital weakens discipline and compensates for lack of conviction. Lack of access to capital strengthens the focus on cash flow and profitability and ensures only those with genuine conviction can proceed. The true test of economic cycles presents itself at the peak and the trough. At the top of the economic cycle, it is a test of character to see if we can walk away when everyone wants to give us money. Only we can properly assess our ability to take it and put it to productive use. In the last economic cycle, too many chose to take the mortgage from the bank even though they had no capacity to repay. Too many built their personal and business decisions on the assumption that money would remain easily accessible, that asset prices would only go up and that the future could only be brighter. Others, like Lehman Brothers and a multitude of real businesses from Toys R Us to pharmacy chains like CVS in the US, chose to take on more debt than their company could ever service. At the bottom of the economic cycle capital disappears and even the most successful businesses find it hard to raise money.

Team Brawn

When the economy pits character against capital, we see inspiring stories unfold. Consider the short story of Team Brawn in Formula 1 racing. F1 has never been a big success in America, but worldwide it draws one of the largest audiences for any spectator sport. By the time of the financial crisis in August 2007, F1 had become a frenzy of free money being thrown at teams and technology. Firms including Vodafone and Orange were paying $75 million annually to sponsor F1 teams. Honda and Toyota spent nearly $1.5 billion in 2008 alone. Honda had offered Ross Brawn the top job, "team principal", in November 2007, asking him to sever his ties with F1 to form a new team just three months after the financial market crisis began.

Brawn was a highly acclaimed former technical director and racing strategist for Benetton and then later for Scuderia Ferrari. He helped the acclaimed F1 driver Michael Schumacher win many world championships. A few months after the financial crisis unfolded, it suddenly became clear that Honda's sales had collapsed and the company could not afford to remain an F1 sponsor. Some say it had already decided to get out and the financial crisis provided the excuse. Either way, Brawn was suddenly without a backer or a team. So, he decided to buy the team himself and find new backers. Brawn GP "Team Brawn" was launched in November 2009 and went on to raise enough cash here and there, from Virgin and from QTel (the Qatari Telecom firm) and a few others. They had enough cash to make it to the next race – just – which meant they had to win or fold.

There are only two prizes in F1 racing – best driver (World Drivers' Championship) and best car (Constructors' Championship). In 2009, Team Brawn won both. This had never been achieved by any other F1 team operating in its first year of existence let alone by a team that was operating on a shoestring of cash. Keep in mind that F1 racing is not only extremely expensive but is also a technical undertaking in which the driver is only as good as his car. These races are won more in the garage than on the circuit. The technical engineers who construct these machines are pushing the boundaries of physics, constantly balancing the need to shave off another gram of weight without sacrificing the structural integrity of a car that will be driven at such speeds that a sudden need to brake would snap the neck of any untrained driver. This is expensive and arduous edgework.

What led to their success? No doubt, Ross Brawn's personal conviction and firm view that they could and should accomplish their goal in spite of the obvious obstacles played the greatest part. Maybe they won *because of* the financial obstacles rather than in spite of them. The point is, when confronted by a problem, those without capital have no choice but to rely on character.

Born to win

Similar stories are told by John Bertrand, the Australian yachtsman who won the America's Cup in 1983, and also by Ernesto Bertarelli, whose team, Alinghi, won the America's Cup in 2007. Both said lack of capital forced them to rely on other means of winning. Bertrand explains in his book, *Born to Win*,[27] that he hired a team psychologist, in spite of overwhelming ridicule. This helped create such deep knowledge of the strengths and weaknesses of each team member that the group won principally through teamwork rather than through technology. Bertarelli similarly describes having to rely on teamwork because he did not have the cash to rely on technology.

It is character that tips us over the edge of the boom and into the bust. And character is what leads us out of the bust and into the next boom. Innovation, indeed the vision from which innovation springs is a function of having the character to strive for something that is beyond one's reach or beyond the limits of imagination.

Joy

Consider the story of the classic French perfume, Joy. The crash of 1929 and the subsequent depression devastated the economic landscape. Jean Patou owned a couture house in Paris that had invented the designer tie and sports knitwear and launched

---

27 *Born to Win* by John Bertrand and Patrick Robinson (William and Morrow, 1985)

a series of fragrances in the 1920s. The crash wiped out most of his clientele. He took a dramatic decision and closed the clothing business. Patou and his head perfumer, Henri Alméras, then took a bold leap of faith. They together concluded that there would always be someone who would figure out how to make money no matter the condition of the world economy. As a result, they decided to launch the most expensive perfume ever made: Joy. Every 30mls contains more that 10,000 jasmine flowers and the petals from more than 300 roses. It has been almost as successful as Chanel No5 and continues to be one of the best-regarded perfumes, in part because of its commitment to luxury.

It would take a strong character to launch the most expensive perfume in history in the midst of an epic economic crisis. Thank goodness for that courage though, because it created untold jobs in the perfume industry that exist to this day and also offered a vision of hope that inspires some eight decades later.

A reply to the Queen

On the 9th of November 2008, I imagine that Queen Elizabeth II woke up thinking about the speech she would deliver later that day at the London School of Economics to mark the opening of the new £71 million lecture theatre. In my mind's eye, I can see her sitting upright in bed, no doubt ramrod straight, given what we have seen from photographs and paintings of her character and her poise, as she asked the question that lurked in everyone's mind: "Why did no one see the crisis coming?"

She decided to ask the economists of the world who, after all, one would have expected to warn us of impending danger. Shouldn't they have seen all the signals? The Queen observed that the crisis seems to have involved "a failure of the collective imagination of many bright people", who were all "doing their job properly on its own merit". A response to her question was posted in the *Financial Times* by members of The British Academy on the 22nd of July 2009:

When Your Majesty visited the London School of Economics last November, you quite rightly asked: why had nobody noticed that the credit crunch was on its way? The British Academy convened a forum on the 17th of June 2009 to debate your question, with contributions from a range of experts from business, the City, its regulators, academia, and government. This letter summarises the views of the participants and the factors that they cited in our discussion, and we hope that it offers an answer to your question.

What did members of the Academy cite as the true cause? "Principally a failure of the collective imagination of many bright people, both in this country and internationally, to understand the risks to the system as a whole."[28]

Imagination does indeed lie at the heart of the matter. Here is the belated reply I would like to have sent her, on the very timely, apt and profound question she posed.

Her Majesty The Queen
Buckingham Palace
London SW1A 1AA
United Kingdom

Your Majesty

In answer to your question, "Why did no one see the crisis coming?" the answer is simple and unsatisfying: Some never do and never will. Some did and always will. What follows is an explanation and a remedy.

We can no more prevent economic crises any more than we can control the advent of storms on the high seas. John Kenneth Galbraith observed that financial market experts are usually very rich (financiers) or powerful (economists), and therefore held in awe, surrounded by the most skilled staff and able to access

---

28 The letter to the Queen includes the following as the address for correspondence: Professor Geoffrey M. Hodgson, The Business School, University of Hertfordshire, Hatfield, Hertfordshire AL10 9AB

the best information. Thus the "experts" are "endowed with the authority that encourages acquiescence from their subordinates and applause from their acolytes and excludes adverse opinion". This leads to an assurance of "personal mental superiority" that "in turn diminishes self scrutiny". This fact about humankind cannot be changed. The "experts" will always lead us down the wrong path and we will always willingly follow the path, so brilliantly lit with genius, to supposed riches. The rule is simple, Galbraith notes: "Financial genius is before the fall."

So far, no economist has come up with a reliable theory that allows us to predict a crisis or even when the cycle will turn for better for worse, as all the economists confirmed when they wrote back to you. The American economist Hyman Minsky wisely noted that things tend to change very suddenly. But even he left no formula for knowing when this will happen.

So, here is a dark joke for you, Ma'am. The three best jobs in the world are:

1. *Designated hitter for a major league baseball team*
2. *Meteorologist*
3. *Economist*

In what other profession can you fail 79% of the time and still be considered good at your job? It's an old joke. "The only function of economic forecasting is to make astrology look respectable."[29]

Barring some extraordinary innovation, let's forget prediction. Even if we cannot predict, however, we can still prepare. Participants in the world economy can be better equipped to manage these storms when they occur. A few specific undertakings

---

29 I conferred with James Galbraith on this quote and discovered that his father, John Kenneth Galbraith, "never said it". "The remark was made by some less-well-known figure, and because it was clever, the Internet decided to credit Dad."

would shore up every man and woman so that they can captain their own ship in spite of the storms, instead of being subject to fate, whose turn can be apparent before action needs be taken instead of only in retrospect, as has been the case for too many.

There can be no sustainable economic and financial innovation without financial education. By this I do not mean the often paltry efforts of banks and finance ministries to help schoolchildren learn how to understand how the interest rate on a mortgage is calculated, critical as that may be. In addition, people must learn that there are signals in the world economy, interpret what they mean, and act on them.

Investing in oneself, in the markets, in the future, all require risk. If there is no risk, there is no reward. So, there is little point in trying to devise new rules or even institutions that can prevent bad outcomes. The SEC, the FSA and other financial regulators can never protect us from fraud. No regulator can save us from having to do our own homework. Loss is a normal part of the world economy and indeed progress cannot occur without it.

The signals are there and it is our job to see them and act upon them. For example, the bank that pays the highest rate of interest is the one with the least trust. That's why they have to pay more interest than their competitors. And yet, throughout history, people seem to be happy to place their life savings in the bank with the highest interest rate. Many pension funds in Britain placed virtually all their assets with Icelandic banks, which were paying higher rates of interest than British banks in the run-up to the financial crisis. Why is it not understood that a bank has to pay over the odds to attract deposits only when it suffers from a lack of trust? Instead, it seems that the firemen and police wanted to get paid the most they could be paid for their deposits and did not consider or appreciate the risks. Interest rates are one of many signals. People need to know these signals and understand how to respond to them as surely as we expect a person to stop at a red light on and go on a green one.

Volatility and the economic cycle cannot be outlawed or prevented, but we can cushion against them by encouraging a greater diversity of opinion and endeavour in the world economy. Ironically, in financial markets it is believed that the one "free lunch" is diversification. Yet we do not encourage diversity of opinion or diversification of economic activities in our societies. Those with a contrary view from the consensus are given air time by the press only after the fact and only if they were right. Instead, a diversity of opinion ought to be expressed regardless, so that we can consider the risk that the experts might be wrong and therefore prepare for such a possibility.

Whenever the majority of the population seeks to pursue the same idea at the same time, it usually ends in tears. Just as it is a sure sign of trouble when 85% of the graduates of business school want a job in the financial markets, it is a sure sign of trouble when everyone buys the same investment ideas at the same time (tulips in 1637, railroad stocks in the 1800s, internet stocks in the 1990s, homes in the 2000s) instead of diversifying away from the crowd. There is wisdom in crowds, no doubt, but there is also safety in forging a different path from the crowd so that when the crowd turns we are not trampled to death. Countries benefit from diversification as much as portfolios.

We should be encouraged to be more eccentric in our edgework and our life experience. Eccentricity is essential to restoring diversity in the economy. The greater the diversity of opinion and activity in the economy the better cushioned we are to managed the inevitable ebbs and flows in the world economy. Why? Because events can be managed better if we pursue different opinions, different businesses, different activities and different visions of the future, rather than all leaning the same way at once.

The more we forge our own eccentric and edgy path, the greater our strength of character will be; a strength of character essential for managing the economy's inevitably changing tides. In this way, we can begin to appreciate the opportunities that fall out of the top and the bottom of the economic cycle. After all, it is typically when the economic cycle sinks into crisis mode that assets are shaken free from the privileged hands of their current owners and shift, at much lower prices, into the hands of aspiring owners. And, it is typically at the top of the economic cycle that the opportunity to take one's profits home presents itself. But that is precisely the moment that it is hardest to sell.

It takes vision, conviction, character and preparedness to sell at the top and buy at the bottom. Back to that adage about bulls, bears and pigs. What it means is that pigs lack the necessary character and judgement to prevent hubris from overpowering them to such an extent that nemesis is given easy access to their lives. "Pigs" do not invest. They do not have a view with any conviction. Pigs merely follow the crowd and the seemingly easy money. I find myself in agreement with the 19th-century English philosopher and economist John Stuart Mill, who wrote, "That so few now dare to be eccentric marks the chief danger of the time" and, "All good things which exist are the fruits of originality."[30]

The solutions here are simple. We must be encouraged to reach for something that is just beyond our grasp; to do edgework instead of remaining comfortable and therefore more vulnerable to the random upheavals that global economic cycles inflict. The solution is definitely not to meet every crisis and economic downturn by throwing unlimited amounts of capital at the problem. Capital, as with all things in the world economy, is subject to supply and demand and has a price. Sometimes capital is cheap and easy to find, sometimes it is expensive and in short supply. It is not a shortage of capital that holds back the economy during times of economic weakness; it is a shortage of good ideas and the character to pursue them that holds it back. Free money alone does not generate growth. If anything, it weakens the discipline with which we apply our convictions. When circumstances pit character against capital, character usually wins.

---

30 Both quotes from *On Liberty* by John Stuart Mill (1859)

If we were to guess the rightful resting place of a crystal ball in this world, we might venture to think that it is somewhere among the possessions of a Queen. But, I am guessing even you have not found a crystal ball among your many vaults and closets. Happily, we don't need a crystal ball, because another Queen has given us this useful insight. The Queen of Hearts advised Alice in Wonderland to try to think of at least six impossible things before breakfast. Why, you may ask? Because it improves preparedness. It leads to greater care in our protection against uncertainty and greater conviction in our dreams. Lest we forget, the 19-century American philosopher Henry David Thoreau reminds us that, "Dreams are the touchstones of our character."

Preparedness for possibilities is the right goal, not prediction. Greater imagination allows us to see that there are benefits to success and adversity, to the boom and the bust alike. Successful navigation of the world economy and its inevitable cycles requires calculated risk taking. Instead, our task is to learn to prepare for the inevitable storm and the interesting opportunities that spill out from the highs and the lows, and to benefit from their diverse treasures. This means we need to be better at reading signals, and debating them with the greatest robustness. The rest of this book is written to that end.

Sincerely,
Pippa Malmgren

The Algorithm Made Me Do It

"This is bullshit!" the motorcycle mechanic blurted out with frustration, as he glared at the coloured LED screen on the digital multimeter he was using to measure the width of an engine part that needed replacing. The screen kept flashing different numbers and would not settle on a precise measurement. In engine construction, precision matters. An imprecise measurement is dangerous because a misfitting part can cause the engine to jam, burn out, or blow up, possibly injuring someone in the process. In the old days, motorcycle mechanics used a mechanical caliper to measure the exact size of a part that needed replacing. Today, everything is computerised and mechanics have "upgraded" to LED instruments that measure the size of components. Except it turns out that sometimes the old-fashioned measure of reality can be more accurate. This is as true for motorcycle parts as it is for the world economy, as the cultural commentator Matthew Crawford points out in his book, *Shop Class as Soulcraft* (2009).

We now trust computers, numbers, algorithms and mathematical models more than we trust people, qualitative inputs and human judgement. We now put more faith in standardised tests that measure a child's progress in school rather than relying on the opinion of a potentially cranky teacher the child happens to be assigned to in the classroom. Many feel more confident knowing a computer is flying the plane than a pilot whose human error could threaten lives. Still, there are some who still trust the pilot and hope he can override the computer if he has to.

This is the essential debate in modern economics: Whether and when to override the system and on what basis. Should we do what mathematical models tell us or what commons sense tells us?

Crawford points out that the financial crisis hinged on such a "this is bullshit" moment – the moment someone realises that the mathematical model we are relying on is directing us to do something stupid that defies common sense. In an article called "Recipe for Disaster: The Formula That Killed Wall Street",[31] the financial journalist Felix Salmon explained how smart people are led to do stupid things by misplaced belief in an algorithm. In short, they become wedded to the elegance of the math at the expense of reality. Reality is messy. You can't quantify it and it does not neatly "fit".

The very moment that common sense and algorithms come into conflict warrants close attention. The mortgage lending officer at the bank has no freedom to override or adjust the computer-generated outcome, just as the owner of a BMW is no longer permitted to reach into the engine simply to measure the oil level. These days, the engine is often encased and locked. If you break into it, the manufacturer will not service your car any more. In a similar manner, the mathematical algorithms in the world economy cannot be easily overridden. At best, in 2006 the local mortgage broker would have reluctantly signed off on my mother's mortgage if he had had a chance to review her financial situation. But he was not there. Banks had fired most of the lending officers in the 2000's on the grounds that the algorithm could do the job better and faster.

The algorithm did not care as I explained to my mother, "If interest rates rise you won't be able to make the payments, and should the value of the house fall in the slightest, you will have negative equity – the house will be worth less than the mortgage." The lending officer would have agreed, which is exactly why he had to be fired. He stood in the way of "progress", defined as more transactions leading to a higher share price for the bank. In the world of finance, a similar signal echoed on trading floors of big banks when credit officers were increasingly not invited to attend the meetings where important investment decisions were being made. They asked too many questions. They had too many

---

31 See *Wired* magazine, 17 February 2009: "Recipe for Disaster: The Formula That Killed Wall Street" by Felix Salmon

objections. Instead they could be found in the corridors, grumbling about not being included in the decision-making process.

By removing bank lending officers and disinviting the credit officers from the meetings, banks showed they trusted algorithms more than people (which was an important signal at the time). It also showed that the volume and speed of transactions, which would have been slowed down by questions, had become the principal driver of a higher share price. I am now alert to a signal that often appears in a booming economy: if the volume of transactions drives the share price up more than the quality of transactions, something is wrong.

Perhaps there was a moment when the closing bell at the stock exchange should have been interpreted as an alarm bell; the moment that the quantity of transactions and deals supplanted quality. Banks, mortgage brokers and mortgage lenders can honestly say, "The algorithm made me do it!" Anyone who pays attention to deteriorating quality at the expense of a rising share price is bound to be batted away, removed from a position of power, or fired. In this sense, the algorithm indeed made them do it.

Bankers, fund managers and the denizens of Wall Street calculate the risk and the reward in their portfolios all day long. They also calculate the risk and reward with the algorithm that pays them. The Queen asked, "Why didn't anybody see it coming?" in 2007. The answer is, they did. The most popular topic of discussion that year was the imminent disaster in the credit markets. Most of my clients spent hours hypothesising about how the inevitable would play out and indeed how to profit from the coming debacle. So, why did they not sell? The algorithm is the simple answer. Being right early means selling when prices are still rising. To be right early means underperforming and therefore to risk losing clients and one's job. In the UK, this is called "the Tony Dye effect". Tony Dye was a British Fund manager who called the crisis correctly (much to everyone's derision, earning himself the nickname "Dr Doom") and sold a year early, which meant he underperformed the market and his peers. He was, therefore, fired. He was also vindicated when the market turned but it was too late to profit from his views by then.

If, in contrast, we know the stock market and asset values are going to fall apart, but we also know that we cannot be blamed or fired as long as we do not underperform our peers, then we may be content to think about sitting tight. If we lose 30% but everyone else does too, we get to keep our job. If we sell too early, we get fired.

The source of the "bullsh**" problem: algorithms and hubris

The economics profession suffers from its desire to jam all human activity into a mathematical model. There is a long history behind this tendency to believe that the entire truth lies in math, which is something the Hungarian-British writer Arthur Koestler called "The Cartesian Catastrophe". Yet the origin of the problem is clear, no better phrased than by the 18th-century physicist Sir Isaac Newton, who said, "I can calculate the motion of heavenly bodies, but not the madness of people." Notably, he said this after losing all his money in a financial market catastrophe: the South Sea Bubble of 1720.

No doubt it is hard to quantify mathematically the "madness of people" but there is grave danger in believing that anything that we cannot ascribe a number to simply does not count. It would certainly make life easier if we could just eliminate the risks we cannot quantify, including politics, policy and geopolitics, not to mention hubris, ego and incentive. These factors don't neatly fit into an algorithm. Markets would be much easier to manage if these risks could simply be removed from the landscape. And so it has become the norm to set aside, diminish or dismiss that which cannot be quantified. The Israeli-American psychologist Daniel Kahneman, who won the Nobel Prize in Economic Sciences in 2002, was named one of the world's top global thinkers by *Foreign Policy* magazine for his work on pushing back against this tendency to quantify, for restoring behaviour as a driver of economic outcomes in his book, *Thinking Slow, Thinking Fast* (2011). Nevertheless, I find that many in the world economy derive far greater comfort from data, algorithms and math than with non-quantifiable risks, in spite of the many warnings from Nobel Prize-winners.

The pretence of knowledge

When the Austrian-British economist and philosopher Friedrich Hayek took to the stage in December 1974 to deliver his Nobel lecture, "The Pretence of Knowledge", he went straight to this point: "Physical scientists can observe and measure the things that drive the systems they are studying." But:

> ... society, and therefore the economy, is not like a physical system: many of the most important factors cannot be seen or measured. Consider the thoughts and intended actions of millions of people at different times, for example. Economists and other social scientists, in their attempt to be scientific, ignore what they cannot measure. Therefore, many of the most important factors affecting the economy are not considered, while some of those factors which can be measured are deliberately controlled. The results are incorrect predictions and actions which positively harm society.

Hayek was specifically railing at policymakers about the dreadful state of the world economy in 1974, when everyone was being crushed simultaneously by high inflation and high unemployment. In short, he concluded that:

> ...the failure of the economists to guide policy more successfully is closely connected with their propensity to imitate as closely as possible the procedures of the brilliantly successful physical sciences – an attempt which in our field may lead to outright error. It is an approach which has come to be described as the 'scientistic' attitude – an attitude which, as I defined it some thirty years ago, is decidedly unscientific in the true sense of the word, since it involves a mechanical and uncritical application of habits of thought to fields different from those in which they have been formed. I want today to begin by explaining how some of the gravest errors of recent economic policy are a direct consequence of this scientistic error. It is as if one needed only to follow some cooking recipes to solve all social problems.

A recipe for disaster

Whatever recipe we've been following, it keeps resulting in a rather unpleasant dish. The public opinion analyst and social scientist Daniel Yankelovich, who founded the original *New York Times*/CBS poll, clearly explained why the essential ingredients were missing from the recipe:

> The first step is to measure what can be easily measured. This is okay as far as it goes. The second step is to disregard that which cannot be measured, or give it an arbitrary quantitative value. This is artificial and misleading. The third step is to presume that what cannot be measured really is not very important. This is blindness. The fourth step is to say that what cannot be measured does not really exist. This is suicide.[32]

Peter Drucker was more blunt: "The computer is a moron",[33] though a helpful moron. He came to this conclusion as, "All a computer can handle is abstractions, and abstractions can only be relied upon if they are constantly checked against concrete results. Otherwise they are certain to mislead."

Alan Greenspan echoed the sentiment:

> "Models do not fully capture what I believe has been, to date, only a peripheral addendum to business-cycle and financial modelling – the innate human responses that result in swings between euphoria and fear that repeat themselves generation after generation with little evidence of a learning curve."[34]

A little poetry

Beneath all the faith in models and math, there is also an element of convenience. After all, math and models can obfuscate the truth as much as they can reveal it. Economists can carry on talking

---

32 From *Corporate Priorities: A Continuing Study of the New Demands on Business* by Daniel Yankelovich (1972)

33 From *Technology, Management and Society* by Peter Drucker (1970)

34 See *The Financial Times*, 16 March 2008: "We will never have a perfect model of risk" by Alan Greenspan

amongst themselves without the general public being able to join in the conversation – and policymakers can hide behind the math and push out policies without being questioned too much.[35] John Lanchester writes in the New Yorker, "The language of money is a powerful tool, and it is also a tool of power. Incomprehension is a form of consent. If we allow ourselves not to understand this language, we are signing off on the way the world works today". Kenneth Boulding, an economist with poetry in his heart, captures this "obfuscation" inclination beautifully:

> If you do some acrobatics
> with a little mathematics
> it will take you far along.
> If your idea's not defensible
> don't make it comprehensible
> or folks will find you out,
> and your work will draw attention
> if you only fail to mention
> what the whole thing is about.

In economics and markets we "commit suicide", by Yankelovich's definition, every few years with, as Hayek says, catastrophic consequences for the general public. Financial and economic crises occur pretty regularly. In recent years, most have arrived as "surprises", including the Savings and Loan crisis, Long Term Capital Management crisis, the Asian financial crisis, Mexico's default and the financial crisis of 2007/8. They are often thought of as "Black Swans", which are, as Nassim Taleb explains in his book of the same name, inherently unpredictable. They come out of the blue. It's no use, he says, trying to think about the "unknown unknowns". Therefore, a Black Swan leaves everyone absolved of the responsibility to anticipate. The model, the math, the computer – all are especially absolved because the Black Swan is an Act of God.

---

35 See "Money Talks by John Lanchester, The *New Yorker*, August 4, 2014

This may not be entirely true, however. Perhaps a Black Swan serves as a comfortable fig leaf in catastrophic moments. What if we could see a signal that an event was likely to unfold? Recast in this light, it would not be a Black Swan, though it might be a "tail event". This means the event might occur on a normal statistical distribution, even though it might be rare. It is unlikely, but not unpredictable. We cannot "know" it will happen but in terms of probabilities, we know it might. We could incorporate the simple idea that the economist Hyman Minsky put forward: "Stability is destabilising" and look for signals that indicate changes are occurring all the time – good changes and bad changes alike. In this way we start to muse about ten impossible things before breakfast and prepare for what the future might bring. But this would mean considering signals that cannot be quantified, in effect challenging the dominance of the mathematical approach.

The two cultures

In 1959 Sir CP Snow, the chemist and novelist, stood at the podium at Cambridge University to deliver the 291st Rede Lecture, "The Two Cultures", on exactly this point. He caused an academic firestorm that rages to this day. He said that the humanities and the sciences had become so separated that neither camp had any ability to solve the real problems society faces. One spoke English and the other spoke math. Science/math people occupy one world and humanities/literary people occupy another, each ignorant of the value the other brings to the game.

> "A good many times I have been present at gatherings of people who, by the standards of the traditional culture, are thought highly educated and who have with considerable gusto been expressing their incredulity at the illiteracy of scientists. Once or twice I have been provoked and have asked the company how many of them could describe the Second Law of Thermodynamics. The response was cold: it was also negative. Yet I was asking something that is the scientific equivalent of, 'Have you read a work of Shakespeare's?'

I now believe that if I had asked an even simpler question — such as, 'What do you mean by mass, or acceleration', which is the scientific equivalent of saying, 'Can you read?' — not more than one in ten of the highly educated would have felt that I was speaking the same language. So the great edifice of modern physics goes up, and the majority of the cleverest people in the Western world have about as much insight into it as their neolithic ancestors would have had."[36]

It is not just that the numbers, the math, and the algorithms are hard for even educated people to comprehend, or that the non-quantifiable risks are hard to manage even for the brilliant. It is also true that policymakers like to get the outcome they want. This is a shocking notion, but it is also true that it is human nature to pick the model that is most likely to give you the result you want. My father was called in to see President Lyndon Baines Johnson in the early 1960s. President Johnson greeted him and engaged in the usual "Relax, I'm just a regular guy" niceties that all Presidents perfect to help people sufficiently overcome their awe to be able to tell them what they need to know. The President then leaned forward and asked my father for his analysis of some international trade figures. My father proudly declared, "The number is X", having spent days preparing for the meeting and being very sure that he was right. The President said, "Your numbers are wrong." Talk about a punch to the solar plexus. My father attempted to defend his data but the President interrupted him. "You're not hearing me. Your numbers are *wrong.*" The President then explained why he could not negotiate the international trade deal the US then needed unless that particular number was a little different. Why would politics demand that the numbers be skewed in a particular direction? Power. Politicians and policymakers want power. They want votes. They want the mathematics to show whatever will favour them in an election. If they want a different answer they just change the assumptions or the parameters of the algorithm.

---

36 From *The Two Cultures* by Sir CP Snow (1959)

If mathematical genius comes not from solving equations but from knowing which equations to solve, then policy genius comes not from manipulation of the data but from knowing which data it is useful to manipulate. Much time is spent in the policy world ensuring the models and the math churn out the answer that policymakers want. They may not always win at this game, but the trying is formidable.

What does all this mean? It means that the conversation about the condition of the world economy involves people with varying agendas throwing a lot of math – often skewed math that is opaque and inaccessible – at a confused public, while ignoring the things that cannot be easily quantified. The public has common sense but cannot easily discern whether the math is right or wrong. Instead the public shakes its head with a feeling that things don't make sense. The public could read *The Financial Times* or *The Wall Street Journal* but the terminology and concepts are presented in a way that is often hard to grasp. "Surely there is someone in a wood-panelled office somewhere in the capital who is smarter than me who is sorting this all out," we hope and believe, not realising that thinking this way means devolving responsibility for our own future to the state.

The ghost of Eric Fromm smiles and nods in recognition of this human inclination to trust that someone else can take control and sort things out. Sir CP Snow warned us about this in 1960 when he wrote, "One of the most bizarre features of our time, is that the cardinal choices have to be made ... by a handful of men who cannot have a first-hand knowledge of what those choices depend upon or what their results may be."[37]

So, to be clear: there is a need to understand the motivations of those who are sending the most important signals in the world economy – policymakers. There is a need to understand our own bias.

And now we stumble upon a philosophical canyon that divides the world of economics as deeply as views on religion divide others.

---

37 Sir CP Snow, "Science and Government", The Godkin Lecture at Harvard University, 1960 (Harvard University Press)

Freshwater and saltwater

Whatever we think about the numbers, whether we believe the numbers are "true" or they reflect the parameters that have been chosen to arrive at the wanted answer, what really matters when it comes to assessing signals in the world economy is whether we are "freshwater" or "saltwater". The journalist and author Peter Kilborn elegantly captured the simple question that hangs over all economics in a *New York Times* editorial, "To tinker or not to tinker?"[38] Should the state intervene in the economy or should the state get out of its way?

There are those who believe that tinkering by policymakers and governments causes markets to become off-balance, veer into crises and then prolong the crises. For others, insufficient or incorrect tinkering by government is what causes and prolongs economic crises.

The first camp, those who blame governments for being the cause of economic problems, are sometimes called "freshwater" because the proponents of this view have tended to come from institutions near the Great Lakes in the American Midwest, such as the University of Chicago. "Freshwater economists are," as American economist Paul Krugman explains, "essentially, neoclassical purists. They believe that all worthwhile economic analysis starts from the premise that people are rational and markets work."[39]

The second camp, those who blame governments for failing to properly contain the excesses of markets, are called "saltwater" because their proponents tend to come from institutions that are near the Atlantic Ocean, such as Harvard and Princeton. Krugman writes:

> Where the freshwater economists were purists, saltwater economists were pragmatists ... They were willing to deviate from the assumption of perfect markets or perfect rationality,

---

38 See *The New York Times*, 23 July 1988: "Fresh Water Economists Gain" by Peter Kilborn

39 See *The New York Times*, 2 September 2009: "How Did Economists Get It So Wrong?" by Paul Krugman

or both, adding enough imperfections to accommodate a more or less Keynesian view of recessions. And in the saltwater view, active policy to fight recessions remained desirable.[40]

It matters which camp you are in because this will define how you will respond to economic signals. Ronald Reagan demonstrated that he was definitively freshwater when he said, "Government is not the solution, it is the problem." So, all his solutions for a weak economy involved lessening the role of government and diminishing its size so as to disempower bureaucrats and empower the markets.

If you believe that the only people who can fix the economy are real people engaged in calculated risk taking, balancing hubris and nemesis as they strive to pursue a dream that creates GDP and employs people, then you are freshwater. If, in contrast, you believe that you could fix the economy by gathering a bunch of really smart people in the nation's capital and empowering them to use the power of the state, then you are saltwater.

A freshwater thinker's version of Hell is putting a lot of smart people in the nation's capital and empowering them with the public's trust and the public's money. A saltwater thinker's version of Hell is giving power to real people in the real economy because you can't trust markets and you can't trust people to figure out how to identify or protect their own best interests.

Put another way, President Bill Clinton was a freshwater Democrat. He supported business and risk taking by individuals and felt the state should be made smaller. President Barack Obama is more of a saltwater Democrat. He wants to tax businesses and risk taking and put more power into the hands of an enlarging state. President GW Bush is a freshwater Republican at heart but got corralled into saltwater intervention by events that threatened to weaken the economy. Ronald Reagan was a freshwater Republican who tried to reduce the size and scope of the government's reach, though even he believed that state

40 *The New York Times*, 2 September 2009: "How Did Economists Get It So Wrong?" by Paul Krugman

73

expenditure on nuclear weapons would bankrupt the Soviet Union, which is a rather saltwater approach. The divide that faces the world is no longer between the left and the right or between the followers of those two titans of economics, JM Keynes and Milton Friedman[41]. The divide is between the state and the citizen and between those who favour strengthening of the one versus the other. Each of us must decide for ourselves where we stand. The choices we make will define the economy we have in the future.

An old argument

The argument is very old, but, as the political and cultural commentator David Brooks once explained in his piece "Bentham vs. Hume",[42] the character of the two sides is unchanging over time. The British philosopher and reformer Jeremy Bentham (1748-1832) believed in a plan for everything. Plans, he thought, could be measured by the greatest happiness for the greatest number. The Scottish philosopher and economist David Hume (1711-1776), felt quite the opposite. He believed the markets and individuals within it were best placed to sort things out. Brooks writes, "Mr Hume's side believe government should actively tilt the playing field to promote social goods and set off decentralised networks of reform, but they don't think government knows enough to intimately organise dynamic innovation."

People like Jeremy Bentham want smart guys, "the best and the brightest", to be locked in a (wood panelled) room, where they can create a plan that will work because they are more brilliant than anybody else. People like Hume have no idea how to fix the economic mess, know that no "plan" will work, and conclude that you have to trust the market to sort out a solution because the efforts of the many pursing their self interest will always produce better results than "bright" people locked in a room.

---

41 JM Keynes (1883-1946); Milton Friedman (1912-2006)
42 See *The New York Times*, 5 October 2009: "Bentham vs Hume" by David Brooks

This was the debate that raged between JM Keynes and Friederich Hayek and later Milton Friedman. It continues today when central bankers say, "We will do whatever it takes" to prevent large institutions from failing, and the Vice Chairman of the Federal Deposit Insurance Corporation, Tom Hoenig, says we should not protect those who have failed. It happens when we hear the Left and the Right argue about whether the solution is bigger government or smaller government, more benefits or fewer benefits, more regulation or less regulation, higher taxation or lower taxation.

Regardless of whether you are freshwater or saltwater or whether you believe that the algorithms are right or wrong, it is important to know that both camps invoke algorithms and math as proof that they are right. It is nigh impossible for members of the general public to quibble with sophisticated models that neither side make readily available to the general public. There is, of course, a cottage industry among those whose skill at mathematics is superb. They lob criticism and insight about the models that drive policymakers back and forth. But this is all well over the head of the average person who simply wants to know what is the right thing to do.

The answer lies in something that I will shortly explore in depth: the social contract. This refers to the "deal" that exists between the citizens and the state. Citizens and their states will decide where the line ought to be drawn between the state versus the market. That line is bound to be in a different place in France than it is in China or the US. There is no "right" or most efficient answer. It all depends on the views of the citizens and their leaders. That is where human qualities begin to influence the outcome.

Goalkeeper science

All policymakers, freshwater and saltwater alike, want to intervene in the economy when pain, volatility and uncertainty begin. The Canadian science and technology writer Clive Thompson wrote an insightful article for *The New York Times* in 2008 that explains why. He reviewed a 2005 academic study called "Action Bias Among Elite Soccer Goalkeepers: The Case of Penalty Kicks" by academics at the Ben-Gurion University of the Negev and The Hebrew University of Jerusalem. Thompson reported, "The academics analysed 286 penalty kicks and found that 94% of the time the goalies dived to the right or the left — even though the chances of stopping the ball were highest when the goalie stayed in the centre."[43]

"If that's true," the academics asked themselves, "why do goalies almost always dive off to one side?" "Because," answers Thompson, "the academics theorised, the goalies are afraid of looking as if they're doing nothing — and then missing the ball. Diving to one side, even if it decreases the chance of them catching the ball, makes them appear decisive." One of the authors of the study, Michael Bar-Eli, explained, "They want to show that they're doing something... Otherwise they look helpless, like they don't know what to do."

Much policymaking is driven by the need to jump in order to avoid the appearance that the policymakers do not know what they are doing. This is also the easiest thing to do when we are tired or don't know what to do: we appear to do something. Policymakers are often tired and without a quick answer. I know. I used to be one.

How the algorithm made me do it

As one of six people serving on the National Economic Council as a Special Assistant to the President of the United States, I have had first-hand experience of being one of the so-called "best and the brightest" locked up in a wood-panelled room trying to solve an "impossible" economic problem. During my time in office, America experienced seven of the nine largest bankruptcies in American history, including Enron, Tyco, and Worldcom. This was just two years after the Dot.com bubble had burst, leaving the national, indeed the world, economy reeling. After 9/11 we had a very specific problem. Two thirds of the global trading capability in US Government bonds had been destroyed. The New York

---

43 See *The New York Times*, 12 December 2008: "Goalkeeper Science" by Clive Thompson

Stock Exchange shut down after the first plane hit the World Trade Centre because the power station supplying all of lower Manhattan was underneath the building. Initially it was on fire. Afterwards, the fire department flooded it. Obviously fire and water are not good for the electricity supply. The biggest practical problem to solve was how to restore the electricity supply to the Stock Exchange so that data could be forwarded to another location where the markets could be opened again.

Far from being a "policy" issue, the problems were entirely practical. Where could a power generator be found? How could it be transported up the main highway, I-95, and across the river into lower Manhattan? How could the few critical New York Stock Exchange personnel travel down to the site so they could flip the switch to forward the data so the stock market could reopen? This last point proved especially difficult. When I was put through on the phone to police officers on the 14th Street barrier, I tried to give them the names of the NYSE staff who should be issued Bio-Suits and permitted to walk down to the World Trade Centre. The officer I was speaking to clearly thought it was a prank call. "Sure you're calling from the White House, lady." Click. They had hung up. I had to get Governor Pataki on the line because at least they recognised his voice and his authority and would not hang up on him. It is sometimes said that policymaking, especially when it involves close proximity to the head of government, is like "drinking from a fire hydrant". In my experience, this is true. Problems are not always philosophical; they are often practical. But the algorithm is clear: problems that rise to the level of the White House or its counterparts around the world must be resolved and resolved in a timely way.

The simple fact is that the only issues that arrive in the White House are the ones that are too difficult, complex, or important to be successfully tackled elsewhere in government. By definition, such issues and the subsequent decisions that need to be made involve sacrificing the interests of one part of the community in order to benefit the interests of another.

Usually decisions have to be made without sufficient time or information to make the decision comfortably. They have to be made, often at great speed, because history, the public and the press corps all require an answer to the question at hand. This situation is a permanent state of affairs. My father experienced it working for four Presidents and I experienced it working for two. Perhaps the best preparation manual for a job at this level of government remains *Thinking in Time: The Uses of History for Decision Makers* (1986) by Richard E Neustadt and Ernest R May, which grew out of a lifetime of work writing and consulting on this subject since the 1950s and for the coursework they set at Harvard's John F. Kennedy School of Government. The best primer on the practical matters of managing the best and the brightest is still the unpublished paper that virtually every President has consulted, called "Some Thoughts for Newly Assigned Senior Political Appointees on the Management of Bureaucracy"[44] written by Richard McCormack, a long-time Presidential Advisor. He explains how we have to take human factors into consideration, like the fact that the staff are not getting enough sleep at any given time – especially in emergencies. Pilots would never be allowed to fly a plane on so little sleep, but we are content to let White House staff navigate the nation's future in this condition.

The algorithm for a politician is simple: you must win to have power. They need policies that are popular and potent in order to win. Usually this means responding to events rather than pursuing an agenda of their own choice. So, the political algorithm demands that policymakers jump to the left or jump to the right. It demands that they are seen to be doing something. It demands that they announce something to the press corps, which waits just outside the door.

Ward Three morality

We cannot quantify the human factor, but we can understand that it exists. If we continue looking at the US, though this applies to every government, the drivers for all those who set or advise on policy are easily discernable.

---

44 20 June 1970, updated 20 January 1992

In an article for *The New York Times*,[45] David Brooks describes the "morality" of the people who live in Ward Three of Washington DC and why it plays an important role in the making of public policy in America. It happens that I grew up in Ward Three, which is the northwest quadrant of Washington DC and centres on Chevy Chase. I speak with the confidence of a local when I say his article, "Ward Three Morality", rings true. The residents there are, by day, senior officials who run agencies, command the military, run the intelligence agencies and can move the markets with their words and by the flourish of a pen. By weekend, they are the neighbours I grew up with: the Deputy Head of the CIA, the Senator, the Head of various Congressional Committees and the like. These people always looked pale and exhausted from their labours, yet had no alternative but to mow the lawn themselves as they lacked the income to pay someone else to do it.

I remember one Senator who always looked perplexed when he could not get the pullstring starter on the lawnmower to work on a Saturday morning. The cash flow problem is especially severe for this powerful group, who arrived in the neighbourhood due to their extensive education or exceptional brilliance. They inevitably have ambitions for the education of their children. Unfortunately, private school fees are extremely expensive in Ward Three, as are house prices, as are the people who can be paid to mow the lawn. As a result, the residents suffer from what Brooks calls "Status-Income Disequilibrium" and "Sublimated Liquidity Rage".

The algorithm, the mathematical calculation that can be applied to them, is clear: work for free now to get paid a lot later. This formula holds true even among the countries that have a permanent civil service. Brussels, Washington, London, Tokyo, New Delhi and Beijing have a thriving community of ex-officials who are paid a good deal to explain policy and influence policymakers.

Who will be chosen for the lucrative post-office jobs? The most influential are chosen first. The second consideration boils

---

45 See *The New York Times*, 2 February 2009: "Ward Three Morality" by David Brooks

down to simpatico. Is the person left or right, saltwater or freshwater? The philosophy and principles we hold define who our employer will be. It's not very likely that a policymaker who opposes bank bailouts will end up employed by Citigroup. It is very likely that a policymaker who forcefully pursued the bank bailout will be rewarded with a significant contract, even if not visible to the public, and possibly a serious role.

As members of staff, we make risk-reward calculations as well. After all, as a member of staff, part of our job is to take a bullet for the President or the institution we serve, should that become necessary. A Secret Service officer might have to jump in front of a real bullet but, as a staffer, we are supposed to jump in front of a political bullet when events might damage the President or the Presidency. Such bullets can cut our career short or even dead.

For me the bullet whistled close by when Enron hit the headlines. This large energy company went bust on the back of fraud. At the time, Senator Lieberman was a leading potential Presidential candidate. He issued the White House with a subpoena with the simple request for a record of any and all contacts between White House staff and Enron. I thought I had none, but it turned out that one of my former contacts in the financial markets had become the Head of Enron in Japan. We met for a single drink (I paid for my own) to discuss the abysmal state of the Japanese economy. I sent in the record of the meeting and asked White House Counsel to inquire whether Senator Lieberman thought he felt that the problem was that we in the White House had done too much to help Enron or not enough to help Enron. The answer came back: "Yes". In other words, whichever outcome would prove more useful for Senator Lieberman would be the correct answer. This is how politics works. Senator Lieberman was right to pursue the subject and to leave his options as open as possible. I was right to accept that my job was to tell the truth, regardless of personal consequences. I might have to take a bullet for the President and be carried away on a stretcher. Luckily, that did not happen. But such events make us realise that the longer a person stays in these roles the more likely they are to be hit by a bullet.

The "revolving door" in Washington DC and other capitals serves a good purpose. It permits talent and experience from the real world to influence policymaking in a positive way. But, it would be naïve to think that people do this work purely for charitable purposes, especially when the bullets start flying the moment that Congress begins investigating one's background. It is sometimes said that even Jesus Christ could not successfully pass through the Senate confirmation process. We would do well to consider the unintended consequences of a confirmation process that excludes many good people. As the Pulitzer Prize-winning columnist Charles Krauthammer memorably wrote in his column for *The Washington Post*:

> If we insist that public life be reserved for those whose personal history is pristine, we are not going to get paragons of virtue running our affairs. We will get the very rich, who contract out the messy things in life, the very dull, who have nothing to hide and nothing to show, and the very devious, expert at covering their tracks and ambitious enough to risk their discovery.[46]

JRR Tolkien vs JM Keynes

Another calculation takes place whenever anyone walks through the doorway of the Oval Office or its equivalents around the world. It has to do with the overwhelming flush of ego that inevitably takes place when people find themselves in close proximity to power. It was not Lord Keynes who came to my aid in the West Wing, or even the great American economist Milton Friedman. It was JRR Tolkien. It may seem like a strange aside, but my mother studied Middle English (medieval English) at Oxford with Tolkien, who wrote *Lord of the Rings* and *The Hobbit* among many other works of fiction. If you recall from my introduction, this was in large part facilitated by a favourable exchange rate at the time between the US and the UK. My mother spent hours with

---

46 See *The Washington Post*, 29 December 1989: Weekly column by Charles Krauthammer

Tolkien and his friend, CS Lewis, author of *The Chronicles of Narnia* and other novels. They loved discussing the imaginary other worlds that initially might seem distant from our own worldly experience, but the things that drive the behaviour of their characters is very human. It is the same in the *Harry Potter* novels. The quest for power is always at the heart of these fantasy stories. Lord Voldemort says, "There is no good or evil, only power and those who are too weak to seek it."

I took a CEO in to see the President one day. On the way he ranted and raved about how all the President's people and policies were wrong. I said, "Great! Tell him. He needs to know what you think." I then watched in shock as his demeanour changed the moment we crossed the threshold into the President's office. I suddenly realised why the Oval Office is round. How many rooms are round or oval? Very few. The unusual shape is a means of conveying the power of this place. It is a ring. And, like the ring in Tolkien's stories, few people can be in the presence of the ring without becoming overwhelmed by the desire to wield its power. This man morphed from a CEO into Gollum, the character transformed from a nice little Hobbit into an ugly evil creature in Tolkien's books. Gollum becomes an obsequious liar in his hope to do whatever is necessary to remain close to power. Gollum is famous for making a dreadful noise with his throat. That's because he holds his tongue and does not speak the truth, just like the CEO. He clearly had visions of being invited onto Air Force One. He suddenly realised he might become the US Ambassador to his favourite country. As such, he wanted to say whatever the President wanted to hear.

M&Ms and tchotchkes

After this alarming episode, I started to take closer note of my colleagues and asked my father and others about their experiences. Who had their eye on the toys, such as Air Force One, Marine One, Camp David, Presidential trips, titles, assignments, or time in the Oval Office? Sometimes the prizes were much smaller but carried very high value, such as the cheap cufflinks with the White House seal that inevitably break when the slightest strain is applied to them or the cute boxes of M&M candies embossed with the Presidential seal that people keep for years after their use-by date. Who would say or do anything to gain access to these toys, these tchotchkes and knick-knacks? The answer is: a lot of people (myself included, which I write eyeing the M&Ms with the Presidential seal which I am too terrified to open now because they are 13 years old). Would people in policy and politics steal ideas from their colleagues in order to increase the chances of being seen to be indispensable to the President? Of course!

They say in politics, your worst opponents are on your own team. The main driver is this simple fact: people want access to power, they like to wield power and they will "kill" anyone who gets in their way as sure as Gollum would kill his best friend and anyone else to secure possession of "My precious" – the ring. This is one reason why the greatest challenge heads of government face is surrounding themselves with those who will tell them the truth.

Once in possession of such power, it is hard for a normal human being to believe that he or she might not be doing the right thing with it. Look at Robert McNamara, the former Head of Ford Motors, who was brought into the US Government as Secretary of Defence from 1961-1968. JFK's express purpose in bringing McNamara in, and others who he called "the best and the brightest", was to capture the mathematical, computer-based analytics that had permitted Ford to turn itself from a company on the brink of bankruptcy to the most successful firm in America. Kennedy hoped that the mastery of algorithms would permit more efficient government. Towards the end of his life, McNamara wrote a heart-wrenching memoir, *In Retrospect* (1995), in which he describes how the infatuation with numbers and models overwhelmed his ability to see or tell the truth about the real situation during the war in Vietnam. In the end, the models did not lead to a more efficient conduct of war but a less efficient, less truthful one. But, his self-belief prevented him from acknowledging this until his later years. His self-belief precluded self-doubt.

The US Congressman Huey Long used to say that every Senator is a person who thinks they should have been President only for some slight accident of history. Every Congressman believes they will be President and it is only a question of time before this happens, barring any accidents. And, to add my own observation, every President has one great fear that drives him – that he will become an accident of history before or after leaving office.

There is a name for this syndrome: Potomac Fever. The Potomac is the river that cuts through Washington DC and which historically carried waterborne diseases that cause the brain to swell. Does Potomac Fever play a part in the making of public policy? I dare anyone in these circles to honestly argue that it doesn't. But how do you add Potomac fever to the mathematical model?

The algorithm made me write it

The media also calculate. Their algorithm is clear: cash flow is driven by stories, especially stories that sell. In order to get stories that sell they need to have sources. In the political arena, there are only two kinds of people in politics as far as the media are concerned: sources and targets. Failure to divulge stories makes you a target. In general, targets get bad press and sources get good press.

Policymakers and politicians know that they have the power to deny access to the media. So, those who write stories that policymakers don't like find that they cannot get a meeting. Their names are dropped from the inner circle. They may get to the press conference but they don't get invited to the drinks party where all the real conversations happen. For those in the inner circle it is perfectly obvious who is in the inner circle and who is a mouthpiece for that circle. For the general public, it is sometimes nigh on impossible to distinguish between objective reporting and such posturing.

When you think about it, the purpose of the news is not to educate the public. The purpose is to generate revenue and income. This is why all print media increasingly use algorithms to write the news stories themselves. *Wired* magazine reminds us, "Every 30 seconds or so, the algorithmic bull pen of Narrative Science, a 30-person company occupying a large room on the fringes of the Chicago Loop, extrudes a story whose very byline is

84

a question of philosophical inquiry."[47] Some three minutes after an earthquake occurred in California on the 17th of March 2014, the first article the *Los Angeles Times* published on the story was generated by a robot. The *LA Times* writer Ken Schwencke had programmed the algorithm. All he had to do was hit the "publish" button, according to *The Huffington Post*, which reacted to this event in an article called, "It's All Over: Robots Are Now Writing News Stories, And Doing A Good Job".[48]

Algorithms are cheaper. Whether and how the objectives of revenue generation, content quality and public education can all be served simultaneously by the media is a constant topic of discussion among those in the media themselves.

The algorithm makes the Fed do it

In conclusion, consider the situation we face today. The financial crisis of 2007/8 threatened to bankrupt the entire global banking system. The problem was not that one large bank was bust, but that virtually every large bank was bust simultaneously. Central banks in the large industrialised countries were compelled to step in because that is the role of a central bank – to be the lender of last resort. Their job is to restore order when markets become disorderly. But, they were further compelled to act because most countries were so deeply indebted that fiscal policy was simply not available as a policy tool. Monetary policy had to bear a greater burden than usual. This led to the historic experiment in which major central banks have resorted to unconventional measures such as Quantitative Easing to push interest rates down and asset prices up. Today the Federal Reserve has emerged as the market maker rather than just a lender of last resort. The Federal Reserve and many other central banks in large economies are doing whatever is necessary to create inflation. As part of the effort, at some point central banks stopped targeting inflation and instead

---

47 See *Wired*, April 2012: "Can an Algorithm Write a Better News Story Than a Human Reporter?" by Steven Levy

48 See *The Huffington Post*, 18 March 2014: "It's All Over: Robots Are Now Writing News Stories, And Doing A Good Job" by Catherine Taibi

began treating it as a tool. They stopped merely providing liquidity and instead started judging success by the level of certain asset prices, like the stock market and property prices.

The Federal Reserve staff have a range of views on these subjects, but it is not uncommon to hear them use the term "The model says…" or "That's not what the model says". Several times I have heard central bankers including Jean-Claude Trichet and Ben Bernanke explain that the reason they did not know exactly what to do when the crisis happened was that they did not have any models to explain it. Some central bankers and their staff will even go so far as to insist that the current situation is not unprecedented or exceptional because this permits them to continue using old models that they are most comfortable with. Others insist that there will be no difficulties whatsoever in exiting from this historic experiment. All the staff deny that they have profoundly altered the balance of power between the state and the market. All will vehemently deny that central bank independence has been jeopardised, even though central banks are now the largest buyers of the sovereign debt of their own nations. They will also deny that their actions will create inflation or that there is any risk of inflation that cannot be controlled, when history suggests that playing with fire results in… fire.

Econometricians: On tap or on top?

This reminds me of the conversation had by US Ambassador Richard McCormack with William McChesney Martin, who chaired the Fed from April 1951 to January 1970. It happened on the 31st of January 1970, which was Martin's last day in office after serving as Chairman under five Presidents: Truman, Eisenhower, Kennedy, Johnson and Nixon. McCormack recalls sitting with the Chairman in his office near the end of Martin's term:[49]

> When I asked him what kind of person we should recruit to head up the new office, he responded: "If you want

---

49 From *A Conversation with Ambassador Richard T McCormack* by Henry E. Mattox (www.xlibris.com, 2013)

this new office to be relevant, do not appoint an academic economist, and particularly avoid econometricians." Instead, he recommended that we recruit someone who "had broad personal reach in the American and global economy, who understood how markets operated, and who was able through a network of personal contacts to anticipate developments before they were finally reported in the official statistics."

He went on to say: "We have fifty econometricians working for us at the Fed. They are all located in the basement of this building, and there is a reason why they are there. Their main value to me is to pose questions that I then pass on to my own network of contacts throughout the American economy. The danger with these econometricians is that they don't know their own limitations, and they have a far greater sense of confidence in their analyses than I have found to be warranted. Such people are not dangerous to me because I understand their limitations. They are, however, dangerous to people like you and the politicians because you don't know their limitations, and you are impressed and confused by the elaborate models and mathematics. The flaws in these analyses are almost always imbedded in the assumptions upon which they are based. And that is where broader wisdom is required, a wisdom that these mathematicians generally do not have. You always want such technical experts on tap in positions like this, but never on top."

It happens that I met with Ben Bernanke on the day he was confirmed by Congress in his role as Chairman. We laughed about the fact that whatever he had just been through that day testifying before Congress, it wasn't economics, at least not the economics that we learned at school. I said, "No Sir, it is political theatre. That's your new job." Central banking is not a purely technical mathematical exercise where one can rely on algorithms or models to answer the many profound questions that a central bank now has to face.

There is a human element to the calculation as well. Having grabbed the steering wheel from a reckless financial market, central bankers are understandably reluctant to relinquish control over prices back to the markets. There is a distinct air of disdain and a palpable disregard for "the market" now. No doubt someone sober needed to grab the steering wheel. But it is possible that policymakers have become punch-drunk themselves with the feeling of control. Failing to cede control back to the market empowers the policymakers. It is quite something to have the entire world economy hang on your words. It is a signal when experienced market professionals such as Stanley Druckenmiller, who ran the Quantum Fund with George Soros for many decades, say, "I can't work in a market where I don't know what Ben Bernanke had for breakfast this morning." But that world permits the Federal Reserve and the regulators and the White House to expand their powers and their reach into the economy. It adds additional weight to every utterance. One can understand the seduction of such power.

The question that stands before us now is this: Who should be driving prices in the market? The Chairman of the Federal Reserve, as advised by the econometricians in the basement, or the market mechanism that simultaneously reconciles the rapidly changing and often conflicting views of all the large and small actors in the world economy? No doubt the markets make mistakes, but policymakers can make mistakes too. It will be a shocking and tragic irony if, in the end, the Federal Reserve makes the exact same error that the financial markets made; if they trust models and are driven by algorithms that turn out to be wrong.

Perhaps the Federal Reserve's models are very good multimeters. But, it can't hurt to consider some common-sense signals as well. Perhaps it makes sense to look for signals that algorithms cannot cope with?

In the end, as La Rochefoucauld wrote, "everything is reducible to the motivation of self interest".[50] That is the algorithm that makes everybody do it.

---

50 From his *Maxims* (1665)

The Social Contract

5
CHAPTER

Why did Lady Godiva ride naked through Coventry? Why did William Tell risk his son's life by shooting an apple off his head from a great distance? Why did Gandhi stand in protest with the salt makers of India, revealing to the world his idea of *Satyagraha* (non-violent protest), which later inspired leaders from Martin Luther King to Nelson Mandela? Why did the citizens of Boston throw their tea into the harbour and thereby help launch the American independence movement? The answer is the same: anger at excessive taxation and the absence of representation. In each case, these people realised that the pain of taxation had become so great, and their voice against it so weak, that it warranted challenging the authorities, even if their freedom or even their lives would be lost.

In the 11th century, Lady Godiva feared for her community when her husband Leofric, Earl of Mercia, then the local ruler, raised onerous taxes on the citizens of Coventry and Worcester. She offered to ride naked through Coventry if he would relent. He accepted but ordered that no one should look at her. Curtains were drawn, windows closed, save for one poor fellow who was caught "peeping" named Tom. Similarly, William Tell, a sharp marksman with a crossbow, objected to the onerous tax imposed by the Hapsburg king, who had invaded what we now call Switzerland. Gessler, the king's representative and tax collector, was outraged by Tell's protests and threatened to imprison him unless he could shoot an apple off the head of his own son, Walter. William Tell shot the apple in two and avoided killing his son. Gessler went ahead and imprisoned him anyway. Tell escaped, came back and assassinated Gessler, thereby helping spur the revolution that led to the overthrow of the Hapsburgs and the creation of an independent Swiss Confederation. Gandhi was also outraged by onerous taxes in India, particularly the British tax on a basic staple: salt. In response to the salt tax, he organised the earliest non-violent protest that ultimately led to the expulsion of the British from India. As for the United States, the Boston Tea Party remains an iconic symbol of the independence movement, which was also a protest against excessive taxation without representation by the British.

Where is the line?

Taxation is inevitable. It pays for the things that serve the collective interest. Over-taxation can call people to arms, however. The line between the two, between taxation and over-taxation, is embedded in what we can call a social contract between citizens and the state. It's a flexible line, and its location changes with time but, in the main, there is usually a reasonably well understood agreement between citizens and their state as to where the line is drawn or at least where it ought to be.

Throughout history, we have paid taxes in exchange for a promise. Sometimes the promise is simply this: pay your tax and you will be allowed to live. The ancient Greeks, Romans, Persians, some feudal kings, modern dictators and organised crime syndicates have taken this approach at times. Democracies and modern forms of government tend to promise that you will be given something valuable in exchange for your tax payment, something beyond your life – a military, a police force, a public school system, a road network, a healthcare system of some kind, a commitment to rely on the ballot box rather than to permit the military to engage in coups, retirement benefits at a certain age, a welfare system for the truly poor, and a promise to maintain an acceptable balance between the interests of the majority and those of the minority, among many possible examples. But, when governments ask for too much of the citizen's hard earned cash, and don't deliver on their promises, protests arise. There are always signals that such events are unfolding.

The current state of the world economy is causing social contracts around the world to break. All around the globe, nations have spent more than they have earned and are turning to higher taxation, spending cuts and breaking promises to save themselves. This means citizens are having to pay more taxes and receive fewer benefits at a time of economic weakness. Naturally, protests have begun. Protests are a signal.

People protest in different ways, as the great 20th-century economist Albert O Hirschman described in his seminal work, *Exit, Voice, Loyalty: Responses to Decline in Firms, Organisations, and States* (1970). Whenever people become dissatisfied with their state they can exit or they can voice their concerns. All are important signals.

Some choose to remove themselves from the state's reach and become independent from their government. For example, there are the folks who buy a large farm upstream from anybody else, fill it with several years' supply of tinned food and load up with ammo and weapons. This might work for a while, but in the end, as Mad Max discovered, even in a lawless, stateless place, you will always pay tax to someone. If it isn't the government it will be organised crime or the mob that will "redistribute" the wealth from the rich to the poor by simply invading your home and taking what they want or by asking for protection money to prevent them from doing so.

Exit strategies

Then there are those who try to remove themselves from the clutches of the state by committing suicide. On the 4th of April 2012 Dimitris Christoulas, a retired pharmacist, protested against the ever-deteriorating situation in Greece by taking his life in Syntagma Square in front of Parliament. Hundreds of other Greeks, Italians, Portuguese and other citizens of indebted countries, including some of the workers who make Apple iPhones in China, have also chosen suicide in recent years as a means of protesting their ever more difficult economic situation. As we shall see, a young Tunisian, Mohamed Bouazizi, sparked the Arab Spring, by choosing suicide as his exit.

Moving abroad or becoming a tax exile is an option some have pursued as a means of escaping the hand of government. Many thousands of people have left Ireland, France, Spain, Greece, Portugal and every other indebted country in the hope of building a new life elsewhere in the world. The wealthy have tried to take advantage of their ability to move their assets abroad. Even in the US, we see people protesting the breakdown of the social contract in California by leaving for other lower tax/higher benefit states such as Texas and Colorado. When California retrospectively raised personal income tax rates to 13.5%, many decided to move themselves or their businesses to other less voracious locations where the state still has the capacity to deliver paved roads and other public services.

Sometimes whole communities start to push for independence from their state, such as Catalonia, Andalucía, Scotland, the Russian population of Ukraine. Even some states in America now see separatist petitions filed by members of the public. My own home state, Maryland, consists of two large territories connected by a very thin bridge of land that barely holds the two sides together on the map. Now that money is in short supply, it is easy to see why East Maryland and West Maryland no longer want the other side to share in spending. So, there is a "Western Maryland Initiative" led by a guy called Scott Strzelczyk, which seeks to allow the West to secede from the East.

All these options involve great personal sacrifices, however. Breaking away from a state always comes at a price. The toughest form of secession is suicide. It is the highest price a person can pay for freedom. Tax exile and immigration have costs too because both mean losing access to one's home. Separatist movements result in the loss of institutions and the history that provides cohesion. Given the costs of departure, it would be so much easier if the state to which allegiances have been pledged would just follow through on the promises that it made – that we receive the retirement and healthcare benefits the government has promised, the social security system payments, that the rubbish will be picked up regularly and that the mail will continue to be delivered six days a week. It would be nice to believe that the social contract is sound, but there are signals everywhere that it has broken. They are simple signals like the announcement that the US Postal Service might only deliver mail only five days a week, or that the British National Health System may start charging for certain procedures or that the state is raising taxes to the point that it becomes more sensible to leave the country than to stay.

The social contract is not necessarily written, but it is understood. It is a fabric woven from the threads of history, formed from the various arguments between the freshwater camp and their saltwater opponents over time, hammered out in the courts or through conflict in the streets, preserved in the institutions including the executive, the legislature, and the military. The burden of debt stresses the social fabric by forcing people to reconsider, if not entirely redraw, the line between the state and the market, between those who pay and those who benefit, between spending and taxation.

Taxation and spending

Ultimately, the world economy exists between two powerful forces: the power of the state to tax and redistribute wealth and GDP and the power of the entrepreneur (or a group of them, which we call a company) to generate wealth and GDP. One might consider the financial crisis as an event that illuminated the fact that governments had over-promised and would be forced to under-deliver on their promises going forward. This was the opening salvo in a new conflict between those who generate wealth and those who want to seize and redistribute it.

The social contract seems strong when there is enough growth, cash and wealth creation opportunities to meet everyone's needs. Prosperity glosses over the growing imbalances between promises and the means of fulfilling such promises. The usual business of governance always requires trade-offs. Louis Brandeis, the American Supreme Court Justice from 1916 to 1939, pointed out that all legislation fundamentally involves the "weighing of public needs as against private desires; and likewise a weighing of relative social values". Prosperity diminished the need to choose and allowed everyone's needs and desires to be met.

But the historic debt burden we face today renders trade-offs much more painful, biting into lifestyles in ways that reveal the fragility and vulnerability of the social fabric. When the economy is growing, and people believe they will get rich before they get old, they have hope and faith that the future will deliver them a better outcome. When the economy is stagnating, they lose their hope and belief that the future will be better. They begin to question the social contract. The state begins to demand more and more and the citizens begin to protest at having less.

When the social contract breaks, when the balance of power between the state and the citizen shifts in favour of the state's interests at the expense of the citizens' interests, a new question presents itself. It is the central question dominating the global economic landscape today: "Why is the wealth and the power in our society being distributed to some other guy and not me?"

The burden of debt is now testing many assumptions about how we have chosen to distribute wealth and the power. The debt burden poses fundamental questions we thought we had answered and which now divide us. It pits those who believe capitalism failed against those who believe the state failed to regulate capitalism properly. It pits the savers against the speculators, the young versus the old and those who contribute to the state's finances against those who benefit from the state's largesse. It also pits states against each other as they seek to control cash flows and assets that would remove the pressure from their own citizens.

The British historian Niall Ferguson pointed out to me that the social contract was a very bad idea written by a man who abandoned his two children, the Genevan philosopher Jean Jacques Rousseau. Rousseau first presented the idea in 1762 in a leaflet called *The Social Contract or Principles of Political Right*. His particular version of the social contract was unattractive, even offensive, for many reasons, but mainly because it put the needs of the many over the rights of the few. The notion inspired reform and the French Revolution, which ultimately destroyed the social contract that had been in place in France till then.

We may not like a particular social contract, but the very fabric of society is always based on some sort of deal between citizens and their state. There are good deals and bad deals. Some social contracts are better than others. Some are more robust than others, no doubt. The public favours some and rejects the rest. There is *always* a social contract, however. And, there are always moments in history when governments go broke and default on their promises to their citizens, thus putting the social contract under severe distress, if not destroying it altogether.

Is there a debt problem?

Yes. The debt problem in the industrialised world is sufficiently large that it is unravelling the social contract. How big is the debt problem? Most people have no affinity for numbers and cannot conceptualise the colossal size of the debt. The British world champion bridge player, SJ Simon (1904-1938), wisely observed that although most bridge players actually enjoy devoting a Friday night to playing with numbers, they are not only mathematically ignorant but mathematically "oblivious". "Mathematical apathy is one of the most fascinating sidelights in the world of cards," he wrote in his book, *Why You Lose at Bridge*, in 1967. Well, government budgets and debt problems are a similar kind of card game, only on a vastly larger scale. The magnitude of the debt is so huge that the human brain cannot process it purely mathematically, as the mathematician John Allen Paulos explains in his book, *Innumeracy* (1998). This is one reason why I will try to explain the debt problem without using any numbers. After all, once we reach a billion or even a trillion, the human mind converts everything to "big". It is not that policymakers and economic experts are any better at this. The Canadian monetary policy expert William White (whose warnings about the imminent financial crisis were ignored by policymakers around the world in 2006 and 2007) once tried to aggregate the value of all derivatives contracts in the world and came up with the number $1.2 quadrillion. Even the experts could not mentally process that.

It is sobering when we realise that the US, the UK and many other indebted nations would still be left with a decade-long debt repayment problem, or more, even if the government taxed every citizen 100% of their income. Flip the coin around: even if all government spending were eliminated – other than interest payments, retirement benefits such as Social Security and the national healthcare system – then the debt would still take a decade or more to pay down, at least.

If you are saltwater, you might say, "Let's just tax the rich more, redistribute their wealth to those with less privilege and, in this way, preserve the social contract and the standard of living as it stands." Steny Hoyer, the Congressman from Maryland, stated this position clearly when he said, "We don't have a spending problem. We have a taxing problem." Of course, the very fact that the state forces the citizen to work longer on behalf of the state, bends, if not breaks, the social contract.

A tax rate of say, 91%, something that the very saltwater Nobel Prize winner, the economist Paul Krugman, has suggested, would force Americans to hand over a much larger proportion of their income than most are comfortable with. Larry Summers, the former Chief Economic Advisor to President Obama and the Secretary of the Treasury, suggested that the tax code be revised to eliminate the distinction between income tax and tax on returns from investments, which are called "capital gains". In other words, he wants to raise the effective tax rate on the wealthy. This alone is a deal breaker for those who think they belong to a society that treasures and promotes freedom of the individual and his enterprise. In France, President Hollande has suggested the state should tax the public 75% of its income. Even in a country that is far more inclined to support socialised outcomes, the French public is revolting against the higher taxes combined with a state that promises to deliver less, not more, in exchange.

If you are freshwater, you might think, "Let's drop taxes to practically nothing, reduce the size of government and encourage the citizens to work harder and be more entrepreneurial." No doubt, entrepreneurs would rush to build new businesses. But, this takes time. Many, if not most, new ventures fail. High technology means that many new businesses won't employ many people, given the availability of automation. Employment, which is a lagging indicator anyway, therefore lags even further behind the economy, which means nobody feels like the economy is improving.

In the meantime, reducing taxes would also reduce the cash flow required to pay the interest on the debt. This means the state would risk being thrown into default anyway. This brings us straight to the point. Taxing citizens 100% of their income would impoverish the public and still require many years to repay the debt burden. If all spending could be cut other than retirement benefits, interest payments and healthcare benefits, the debt would still take more than a decade to pay down. This is true of every major indebted nation, including the US, the UK, Japan, the EU members and possibly even China.

Keep in mind that interest rates in the US, and most of the West, are at the lowest levels recorded since the Roman Empire (or nearly so). The chances that they stay at this historic low level for the next decade are not good. So, the cost of the debt is probably going to rise at some point, potentially worsening the problem exponentially.

Allocating the blame and the pain

If you are quite insane, you might suggest that the debt be paid off. It can be paid, of course, but at what human cost? Paying off a debt this size takes time – at least a generation and maybe even two, as Spain, Portugal, Greece and others are finding out to their great dismay. There is a clear price for agreeing to pay: years of high unemployment, low growth and economic stagnation. Japan made the decision to pay in the aftermath of its stock market crash in 1991. It has still never recovered from that event. The country has endured more than twenty years of deflation and slow growth. So far, no other large democracy has been able to willingly suffer such pain. It is almost impossible to imagine Western democracies enduring such pain silently for so long.

Since tax cuts, spending cuts and paying the debt all result in the loss of a decade or more, it is possible that most, if not all, of the debt in the industrialised world today is very likely to be defaulted upon because the pain of paying it back is higher than the voters in democracies are willing to withstand. In short, it is politically impossible and mathematically difficult to pay the debt now owed by the industrialised nations. Therefore, all the tax and spend discussions are misleading to the public.

Cutting spending typically means cutting the continuing upward trajectory of spending to a somewhat lower trajectory. This is painful enough. Imagine if someone said the spending should simply stop. Democracies would not be able to withstand the hit to GDP.

As Oscar Wilde said, "It's not whether you win or lose but how you allocate the blame." Today the public policy arena is entirely consumed by the need to allocate the blame and the pain. Someone has to pay for the loss. The social contract has to break. The only question is who will bear the loss and the pain? This depends on how the debt will be defaulted upon and therefore how the social contract will be broken.

The public debate about cutting a little here and taxing a bit more there is a deep disservice to the general public because it creates the impression that something significant is being done. At best, most governments consider any decline in the upward trajectory of public spending, however temporary, as a victory when in fact the nation remains on an unsustainable path. The economists Ken Rogoff and Carmen Reinhart put it neatly: Once the ratio of debt to GDP exceeds a certain level, growth simply cannot occur. There is loud disagreement about what that level is – 80%, 90%, 70% – but many agree that the higher the number, the more likely a nation tips over into a default situation, like a ship that takes on too much water. It now seems that Rogoff and Reinhart made some minor and simple errors in their mathematical calculations that has given their opponents a great excuse to dismiss their premise. But, in the end, everyone understands there are limits to the debt a nation can carry without damaging its growth prospects.

Martin Wolf, the Editor of *The Financial Times*, points out:

In 1816, the net public debt of the UK reached 240% of gross domestic product. This was the fiscal legacy of 125 years of war against France. What economic disaster followed this crushing burden of debt? The Industrial Revolution.[51]

---

51 See *The Financial Times*, 23 April 2013: "Austerity loses an article of faith: The UK industrial revolution shows the Reinhart-Rogoff thesis on debt is not always right" by Martin Wolf

He is arguing that innovation can create GDP, which is true. He is hoping that some anonymous person(s) or process suddenly becomes wildly successful and we find ourselves with a revolutionary new economic engine. I believe this can happen given my confidence in the ability of the common person to innovate and navigate the complexities of the world economy. There are many examples that such innovation is already underway, as we shall see in Chapter 10. The greater the economic pressures, the greater the capacity for innovation and reinvention. But, just because a new Industrial Revolution is possible does not mean it will happen. And even if it did, it does not absolve governments of the need to sort out their financial messes in the meantime, especially because the debt, sadly, is not static. It is alive.

Compound interest: the eighth wonder of the world

The debt grows even if you don't feed it. It gets bigger over time due to interest. Like all borrowing, it has to be repaid with interest. It compounds. Compounding is something we only really learn about when we feel it bite. Einstein said, "Compound interest is the eighth wonder of the world. He who understands it, earns it... He who doesn't... pays it," which explains much of why I have written this book. Those who will pay, and that would be most of us, dear readers, unless we take care, need to be informed of this fact so we can prepare for the consequences.

There are a few exceptions no doubt, but, in the main, schools do not teach basic financial concepts. They don't teach us how interest rates change the price of a mortgage or the APR rate on a credit card over time, let alone how the national debt compounds. So, here is a fascinating parable about compound interest, as told by the economic policy analyst Stephen Moore:[52]

The Emperor of China was so excited about the game of chess that he offered the inventor one wish. The inventor replied

---

52 Originally published in *The East Valley Tribune*, 24 January 1999, and reproduced on The Cato Institute website (www.cato.org): "Tapping the Power of Compound Interest" by Stephen Moore

that he wanted one grain of rice on the first square of the chessboard, two grains on the second square, four on the third and so on through the 64th square. The unwitting emperor immediately agreed to the seemingly modest request.

What the Emperor did not understand is that by the 30th square, the number adds up to a billion grains of rice. "Two to the 64th power is 18 million trillion grains of rice—more than enough to cover the entire surface of the earth," as Moore's version of the parable points out. Do not forget that there are 64 squares on a chessboard, unless you count the whole board and all other squares that are made of groups of squares, in which case there are 204 squares. The Emperor did not have enough money to provide the rice. By then he had bankrupted his kingdom with his promise. Of course, the Emperor had a clever solution, and used the power of the state to solve the problem. He had the bright inventor executed.

What is the current account deficit?

This is the problem today. We have spent more than we have earned and we have borrowed from others to make up the difference. It tends to become harder to keep borrowing once lenders are aware of the magnitude of the debt and are therefore unsure of the ability or willingness of an individual or nation pay it back, including the interest, which is compounding every moment of every day. The government can force us to pay for the debt by threatening us with "execution" in the form of taxes and/or higher inflation or many other methods that leave you worse off.

It is hard for people to understand the debt problem because many don't realise they have borrowed any money. When I was working in the White House in 2001 and 2002, I remember imploring two US Congressmen to not persist with more fiscal spending – an argument I decisively lost. The conversation went like this:

PIPPA
If we keep spending like this, the current account deficit will get much worse.

100

CONGRESSMAN 1
(*Frustrated*)
You economists are always going on about the current account deficit. What is the current account deficit?

PIPPA
(*After a moment of hesitation, realising the gravity of the question. After all, how can we expect politicians to resolve a debt problem if they do not realise they have one?*)
Sir, it means we have spent more than we have earned and have been borrowing money from foreigners, mainly China, to make ends meet.

CONGRESSMAN 2
(*Leaning forward rather aggressively*)
There's not a single member of my district borrowing any money from the Chinese.

This conversation will leave market experts incredulous. But, the point is that Congressman 2 was right. No one in America goes to a Chinese bank to get a loan. Nobody registers that when foreigners buy US government bonds, the US is "borrowing" the money. Therefore, it is hard to be surprised that people are surprised by the magnitude of the debt problem. This is also true for every other indebted nation, from Britain to Europe to Japan.

How can any politician tell the public that it will have to endure perhaps twenty years of pain, as Japan did, for a problem the public doesn't appreciate even exists? The math does not add up. Why would you risk the votes and your political career on something people cannot even imagine, let alone comprehend? You would not.

Add another dimension to the problem: the free money from the Federal Reserve, the quantitative easing, and the super-low interest rates all subsidise the government's debt problem. President George W Bush's economic advisor, Larry Lindsey, and the former Head of the Office of Management and Budget, David Stockman, among others, ask, "Why would Congress do anything about the debt problem when the Federal Reserve is funding the debt so cheaply?" There is no incentive to act.

All this helps explain why American policymakers chose to jump in one direction when the financial crisis came. They chose to bail out the broken banks rather than to let them fail. They realised that the consequences of failure were vastly larger than the public could possibly comprehend. They made the decision to manage the debt in a way that the public would only comprehend years later. The combined effort to use fiscal policy, monetary policy and regulatory policy all amounted to moving the losses from the speculators to the government and then to the taxpayers.

One can debate whether or not this shift was in the public interest. No doubt this was done with the good intention of protecting the taxpayers and the voters from the horrific consequences of the economic downturn that might have occurred if these institutions and the financial system as a whole had been permitted to fail, although even this is debatable. I had too many clients who would have been prepared to buy the businesses, the buildings, the hotels, and the stocks and bonds that the banks and other owners would have been forced to sell had the government not bailed out the banking system. They would have invested new capital, too. But at the time, in the midst of the emergency, few were prepared to trust the market. They trusted the state.

What's done is done, except that many do not understand what was done: the losses were moved from the banking system to the government's already over-indebted balance sheet, thus pushing the losses onto us, the public. The losses were "socialised". Put another way, the global banking system was "saved", but what was never mentioned was the price, the true cost. The price is this: we, the citizens, whether we live in an indebted country or not, will have to pay for it by retiring later than we expected and endure a lower standard of living than we imagined. We will have to accept that the state we live in will provide us with less along the way – less GDP, less public services and less income due to higher taxes. The price is that we saved the banking system at the expense of the social contract.

For anyone who thinks the debt story applies exclusively to Americans, let us be clear. The same thing occurred when the British Government sought to save the Royal Bank of Scotland, Lloyds TSB and HBOS, to name a few. It happened in France when the French Government sought to save BNP Paribas and Société Générale, and to the Swiss in regard to UBS. The Irish had to save Anglo Irish and the list goes on.

Breaking the social contract

One of the most important outcomes of all is that the debt burden in the West damages the hopes, aspirations, and beliefs of people everywhere, even in emerging markets that don't have a debt problem themselves. Emerging-market workers now rightly question whether they will get rich before they get old. This undermines their confidence in their leaders. It makes them question the seemingly unfair distribution of wealth in their country. It brings into question the social contract where they live.

If the purpose of all the government action was to save us from another Great Depression, then fine. But, no one ever says what the price was or will be. The price is that the social contract will break, like it or not. The state simply cannot absolve the financial sector of all its substantial losses and remain solvent itself. Something has to give. The state has to break and renegotiate the social contract to survive.

Here are the two inescapable choices that sovereigns and citizens of indebted countries face:

1. Pay off the debt.
2. Don't pay off the debt.

There are those who believe that the debt problems in the industrialised world are not that bad and are solvable by policy measures. The main argument is that these states – the US, France, Britain, Belgium, Portugal, Greece and others – are not insolvent but are simply "illiquid". It's just a cash flow problem. If someone would just lend them a bit more cash, or if they simply taxed the rich more, or cut spending a bit harder, then eventually the economy would recover and then they would have enough cash to pay everybody back and deliver on their promises. Herein lies the crux of the problem. The debt load is so heavy that it squashes GDP and inhibits calculated risk taking.

There are some inescapable facts:

1. You cannot solve a debt problem by borrowing more money. You can postpone it and exacerbate it, but not solve it.
2. All sovereign defaults have the same sequence: the government denies, denies, denies and then either says, "Bring the defibrillator – we're defaulting", or it just continues denying.
3. When government promises more than it can afford to deliver, the government's power to tax is pitted against the citizen's power to generate a profit. If the government tries to take too much, it kills the golden goose and destroys any hope of recovery.

The inevitable defaults

Here are the five principal ways in which governments typically default on their creditors.

1. Argentine/Russian-style default

We can wake up one day to hear a government simply announce, "We are never going to pay you back. Ever." This is called an Argentine-style default because that is exactly how Argentina defaulted in 2001. Such an approach is violent, sudden and involves defaulting on the foreigners who have lent money to the nation. That's what Russia did in 1998. The consequences of such a default are typically the following:

i) The currency suddenly falls in value and immediately prevents citizens from buying more from abroad.
ii) It makes exports much cheaper, thus increasing foreign sales. This immediately reduces the need to borrow from abroad.
iii) There is a risk that no one will ever invest in your country ever again after you bite the hand that feeds you that hard,

since creditors are not likely to lend more to someone who has defaulted on them so bluntly.

2. Haircuts

A government can say, "We are definitely going to pay you back but a little bit later or a little bit less or both." This sounds a lot nicer. Today *The Financial Times* and *The Wall Street Journal* describe this kind of default as if nothing problematic has happened. The country merely "extended the payments" or "restructured" the debt. But, one penny late or less is still a default when it comes to debt.

A "haircut" does not sound so bad. The most recent examples of haircuts were in Dubai, Greece and Ireland. In each case *The Financial Times* and other media said that Dubai's leadership had decided to "extend the payments". Greece has "restructured" its debt many times since this last debt crisis began. Ireland "successfully extended the payments" with the backing of the European Central Bank. All sound perfectly okay to the untrained ear. But, all have enormous consequences for those who have lent the country money – the bondholders.

Just to be absolutely clear, we are talking about how a government defaults on its debts. It usually acquires the debt by handing out little pieces of paper in exchange for cash. We call these "bonds". These IOUs (I Owe You) are promises to pay the lender back at some future date in full and with interest. So, when we buy a government bond, or our pension fund or mutual fund does, we expect to not only get our money back but to also get paid for taking the risk of making the loan. The interest rate is the purpose of the investment.

When we give or lend a government cash, in exchange it says, "I owe you". It promises to return the cash at some future date along with interest; we expect that we will get all of the investment back and on time. These pieces of paper are very popular investments for another reason. The value of the piece of paper will go up and down depending on the level of interest rates. The higher the interest rate goes, the less the price will be and the lower the interest rates go the higher the price will be. The yield (the interest rate) and the price are inversely related. But, no matter what, if we don't get all our money back on time, then the bond has defaulted. From an accounting point of view, a default occurs if we are paid back one minute or one penny late.

3. Austerity

A state can default on the promises it made to its citizens. This is called austerity. When there is a massive debt burden, the government discovers that it cannot find the money to fund our retirement at age 55 and might not even be able to fund retirement at 65, so it asks us to work longer by increasing the retirement age. It cannot provide public transport and healthcare at the same price as in the past, or to the same extent, because it is now broke, so it asks its citizens to pay more out of their own pocket for these things. The fare for the Tube in London, the Subway in New York City, the Metro in Paris, Madrid, Milan and Brussels all rise. Airport taxes go up. Train fares rise. Tolls on bridges become more expensive and the police write tickets for driving three miles an hour over the speed limit instead of giving you the old latitude of, say, 10 miles an hour because they need the money. The government raises our taxes and reduces the services it delivers to the public.

Austerity is not just when the government reduces spending. It is when the government says, "We promised to do certain things, like collect the rubbish twice a week, deliver mail six days a week, but now we cannot pay for these things, so your rubbish will be picked up once a week and if you want more you have to pay for it yourself, and the mail is only going to be delivered on weekdays."

4. Devaluation

The government can also allow or force the value of the currency to fall against other currencies so that our nation's goods and services become cheaper, letting us earn more from sales abroad. It also makes imports more expensive, thus compelling us to stop buying imported goods. Devaluation may or may not be in the government's control. The Americans, British, Australians and

Canadians might prefer a cheaper currency but cannot make it happen easily because these currencies are seen as safe havens in a world troubled by the Eurozone, and given the low growth and rising social protests in emerging markets. Investors buy these currencies due to their fear that other nations seek to devalue.

Devaluation is also a sub-category of inflation because imports become more expensive when the value of the currency weakens. When currencies devalue, inflation almost always goes up. When Argentina devalued by 23% in January 2014, Whirlpool, which makes washers and dryers, and other companies that import into Argentina immediately announced a 30% increase in their prices.

5. Inflation

Inflation is the most invisible and immediately painless option (the pain comes later). All the government has to do is "print" more currency and/or more bonds, and reduce interest rates to practically nothing so that the cost of money – the interest rate – is free, at least "free" to the banks. This usually causes asset prices to rise, which is the point of the exercise. This is why Chairman Bernanke and Yellen claim credit for the fact that the US stock market went up after he introduced quantitative easing. The purpose of money printing is to make asset prices rise and thereby entice investors back into the market.

When governments push down the cost of money to very low levels and make it practically free – at least free to the banks – they are forcing the participants in the economy to speculate. If cash pays very little and costs little to borrow, then the government is able to incentivise citizens to overcome their fear of debt and instead begin to speculate and invest in assets again.

However, as the eminent Swedish economist Knut Wicksell repeatedly pointed out during his long career, the interest rate is a kind of democratic instrument that balances the interests between the borrowers and the lenders in a society. That balance should be "just". Injustice is done when interest rates are artificially suppressed because it assists the borrowers at the expense of the lenders, who are the savers. It shifts the balance of power in a society because inflation is a form of taxation, if not expropriation and confiscation. It is a means by which the state steals money from the savers and the weaker members of society in order to serve its own interests and those with vested interests. When governments assist savers or borrowers at the expense of the other, they change the nature of the social contract, whether the citizens like it or not.

John Maynard Keynes reached the same conclusion in 1919. He leaned heavily on an insight offered by the father of Communism, Vladimir Ilyich Lenin, and wrote the following in his book *The Economic Consequences of the Peace*:

> Lenin is said to have declared that the best way to destroy the capitalist system was to debauch the currency. By a continuing process of inflation, governments can confiscate, secretly and unobserved, an important part of the wealth of their citizens. By this method they not only confiscate, but they confiscate arbitrarily; and, while the process impoverishes many, it actually enriches some. The sight of this arbitrary rearrangement of riches strikes not only at security, but at confidence in the equity of the existing distribution of wealth. Those to whom the system brings windfalls, beyond their deserts and even beyond their expectations or desires, become 'profiteers' who are the object of the hatred of the bourgeoisie, whom the inflationism has impoverished, not less than of the proletariat. As the inflation proceeds and the real value of the currency fluctuates wildly from month to month, all permanent relations between debtors and creditors, which form the ultimate foundation of capitalism, become so utterly disordered as to be almost meaningless; and the process of wealth-getting degenerates into a gamble and a lottery.

If anything captures the zeitgeist of the world economy today it is this sense that we are now in a lottery; we are gambling and the only known factor is that the "house" – the government – decides the outcome. One of the most successful hedge fund mangers in the world returned some $2 billion to his investors, saying that it had become "too hard" to manage the money because he and his team could not guess how the Chairman of the Federal Reserve was feeling that day. In other words, the market no longer depends on market prices: it depends on decisions by policymakers.

In an interview with Goldman Sachs, Stanley Druckenmiller said:[53]

> Part of my advantage, is that my strength is economic forecasting, but that only works in free markets, when markets are smarter than people. That's how I started. I watched the stock market, how equities reacted to change in levels of economic activity, and I could understand how price signals worked and how to forecast them. Today, all these price signals are compromised and I'm seriously questioning whether I have any competitive advantage left.

He is making us aware that governments have not only broken the social contract but now governments have emerged as the most important price maker and player in the market. That means the line between the state and the market has moved in favour of the state's interests and against those of the individual. The widely respected British historian and international relations theorist EH Carr (1892-1982) put it another way, writing at the time of the Second World War: "Everyone defaults, calls it something else and excoriates others for doing the same."

This gives rise to a world where citizens are challenging their leaders and repeatedly asking, "Why is the social contract being broken or changed?"

The Eurozone

At the heart of the Eurozone in central Europe lies a profound social contract problem. After the devastating wars between France and Germany in 1871, 1914-1918 and 1939-1945, the two countries decided to band together and collaborate on the economic resources that they had been competing over: coal and

---

53 As reported on Zero Hedge, 14 June 2013: "Stanley Druckenmiller On China's Future And Investing In The New Normal" by Hugo Scott-Gall

steel. Robert Schuman, the French Foreign Minister (in 1948), proposed a European Union as a means of preventing any more war. He said:

> "Franco-German production of coal and steel as a whole can be placed under a common High Authority, within the framework of an organisation open to the participation of the other countries of Europe. The pooling of coal and steel production should immediately provide for the setting up of common foundations for economic development as a first step in the federation of Europe, and will change the destinies of those regions which have long been devoted to the manufacture of munitions of war, of which they have been the most constant victims."

This was the foundation for what has evolved into the European Union. On the 1st of January 1999 some members joined the effort to launch a common currency called the Euro, which it was believed would further consolidate Europe. This new currency gave the poorer, weaker countries in Europe, such as Greece and Portugal, access to capital at the same interest rates as stronger and wealthier countries such as Germany and France. With the newfound easy money, local politicians committed to new spending without having much incentive to pay attention to revenues and taxes. As long as the world economy was booming, the social contract could be fulfilled. The state could make or increase payouts while not demanding the citizens pay more in tax.

The 2007/8 financial crisis revealed that the spending was exceeding income by such a large amount that many European nations and financial institutions were certainly illiquid, could not meet their cash-flow requirements if they were not already insolvent and needing a bailout.

Now countries in the Euro are being forced by their financial troubles to renege on their promises. Greece and Cyprus have been forced to seek bailouts and default on their debt. The European Union, with the backing of the International Monetary Fund, forced the Cypriot government to take 47.5% of some its citizens' private savings directly from their bank accounts to help fund the loss (as long as there was more than E100,000 per person in the account). There can be few greater breaches of any social contract than when your government simply takes your money directly out of your bank.

In Portugal in 2011 and Poland in 2013 these governments expropriated private assets by effectively nationalising private pensions. The promise is that the employees of Portugal Telecom will still get their pensions, but now the government will be paying the pension, which assumes the government can make the payments. Of course the whole reason for expropriating the pension assets was to shore up the government's balance sheet and reduce the loss it faced in order to qualify for further bailout money from the EU.

There are only a few Eurozone members that have a positive cash situation: Germany, Finland and Holland. Naturally the citizens of these states do not want to write a cheque to the "peripheral" states, which include Greece, Portugal, Cyprus, Ireland, Spain, Italy and possibly even France and Belgium. Why should those who were fiscally sound underwrite the losses of those who were not?

Past trauma

The social contract problem goes much deeper, though. In short, the social contract in Germany insists that no leader ever manage a debt problem by using inflation. Germans are still burned by their traumatic experience with dramatic hyperinflation in the 1920s and 1930s. Many believe that the hyperinflation caused the population to turn to a new leader who promised to protect them from its ravages, which opened the door to Adolf Hitler.

The central problem today is that any effort to monetise the debt (to use inflation to diminish it) – such as issuing European-wide Euro bonds, printing money or having Germany write a cheque to cover the losses – would be considered an inflationary step by most Germans. It would break the German social contract. In contrast, failure to monetise the debt or bail it out will break the social contract in the indebted countries.

This is why we hear the Head of the European Central Bank,

Mario Draghi, say, "We will do whatever it takes" to fix the problem. Such words make the stock markets go up. But then the Germans say "No", they have not agreed to an ECB that can simply print money to fix the problem. They have not agreed to bail out or inflate. They quote Draghi's whole sentence, which was, "Within our mandate, the ECB is ready to do whatever it takes to preserve the Euro." The mandate does not include permitting inflation, say the Germans.

In the meantime, the bailouts in Europe have gone directly to the lenders – the banks. The defaults have left the public in Greece and Cyprus no better off. The stark choice these countries face is clear. If they stay in the Euro, they have to accept the rebalancing of income versus expenditure. That means losing a generation or two while taxes go up and state benefits go down. This means enduring deflation and stagnant growth as they slowly pay off their debt.

Should I stay or should I go?

A country could leave the Euro (though stay in the EU, which would make them similar to the UK). In other words, they could make their currency cheaper through devaluation. Or, at the very least a country like Scotland, for example, if they pursue independence, could gain greater control over their own finances by leaving the UK, even if devaluation was not possible.[54] As the public begins to understand the starkness of the outcomes, populists gain greater sway. In Greece we see the rise of the far-right party, the Golden Dawn, and other extremist groups elsewhere in the Eurozone. They promise to restore the social contract by opting out of the Euro. In Spain the separatist movements in Andalucía and Catalonia promise the same, as does Scotland in its effort to further devolve from the United Kingdom. So far, the public in most Eurozone countries has voted decisively against any leader who promised to do what Germany wants. To be clear, Germany wants each European citizen to be more

---

54 Scotland can only devalue its currency if it introduces its own currency. The Eurozone has firmly ruled out Scottish membership in the Euro.

careful about public finances (meaning they want Greeks and Italians to behave more like Germans, which seems unlikely and probably undesirable). As of 2010, Germany has more or less said that it could support writing a cheque to bail out Europe if the following conditions were met:

1. Each Eurozone member hands over some of their fiscal sovereignty to a central authority in Brussels;
2. Each Eurozone member agrees to the creation of a common federation in which there will be one single Foreign Minister, which of course means there will be one single Finance Minister as well.

So far, every European leader who has supported this fundamental change in the social contract has been decisively thrown out of public office. It is not surprising that no one wants to vote for a system of government that involves handing over sovereign authority to unelected officials who are probably coming from other nations. But EU officials believe it is only a mater of time and explanation before the public realises that the new European Federation social contract will better their interest more than the old *national* social contract.

Democracy and the social contract

There are those in Brussels and European capitals who believe that the old social contract may have evolved around democracy, but the new social contract in Europe may have to be imposed on the people. After all, according to these elites, the public doesn't know that this is in their best interest. As it stands, bailing out most of the Eurozone will break the social contract in Germany and failing to do so will break the social contract in the periphery. Reconciling the two may not be possible.

In my humble opinion, Germany seems to make every effort in public to extend a half-hearted helping hand to the periphery so that it can be seen to be trying. But, Germany's leaders fully understand that countries such as Greece and Cyprus cannot viably remain inside the Euro. The Greek public is only just waking up to the idea that a full default on its debt (and it has defaulted on 90% of its debt as I write) still leaves it dead in the water for many years to come. The Greek economy still can't grow, in spite of the debt burden being relieved by default.

In Greece, the inability of the government to provide law and order due to its financial constraints has encouraged citizens to consider alternative mechanisms for protecting individuals and maintaining community order. As a result, the Golden Dawn came to control many neighbourhoods in Athens and elsewhere. Organised crime also gets a foothold when governments lose the means to enforce the law. It is perhaps unsurprising that we should then hear military voices in Greece again calling for a coup in order to restore law and social order. Greek Special Forces floated this idea in September 2013 and ended up being arrested. The rise of the far right all over Europe is a signal and not a good one. It is a response to the failure of the current state to sort things out and reflects a belief that the state could fix everything if only someone else, someone tougher were in charge.

The only ways out are to create new GDP or to devalue the currency enough to render Greece competitive again. No one can imagine how Greece can create the new GDP. And, it will only devalue if it leaves the Euro. It would therefore be smart for Germany and all Euro supporters to plan for such an outcome. This is perhaps one reason we see Germans reaffirming their commitment to protect the European Union (EU) at all costs, but separate the Euro issue from the EU. Instead, the idea is growing that the Euro can be made more flexible and fluid. New countries are preparing for entry, such as Latvia, while existing members such as Greece and Cyprus are being forced into leaving by circumstance. So, some may come and some may go, but the Euro will still exist. In fact, the Euro will only be a stronger more confidence-inspiring currency if these weaker members leave. Germany cannot force them out, however. Instead, these countries must choose to leave. It is increasingly clear to these societies that the human cost of remaining inside these constraints is probably going to be too high to bear.

The social contract is also being renegotiated in Britain. The government has chosen to rely on lower interest rates, devaluation of the currency, and austerity as the principal means of restoring growth. In other words, they hope to generate more inflation while rebalancing finances by having the state spend less and the citizens taxed more. Some breakage of the social contract is visible to the general public. It is fairly obvious when the British authorities announce that the National Health Service will no longer provide certain types of surgeries without applying a personal surcharge, meaning the citizen must now contribute to the cost.

The French take flight

There are many signals in the UK of substantial changes to the social contract. Here is an interesting signal. When I walk into Battersea Park in London, half the people there now speak French. With tax rates in France rising to 75% (and once you add in death taxes, some are finding the real rate is 100%), many enterprising French people are moving to London. The main French school in London, the Lycée Français in South Kensington, is completely full. So, a few entrepreneurs have gone to the local London Council in the Borough of Wandsworth and leased some large local government buildings with the intention of turning them into new French schools. This gives the local government more cash. It brings jobs to the Borough. And, it helps raise the value of properties nearby. It also means the children of these new emigrés can be brought up in their chosen education system. In addition, I'd say it is pretty likely that the neighbourhood will soon have French bakeries and restaurants, which it currently sorely lacks.

The Spanish, Greeks and others also flee to the UK. An interesting signal is that you almost need to be multi-lingual to order your food in a London restaurant due to the large number of Continental European employees. You say "California roll" and they say "Que?" because they speak Spanish, not English, and don't recognise the words.

Part of what makes Britain more attractive is that it is outside the Euro, which means it still controls its own monetary policy, interest rates and its own currency, unlike the Eurozone members.

But tax is another issue. Britain, France, Germany and the US have made immense efforts to close down offshore tax havens so that they can retrieve tax payments that their citizens might otherwise be avoiding (legally or illegally). Such pressure has been imposed that Switzerland, for example, no longer protects information about who has money on deposit in Switzerland unless they are legal residents. Switzerland has concluded that it is pretty dangerous when the financial services sector dwarfs the rest of the economy, so it has taken steps that make it more difficult for foreigners to deposit their cash there or do their financial transactions there. As smart investors look around the world, they see that the UK now has the lowest tax rates relative to everywhere else, where taxes are rising. In addition, the UK now offers rule of law in a world where the social contract is breaking down. Other places may have separatist movements, coups, years of deflation and the like, but the UK offers a relatively safe haven.

For wealthy families in emerging markets, Britain offers a refuge where they can trust the rule of law. It's a safe place where they can escape if the social contract back home really comes unstuck. This has led to unprecedented demand for residential property in London and the rest of the UK. Real estate agents in London have hired Mandarin, Arabic and other foreign language speakers to help cope with overwhelming foreign demand. The presence of such staff on the payrolls of property brokers is a telling signal.

So, even though the British may be angry about the breakdown of the social contract they thought they had, many foreigners are finding that the new British social contract beats the one they have at home.

"In God we trust"

The social contract in the United States is also changing, and at many levels. Local authorities such as Detroit have sought to default their debt. This means they also seek to default on the promises that have been made to their pensioners. California seeks to keep the deal with its pensioners by breaking the deal with its taxpayers. The state can keep the pension payments as they were but then has to raise personal and corporate income tax rates retrospectively to cover the cost. On this basis the social contract offered by Texas may appeal. Nationally, tax rates are rising while benefits are falling, although austerity is not as pronounced in the US as in the United Kingdom. But this is because America is able to pursue a monetary and fiscal policy that is much riskier than most governments can.

The fact that America is a reserve currency allows it to experiment with unprecedented loose monetary and fiscal policy. A reserve currency is one that people put their faith in regardless of the immediate condition of the economy. Whenever there is trouble in the world or in the markets, people are prepared to believe that the US will always recover, always pay back its debt, always succeed in protecting and pursuing its own national interests. America retains full control over all aspects of economic policy. It controls interest rates, monetary policy, fiscal policy and has the ability to generate growth without much help from abroad. Roughly only 10% of America's GDP comes from exports.

Nonetheless, there are many people in the US who are increasingly uncomfortable with the ever-greater presence of the US government in the market. The balance of power between the state and the market has shifted in favour of the state. Then again, there are others who welcome a state that provides a bigger safety net and seeks to take more taxes from the rich rather than cutting the benefits that go to the poor. The rising presence of potholes in the road and cracks in the sidewalks signal that the state can't or won't deliver what people have taken for granted.

In each case, all over the world, as the social contract breaks or changes, the public begins to ask that simple question. "Why is the state making decisions about how to distribute wealth and power in my society in ways that don't benefit me?" This pits the government against the citizens and the citizens against each other, which is something that will affect everyone.

The Perfect Circle

6

CHAPTER

Buddhists say that suffering is what happens when you have an argument with reality. So, your perception of "reality" matters. After an economic crisis there is bound to be nostalgia for the past. We knew how to make a living in the old economy, so we want to go back to the good old days. But an economic crisis, rather like an avalanche, does not just wipe away our savings and damage our confidence, can permanently alter the landscape.

Rather than wishing for past circumstances that cannot be recreated, we have to stop arguing with reality and instead survey the new landscape; assess the reality of the world economy as it stands today and evaluate what it means for everyone in it. This means avoiding the human tendency that Winston Churchill so aptly described: "Men occasionally stumble over the truth, but most of them pick themselves up and hurry off as if nothing ever happened."

We used to have a kind of "perfect circle" in the world economy. Put simply, the perfect circle was created when investment from the industrialised world went into the emerging markets, thus creating new capacity, new factories and a new supply of things. The emerging markets sold these things to the industrialised world at places like Walmart. They took the cash they earned from the sales and placed a good deal of it in the bond markets of the industrialised countries. Why? In part because exporting the profits would prevent an unhelpful appreciation of their currencies, which would have made these goods more expensive and thus reduced the cash flows to these emerging-market workers. This policy also protected these economies from inflation. More cash for the workers tends to mean higher prices at the grocery story as more cash chases the same amount of goods. This is how China emerged as the largest buyer of US government bonds. This is also how China became the largest lender to the United States and many other industrialised nations.

The export of capital from the emerging markets also made it cheaper for industrialised country-citizens to borrow money at cheaper prices. As emerging market investors buy more bonds in the industrialised countries, it pushes the interest rate down. China and others bought not only US Government bonds but also other US Government debt instruments, especially Fannie Mae and Freddie Mac, the US home-loan companies. Foreigners especially loved Fannie Mae and Freddie Mac because they believed such debt was effectively backed by the US Government, so it was as good as a Treasury bill, but it paid a little more.

More purchases of Fannie and Freddie debt lowered the mortgage rates for millions of Americans and others who could now buy more and bigger houses, which needed to be filled with more of the things that emerging-market workers were making for ever-cheaper prices.

Yes, there were some negative side effects of the perfect circle. Jobs moved from the industrialised world to the emerging markets, from the US to China. This created friction and political pressure. The US began to demand that China revalue its currency so that Chinese goods became more expensive and less competitive. A stronger Renminbi would also lessen the inflation pressures for China and lessen the flow of money into an increasingly overheated US Government bond market. China complied to a degree but, in the main, the forces driving the perfect circle persisted until the financial crisis began in 2007.

This perfect circle gave rise to views that many hold today. It stands behind the idea that, "All the jobs have moved to China, China is the future and America is finished." This has been a popular view in recent years, taken as a given in the popular media, regularly dropped in dinner party conversations and the foundation for a good deal of investment. It's a signal when the wealthy hire Mandarin-speaking nannies for their children and people invest in Mandarin classes. And yet, if we just look around, we see that manufacturing has been moving back to the US and the West very rapidly over the last few years. The signals of this change are everywhere.

Coming home

It now costs less to manufacture steel in the US than in China, according to Price Waterhouse Coopers in a recent report, *A Homecoming for US Manufacturing? Why a Resurgence in US Manufacturing May be the Next Big Bet.*[55] Firms from GE to the Otis Elevator Company to Caterpillar to Brooks Brothers to Tiffany have all brought production back to the middle of America. Even Wham-O is now producing more Frisbees and Hula Hoops in the US than overseas. Mexico, Eastern Europe and some parts of Asia beyond China are also beneficiaries of the changed landscape. Tellingly, Chinese firms are beginning to open manufacturing facilities in America. Zhu Shanqing of the Keer Group, which owns yarn-spinning factories in China, announced his intention to invest $218 million in a new yarn factory near Charlotte, North Carolina. *The Wall Street Journal* reported, "The new plant will pay half as much as Mr. Zhu does for electricity in China and get local government support." Plus, he will lose the overseas shipping expenses.[56]

Similarly, the perfect circle caused people to believe, at least in the industrialised world, that the greatest economic threat on the landscape is deflation. This is not surprising if you think that emerging markets will always drive inflation down because their workers will always do things for less money than anybody else. Putting this simply, you cannot charge fifteen dollars an hour to make a toy if someone elsewhere will make the same toy for only one dollar an hour. The market will always buy the cheaper

---

55 See www.pwc.com: "A Homecoming for US Manufacturing? Why a Resurgence in US Manufacturing May be the Next Big Bet", by Robert W McCutcheon, Robert Pethick, Michael Burak, Michael Portnoy, Anthony J. Scamuffa, Sean T Hoover, Robert B Bono and Thomas Waller
56 See *The Wall Street Journal*, 22 December 2013: "Spotted Again in America: Textile Jobs" by Cameron McWhirter and Dinny McMahon

product and thus impose discipline on the cost of labour even if you yourself don't feel you are affected by the global economy.

If you see the world this way, based on the perfect circle, then the risk is that we end up like Japan, with years of slow growth, falling prices for everything – from food to houses – and de-leveraging, which means banks and other financial institutions will be selling assets for which there are few buyers. As such, it is argued, we must do everything possible to avert such a crisis, including relying on governments to hold up the prices of falling assets such as houses and bond markets and to spend and print money (quantitative easing).

Yet, if we look around the world, we see many signals that tell us that inflation is affecting the emerging markets and rendering them less and less competitive, while prices and the cost of living may be rising even in the industrialised world in spite of deflationary pressures. After all, the whole point of quantitative easing and stimulus is to re-ignite inflation.

I keep stumbling across an interesting signal in my travels. At every dinner party, every barbecue, every social event around the world, the conversations are deeply divided. On one side are bankers and business people who fully understand how great the losses have been in the financial crisis. They fear that without state support, quantitative easing, and fiscal stimulus, the economy would collapse under the weight of bad debt. For them, there is no inflation and no risk of it. The other group tends to be made up of their spouses, entrepreneurs (who are responsible for their own overhead costs), and sharp observers of reality whose first and favourite topic of conversation is the relentless increase in the cost of living. The increase in energy and transportation costs, grocery bills, school fees, health care and the like dominate the conversation.

Inflation or deflation?

Is the perfect circle still with us or is it broken? Is there inflation or deflation? Where does reality lie?

Ben Bernanke and his successor Janet Yellen fear deflation. This is why the recent Heads of the US Central Bank have been busy doing their best, adopting unorthodox and historic measures to conjure forth a much-dreaded old nemesis called inflation. They see it as a strong "animal spirit" that can pull us out of the ditch of deflation. If we should succeed in bringing this dangerous creature back to life, and it starts to threaten us again, then we will just kill it. Central bankers believe that this is easy. Deflation is very difficult to address. There are virtually no academic theories or practical experiences of successfully reversing a deflation. Inflation, in sharp contrast, is well documented. There have been many such episodes in history. The solution is simple. You just raise interest rates or at least stop printing new money.

Then there are those who say there's no such thing as just a little inflation. It's not like spilled milk. Stimulus, especially on this extraordinary scale, is like accelerant. You throw cash around (liquidity, it is often called) precisely because it behaves like gasoline. Its very purpose is to re-ignite the economy. So, being flammable, we cannot be surprised to find that it is not so easy to clean up. A little goes a long way and we have indulged in the largest monetary policy experiment in *history*, not just the largest in the history of the United States. Never before have so many large economies other than the US thrown record amounts of stimulus at the world economy in unorthodox ways, let alone done so simultaneously.

Hard to control and reverse

The last man who had to kill inflation is Paul Volcker, the Chairman of the Federal Reserve under Presidents Jimmy Carter and Ronald Reagan. In the 1970s in the United States he wrestled inflation down and strangled it into unconsciousness principally by pushing interest rates up to 21%. This landed him on the cover of *Time* magazine as the most hated man in America for administering the painful but necessary medicine at that time. He has since come to be revered as the Bruce Willis action hero of economics, the man who saved us from the ravages of inflation through sheer tough mindedness.

In May 2013 he told the Economic Club of New York, "Credibility is an enormous asset. Once earned, it must not be frittered away by yielding to the notion that 'a little inflation right now' is a good thing to release the animal spirits and to pep up investment."[57] This would be pure hubris in light of historic experience. He says we should be wary of "the implicit assumption behind that Siren call", which is "that the inflation rate can be manipulated to reach the economic objectives – up today, maybe a little more tomorrow and then be pulled back on command." Just to emphasise his point, he hammered home the message with this blunt statement: "All experience amply demonstrates that inflation, when fairly and deliberately started, is hard to control and reverse."

The big question is whether all this pertains to the future or whether it is an issue today. Volcker rightly hints that central bankers need to act, and indeed usually act, well before the signs and signals of inflation are apparent. The rough rule has always been that the central bank should start restraining the economy some eighteen months before the action needs to take effect. But, today the supporters of Mr Bernanke and his Federal Reserve believe that we should wait until the US economy reaches at least 6.5% unemployment and achieve a certain momentum before changing course. Around the same time that Janet Yellen was confirmed as the new Chairman of the US Federal Reserve Bank the senior staff of the institutions announced the goalpost was being moved. In a paper presented to the International Monetary Fund, *The Federal Reserve's Framework for Monetary Policy – Recent Changes and New Questions*,[58] the Fed gently implied that the acceptable inflation rate should no longer be 2.0% but 2.5%. Yellen has also implied, or the markets have inferred, that she believes inflation has been below average for so long that it should

---

57 Read the transcript at http://econclubny.com, 29 May2013: "Central Banking at a Crossroad– Remarks by Paul Volcker Upon Receiving the Economic Club of New York Award for Leadership Excellence"

58 Read the transcript at www.imf.org: The International Monetary Fund's 14th Jacques Polak Annual Research Conference, 7-8 November 2013, "The Federal Reserve's Framework For Monetary Policy – Recent Changes And New Questions" by William B English, J David López-Salido, and Robert J Tetlow

be permitted to rise above average for a while. In a Federal Reserve meeting in 1995 she was quoted as saying, "when the goals conflict and it comes to calling for tough trade-offs, to me, a wise and humane policy is occasionally to let inflation rise even when inflation is running above target".[59] In short, the Chairman is signaling that there will be no practical inflation target until all risk of deflation has firmly past.

The reluctance to act at all is not too surprising given that the market responded violently at that time to any suggestion that the level of liquidity might be reduced at some future date. Some liken quantitative easing to free drugs. It's like giving morphine to a recovering heroin addict. The addict becomes agitated when his fix is reduced. Jeffrey Lacker, the President of the Richmond Federal Reserve, who repeatedly dissented against continued QE, pointed out that the central bank had not even begun to talk about reducing QE. He said, "The Committee will be reducing only the pace at which it is adding accommodation. In other words, the Federal Reserve is not only leaving the punch bowl in place, we're continuing to spike the punch, though at a decreasing rate over the next year."[60] This analogy derives from something once said by the longest serving Federal Reserve Chairman ever, William McChesney Martin. During his term in office, from 1951 to 1970, he memorably stated, "The Fed's job is to take away the punchbowl before the party ends." The central banks around the world are, in the main, still adding more free drugs to the punchbowl rather than taking them away.

This brings us to a second aspect of this same issue: Where will we see signals of inflation? Most central bankers are trained to consider only their own economies. They won't look for signals outside their own borders, and there are good reasons for this. Monetary policy is a political function, not just a technical one. Its

---

59 See *The Wall Street Journal*, 6 August 2013: "Janet Yellen's Record" by Mary Anastasia O'Grady

60 Read the transcript of his speech at www.richmondfed.org: "Economic Outlook, June 2013" by Jeffrey M Lacker, 28 June 2013, Judicial Conference of the Fourth Circuit, White Sulphur Springs, West Virginia

role is to preserve the integrity of the currency on behalf of the citizens. Otherwise, politicians would just keep printing money to fund all their favourite and vote-winning pet projects.

The citizens make their own choices about who to elect and which policies to pursue, and need to live by the consequences. No one in America ought to be held to account for Zimbabwe's decision to print so much money that hyperinflation was provoked and its currency became worthless. Imagine if the Federal Reserve said, "We are raising interest rates because inflation in Zimbabwe is increasing." The public would be incredulous and then outraged. And yet, common sense tells us that we live in a global economy, which functions as a single global market. This too brings consequences. One of the consequences over the last quarter of a century was the so-called "Great Moderation of inflation". Paul Volcker set the stage for lowering inflation in 1979, but the thing that really killed inflation was the fall of the Berlin Wall in 1989. The weight of that event crushed inflation just ten years after Volcker began to slay the beast.

The fall of the Berlin Wall

Most people who are responsible for the world economy today are under the age of 50, which means they hardly remember the Soviet Union and the Cold War. Most of them were born after 1961, when the Communist Bloc erected a vast wall that cut Berlin and indeed Germany into two disconnected parts. The wall was not only physical but also marked the psychological and ideological border between Capitalism and Communism. It was known as the "Iron Curtain", separating East from West Germany. At the time the Communist leadership described its purpose as a means of protecting the public from anti-socialists such as Fascists and Capitalists who sought to undermine the "will of the people" in their effort to build a socialist state. In fact it served to prevent emigration, defection and other means by which East Germans might try to escape the new social contract that Communism imposed on them.

By 1989 it had become clear that the Communist approach could not fulfil the promises of its social contract. After years of

125

economic hardship, having to line up for limited or rationed goods and food, the citizens within the Communist world began to revolt. It became "the will of the people" to take hammers and sledges to the Berlin Wall on the night of the 9th of November, 1989. This event, in retrospect, marked the end of Communism not just for East Germany, but also for every other Communist state around the world. The Soviet Union morphed into Russia, or more precisely into Russia and other members of the CIS, the Commonwealth of Independent States, of which Russia emerged as an equal member but with far greater influence. Soviet dependencies including Poland, Estonia, Georgia and Ukraine morphed into independent nations.

China started on a path of reform in 1980, permitting private farm ownership after decades of disasters from collective farming, which paved the way for the privatisation of many economic activities. This launched China into the world economy.

India too was forced by the demise of the Soviet Union to move away from a state-controlled economy. India had sold the Soviets many goods, from cotton to food. When the Soviet Union ceased to exist, it defaulted on the debt it owed India. This left India with a massive financial crisis.

I went to India in 1992 to interview the then Finance Minister, Dr Manmohan Singh, who would go on to become the Prime Minister in his later years. I remember the look on his face. He was clearly being pulled between feelings of overwhelming resignation and the flickering flames of hope as he said that India had no choice but to open the economy to market forces. "We have no money," he told me. He explained that India would have to open the economy to market forces because "we have no money" to choose any other option.[61] That is the problem with Socialism. As Margaret Thatcher once said, "The problem with Socialism is that you eventually run out of other people's money." At the heart of it, that was the economic force that caused the

---

61 See *International Economy*, 1 May 1993: "Singh's Song: an exclusive interview with Manmohan Singh, Finance Minister of India" by Philippa Malmgren

Soviet Union to fail. Tax revenues were insufficient to keep up with the state's expenditure.

Even in Latin America, after the Berlin Wall fell the pro-market right came to power more forcefully than ever before. With the demise of the Soviet Union, defenders of Socialism and Communism were silenced. Francis Fukuyama wrote that it was "The End of History". Capitalism had won the argument. The economic consequences were formidable.

I first heard Alan Greenspan explain the importance of the Berlin Wall at a meeting in the White House long before he wrote about it in his book, *The Age of Turbulence* (2007). He said that following the end of partition between East and West Germany, billions of new workers from China, Bangladesh, India, Africa and Latin America suddenly entered the world economy. This pushed down wages and prices all over the world. That meant that prices could not rise because some new emerging-market worker was always around the corner prepared to make whatever you needed for less. This brought about a "great moderation" of inflationary forces, as economists now call it. It created a world where growth mainly went up and inflation mainly went down.

Today, the majority of people who are running businesses and managing assets grew up in a post-Berlin Wall world. We think growth mainly goes up and inflation mainly falls. We think this is normal, when in fact it was created by an exceptional set of historic and probably temporary circumstances that no longer exist.

Most emerging-market workers are now clamouring for wage hikes that render them and their nations uncompetitive. The jig is up.[62] They are not prepared to work for next to nothing anymore. Meanwhile, the terrible pressure brought to bear by the financial crisis has given rise to great innovation in the industrialised world. People have reorganised their personal and professional business models and their activities in ways that render the industrialised world competitive with the emerging markets once again.

---

62 I am grateful to my friend Elizabeth Dempsey, who summarised my long-winded explanation with this pithy sentence.

The perfect circle was temporary

It is hard for us to recognise that the last 25 years were not "normal". It was a very privileged period of history during which we were blessed with an especially favourable set of circumstances. This exceptional situation is highly unlikely to be repeated.

Some will take issue with this, arguing that there have been many bumps in the road during this period. No doubt this is true. The landscape of the last 25 years is rife with economic catastrophes. There was the US Savings and Loan Crisis of the 1980s and 1990s, which kicked off when Volcker raised interest rates and more than seven hundred Saving and Loan companies went bust. There was the Scandinavian banking crisis of the early 1990s and the Mexican Peso crisis in 1994. Few remember the former but the latter caused a firestorm when Mexico required a bailout. The Asian financial crisis ensued in 1997, which culminated in a default by Russia in 1998. Argentina defaulted in 1999. Financial institutions including the Connecticut hedge fund, Long-Term Capital Management, got caught up in the price movements caused by these events and also began to threaten the stability of the world economy. The recent financial crisis began in September 2007 but became visible to the public when Lehman Brothers defaulted in 2008.

From such a list one might expect that people would assume the world economy is a volatile and dangerous place that forces one to prepare for the worst at all times. But no, this seems not to be the case. Perhaps because each of these episodes of economic distress and crisis were met with policy responses (government bailouts), each trauma passed and all were followed by a return to happy growing conditions. People seem to think about the last twenty-five years as good times with brief interruption instead of as bad times with brief moments of growth.

It may be that for someone who is now 50 years old the economic circumstances have been volatile and unpredictable, but there is no doubt that many people seem to believe that growth is usually dependable and prices generally fall. They believe that they can plan for the future based on their experience of the past.

They still want to pick the bottom of the stock market and believe that the stock market will deliver their retirement intact. They are still quick to borrow tomorrow's income and spend it today, as is evidenced by the record personal and sovereign debt in the world today.

It is an irony that in the financial markets we are required (by law) to repeatedly explain that "past returns are no guarantee of future performance" and yet many people assume their past experience will continue to define their future. Therefore, it is worth describing the economic forces that many now believe to be "normal". These things may seem blindingly obvious to well-informed economists and historians but, in twenty years of speaking to audiences around the world, I have found that it makes sense to explain the "bleedin' obvious", as the Brits call it, because it usually turns out that not everybody actually understands what happened in the past or what it means for them. Let's face it, libraries are filled with books with competing views about what happened in history and why, so why not spend a moment reviewing some of what happened and why, so that at least a few more of us can be ready to join the spirited punch-up about why the argument is right or wrong, relevant or irrelevant.

The end of Communism

The fall of the Berlin Wall triggered other forces that contributed to the perfect circle. These forces moderated inflation and enhanced growth: the end of centralised state control and the end of the Cold War.

It is hard for young people today to imagine, and hard for older people to remember, a "command economy" world in which Communist leaders decided how much steel would be made and how much milk would be available in Moscow or St Petersburg. It is almost impossible to imagine or even remember that the Communist style of asset allocation put all the power in the hands of bureaucrats who chose where things would be made, who would be allowed to buy them and what the price would be for everything, from a pencil to a steel beam to a potato. Under Communism, the state decided who got what. It determined what you would be allowed to study, which job you would be allocated and how much bread you could buy.

The peace dividend

The demise of the Soviet Union and the end of Communism brought another significant deflationary economic force: the peace dividend. Again, it is hard for many people today to remember the zeitgeist of the Cold War period. As a child growing up in Washington DC in the 1960s, I experienced the nuclear alarm once a month or so at Chevy Chase Elementary School. While in the event of a fire alarm we children had to exit the building as quickly as possible, with a nuclear alarm, in contrast, the trick was to dive under the desk as quickly as possible. I still don't know why anyone thought being under a desk at the moment of a ground-zero nuclear event would have made the slightest bit of difference, but it certainly instilled a deep fear of a nuclear exchange. The generation that grew up with that fear was more than prepared to spend on nuclear deterrence, Mutual Assured Destruction as it came to be known, and more than delighted when such spending was no longer required.

From the end of World War Two, the United States and the Soviet Union were locked in a contest for power and deeply entrenched in an arms race. Put simply, a good deal of GDP was diverted into the prevention of and preparation for war. The spending that was channelled towards unproductive resources such as nuclear arsenals, border guards at Checkpoint Charlie on the Berlin Wall and wars against Communism in various parts of the world such as Vietnam, was now free to be redeployed into more productive use in the real economy.

In America, President Johnson and President Kennedy had tried to have both "guns and butter". They paid what was required to beat the Russians in the arms race. But they also wanted to pay for what was required to lift millions of Americans out of poverty, including African Americans who had been denied access to the fruits of citizenship before that. That was the purpose of the "The Great Society" programme. While obviously necessary, it proved an expensive approach. It was expensive deploy defence money on wars while also funding newly expanding social safety nets such as Medicare and Medicaid and welfare payments for the poor. It was so expensive that it was decided to just print and spend money. This is when America's debt problem began to compound. The Federal Reserve estimate is that the great inflation of that era, the one that Paul Volcker had to kill in 1979, actually started in 1965. Once it was dead, around the time that Ronald Reagan came to power, policymakers everywhere remained respectful of inflation. Once the Berlin Wall came down, it began to wipe away the memory of inflation altogether. As the great moderation of inflation and the peace dividend together progressed, it created a sense of belief that growth mainly went up and inflation mainly went down while defence issues mainly receded and social benefits could mainly be expanded. This gave people everywhere a belief that the system would not only supply everyone's needs, it would also make people rich before they got old.

The baby boom

Demographics played a large part in creating the foundation for the perfect circle as well. In the West, the appearance of the "baby boomers" (the children of the sudden population increase that occurred at the end of World War Two in the US and Europe) meant that the young far outnumbered those that retired ahead of them. This meant that the amount of money coming into government, from taxes, Social Security and other state programme payments, was larger than the amount that needed to be paid out. Demographics from the late 1940s onward created the illusion that the amount of cash coming into government coffers would continue rising and therefore governments could continue increasing the pay-out of benefits to their citizens. In addition, it created the belief that growth could be relied upon and that one could spend tomorrow's tax receipts today.

The perfect circle caused an important signal to become more pronounced – debts rose as people became more and more confident that they could safely stop saving for tomorrow. Indeed they could even spend money they expected to earn in future. Usually it makes sense to save for tomorrow in preparation for uncertainty. Instead, belief in the perfect circle gave rise to a benign landscape that provided a clear vision of the future. This "clarity" caused governments and individuals alike to assume that they could indulge in leverage (borrowing) and borrow from the future to pay for the present. We built our national and personal budgets, our corporate and family balance sheets, and our personal lives on this false and ephemeral foundation: the perfect circle.

The financial crisis of 2007

At first, it was assumed the losses were in the banks alone and that they could be saved from certain demise through government bailouts of various sorts – low interest rates, cash, government support for certain assets such as mortgage-backed securities and European Sovereign Debt and semi-nationalisation, among other things. But these efforts proved insufficient. In the early years of the 2007/8 financial crisis a series of decisions were taken that effectively moved the losses from the banking system to the taxpayers. This actually exposed the fact that governments themselves were broke. The business model governments used had also been built on the same idea – agreeing to pay out to citizens today based on tomorrow's expected income. It did not help that the baby boomer era was coming to an end. Suddenly all the promises the government made to pay out to citizens could not be kept because there simply wasn't enough money coming into government coffers. When the economy stalled, tax receipts collapsed and suddenly it became clear that governments had been doing exactly the same thing – spending tomorrow's income today.

As always, when times are good, hubris returns to centre stage. It is a signal when we confuse good luck with skill. Such a signal is amplified when we begin to presume that any particular state of affairs is permanent. Everyone did this in the perfect circle world. The West and the East, America and China, the industrialised world and the emerging markets all expressed their hubris in different ways but hubris nonetheless pushed the perfect circle onto a mutually destructive trajectory. Instead of binding economies together, it began to pull them apart.

The American expression of hubris took many forms. In the West, especially the US, people bought houses without any thought as to the budget that would be required to heat them or maintain them or to continue to own them if they happened to lose their job. Banks lent more and more to less and less qualified borrowers, assuming that all would benefit from the rising tide of national growth and income.

The Chinese did exactly the same thing, but in a different way. Rural workers left their homes to find a job in the big cities without knowing where they would live or how much they would be paid. What they often found were rather horrible working conditions and that their pay would often not arrive in their hands for long periods of time. Employers provided housing, food and necessities for living. Wages were often paid as much as several years in arrears. These itinerant and migrant workers did not spend tomorrow's income today but they did work in the hope that today's income would be paid tomorrow. In other words, they took a big risk too.

Their bosses, the factory owners, displayed the same behaviour as Americans. Instead of borrowing, mortgaging and leaning on credit, this group built their businesses on the assumption that the value of the business was in the market share, the future growth and not in today's cash flow. In fact, Chinese businesses often had negative cash flows. Contrary to the popular image that China was a land of unlimited profits, private equity returns in China were broadly negative from 2000-2007, the supposed boom years. Like the Internet bubble and frankly all other speculative bubbles, people began to believe that performance would come in the future even though profits had not yet appeared. China's economy has now softened and confidence in it its economy has weakened.

Luckily, Western investors seemed more than delighted to provide never-ending Foreign Direct Investment by buying shares in Chinese businesses mainly through the Hong Kong and Shanghai stock exchanges or buying equity in Chinese firms. This new investment filled the gap between the losses and the lack of profits. The focus of Chinese business owners was not on today's cash flow but on tomorrow's exit strategy – the IPO, the sale to a larger firm, the rising share price. In fact, this preoccupation with the future led to an ever-greater willingness to cut costs and skimp on quality. Chinese businesses became less concerned with quality and more concerned with quantity.

This is exactly what happened in the Western financial markets as well. People and businesses became so preoccupied with the idea of an IPO or the sale of a company to a competitor, a rising share price and other ways of exiting the business and taking cash off the table, that they cared less and less about the quality of transactions and more and more about the quantity of transactions.

More risk for less return

The financial community was sufficiently confident that the future would be reliably bright and started to take increasingly risky bets. In short, investors took more and more risk. But the returns on the risk fell as more and more money chased these returns. When everybody is buying Bangladeshi shares because China's assets already seem expensive, when the yield on risky emerging-market debt, such as African bonds, is nearly the same as the yield on a US or European company, then the market is no longer distinguishing between one risk asset and another.

Everything went up in value. The only way to improve the performance was to leverage up the investment. In short, that meant borrowing to make financial bets. In the same way that Americans put less and less money down to buy a house that was larger and more expensive than they ever imagined it possible to own, financial speculators did the same. They put less and less money down to take bigger and bigger financial bets on deals, on equities, on bonds, on foreign exchange markets, on commodities, on everything that would enable them to get "positions" and trades that were larger than the actual cash they happened to have on hand.

Just as Chinese firms became less concerned with profitability and more concerned with market share, Western asset management firms and financial institutions stopped concentrating on stewardship of assets and instead focused on increasing the volume of assets under management. They became less concerned about profitability and more focused on size. More assets under management and more transactions meant more fees and a higher share price or a higher future value of the business.

Business models also began to change as management began to believe that the flow of cash and a rising GDP were permanent and sustainable. In a world where capital was endlessly available, it seemed smart to outsource production to the least expensive locations around the world, no matter the distance. Just in time manufacturing was shifted to the lowest cost locations. We failed to build in redundancy because we assumed that there would always be enough capital to move goods from such places back home. We moved a good deal of the world's production to places that were neither geographically nor socially stable on the grounds that there was always going to be enough capital to throw at fixing any problem.

Many state and local governments as well as national governments built their budgets on the assumption that tomorrow's cash flows would be stronger and higher than today's. They continued to promise increased benefits to citizens and considered it a victory when the value of the benefits went up less than the expected income. Then, the expected income dried up when business transactions fell. Business income was reduced. More and more people became unemployed thus reducing their ability to pay personal income tax. As tax receipts fell, the state ran out of the cash required to pay out the promised benefits and services to the citizens and thus were compelled to borrow.

Consider how American states came to break the social contract. Steve Malanga explains this in an article for *The Wall Street Journal*, "How States Hid their Budget Deficits".[63]

In 2001 the state of New Jersey made a decision "to borrow $2.8 billion and stick it in its own pension funds in lieu of making contributions from tax revenues. To make the gambit seem reasonable, Trenton, a city in New Jersey, projected unrealistic annual investment returns – between 8% and 12% per year – on the borrowed money." Malanga explains that by 2004 the state's

---

63 *The Wall Street Journal*, 23 August 2010: "How States Hide Their Budget Deficits" by Steve Malanga

budget fell short by $2 billion, so it borrowed more money, which, as Malanga so neatly puts it, "is like borrowing on your credit card to pay off your mortgage". If you borrow to fund a pension, you can technically report, as Malanga reminds us, "We have X amount of dollars in that pension, so everything is fine, and we don't need to make any further contributions". But, the fact is that the funds have to be paid back with interest and the state will have to pay in whatever is required to cover the cost of the benefits that will need to be paid out to citizens.

Reversing the perfect circle

In retrospect, it is obvious that the perfect circle caused us to collectively bet on a linear projection of the future. When we lost the perfect circle, it bankrupted the entire system – banks, governments, enterprises and individuals, thus requiring a government response.

The perfect circle began to reverse to such an extent that investors no longer cared about the return *on* their assets. They just wanted the return *of* their assets. Americans no longer cared about buying a bigger house, they wanted the one they owned to retain some vestige of equity (many didn't and some found themselves with negative equity). Bankers no longer cared about their deferred stocks and options, they wanted to simply keep their jobs. Governments no longer focussed on the promises that would be made in the future, they instead started to tax their citizens more aggressively and to reduce their commitments to the citizens in order to protect the government from bankruptcy. Many governments became effectively bankrupt anyway. At a minimum, they wholly depend on the kindness of foreigners who buy their debt in order to allow the gap between saving and spending to be financed. Many prefer not to refer to such a situation as "bankrupt" but as "dependent".

Meanwhile, China's workers no longer cared about the future. They now wanted to be paid the cash they were owed and not have to wait any longer for it. Some actually started frogmarching their factory bosses to cashpoint machines to withdraw money to cover payrolls. By January 2010 some were no longer content to have a job in a high-tech factory like Foxconn, where Apple and Dell products are made, and instead began to commit suicide to protest their plight.

What Now?

Cracked open by the crushing weight of the debt and exposed by the financial crisis, we find the perfect circle now reveals the most important problems of our generation: the conflict between the productive and the unproductive, between the rich and the poor, between the state and the market, between the industrialised world and the emerging markets, between deflation and inflation. The question still hangs: who is right? Mr. Bernanke or Mr. Volcker?

The question will keep passing on to the next generation as well. Esther George, the President of the Kansas City Federal Reserve, has dissented at every single FOMC[64] meeting since she was appointed in 2011 and has demonstrated a spirited defence of Volcker's legacy. Janet Yellen has taken up Bernanke's ideological role but with an even greater willingness to take risks in favour of growth over inflation. Who is right? Esther George or Janet Yellen? Are there signals we should pay attention to, which will help us in this debate? My view is yes. It is an important signal when members of the establishment start to turn away from the consensus view. When Paul Volcker began to warn about inflation, it was easy for Federal reserve staff to dismiss him as an old man who is no longer "in the game" or worthy of our attention. By May 2014, another high priest of the economics profession in the US, Martin Feldstein wrote an editorial: "Warning: Inflation Is Running Above 2%: Research Suggests that unemployment may not restrain wages. If so real trouble may be ahead". He says, "Inflation is rising in the United States and could become a serious problem sooner than the Federal Reserve and many others now recognize". But, there is no need to rely on the words of an expert. Instead, open your eyes and start observing the signals that the world economy is sending. Then a person can make their own decisions and choose what to do about such signals based on their own risk taking capability and skill.

---

64 Federal Open Market Committee

The Vice

Ludwig Wittgenstein and Karl Popper, two of the brightest philosophers in modern history, only met once, on an autumn afternoon in Oxford in 1946.[65] Popper delivered a lecture on the question, "Are there philosophical problems or are there just philosophical puzzles?" Wittgenstein believed there were only puzzles; Popper believed there were only problems. Within ten minutes, Wittgenstein, who was in the small audience, a man famous for his fierce intellect, picked up an iron poker and, according to witnesses, waved it about shouting, "Popper, you are wrong! You are wrong!" Bertrand Russell, another of the 20th century's greatest philosophers, had to intervene and asked Wittgenstein to put the threatening poker down. Wittgenstein apparently stormed off in a huff. The moral of the story is that even extremely intelligent people can find themselves married to a view and no amount of facts or argument will dissuade them of this view. They will wave a poker at anyone who challenges their outlook on the world.

This brings me to a signal I have heard and observed in recent years at the Jackson Hole conference, where the Federal Reserve holds their annual economic policy symposium in August. The President of the Kansas City Federal Reserve invites central bank governors from all over the world to come to this valley in Wyoming, together with a handful of the chief economists from major central banks and a smaller number of independent analysts.

---

65 *Wittgenstein's Poker: The Story of a Ten-Minute Argument Between Two Great Philosophers*, Harper Collins, 2002

For the last few years, the Chairman, Ben Bernanke, has insisted that Quantitative Easing policies would have no spillover effects and would not and could not create undesirable inflation or dangerous imbalances (like artificially high asset prices or resource mis-allocations) at home in the US or anywhere else in the world. Each time he has said this, I have heard two sounds: the uncomfortable shifting in seats and the distinct sound of palms being slapped against foreheads, mainly by emerging-market central bank governors. These faint sounds are a signal of an especially violent disagreement. The rolling of eyeballs by supporters of these policies at those who oppose them merely confirms the seriousness of the disagreement.

Let us try and understand the two opposing views and why the disagreement is so severe. After all, the signals you will observe and give credence to depends on whether you agree with the Federal Reserve's view or the view of many emerging market central banks. The breakdown in the conversation between the two camps occurs because of an impasse over philosophy. Like Wittgenstein and Popper, the Fed and many of the emerging-market central banks see the world so differently that there is little common ground for a conversation. What is a puzzle to the Federal Reserve is a problem for many other central bankers. It feels like both sides would pick up a fire poker at times if one was to be found nearby. The violence with which the two camps attack is palpable. But, they tend to deliver their blows at each other through academic papers, learned journals and through columns found in *The Wall Street Journal* and the *Financial Times*.

The Fed's view

The situation in 2007 and 2008 was so bad that, without action, the world economy would have ended up in another Great Depression. To save the US, and even the world, from such a fate, the US central bank engaged in all kinds of conventional and unconventional efforts to support and stimulate the economy. This lifted many prices: property and stock markets prices especially. These efforts, called Quantitative Easing, have brought no unwanted, let alone adverse, consequences.

The emerging-market view

Emerging-market central bankers do not all hold the same view, but in general, they tend to think that efforts to create inflation by America, Britain, Canada, Japan, Australia and others are certainly working. The problem, from their point of view, is that the inflation is hitting the emerging markets. It is obvious that the rise in the cost of basic needs – necessary food, energy and raw materials – is sparking social unrest across many of the emerging-market countries. It seems fairly obvious to them that cheap money leads to property speculation, since property is a hard asset. The higher property prices go, the higher the prices that must be charged for producing or selling on that property.

The industrialised world is, by their measure, "exporting" its inflation. This is an obvious means of defaulting on the debt that the industrialised world owes the emerging markets. As with all defaults, the governments are bound to deny, deny, deny until later when they will say, "Oh my goodness, inflation happened! That means we are repaying you less than we borrowed. Oops! Sorry about that." Many government officials around the world are old enough to remember the last time the US began exporting inflation, which was in the 1970s. They remember the impact.

There are some who take the opposite view. Some argue the US is exporting deflation, not inflation. That would be true if the US Dollar were falling in value. But, most countries have been doing their best to weaken their currencies against the US Dollar. China, Britain and most emerging markets have seen their currencies weaken against the US Dollar in recent years (inadvertently or deliberately). It is worth noting that the US Dollar has been remarkably strongly supported in spite of Quantitative Easing as investors recognize that the US recovery and US investment opportunities have proved more attractive than anywhere else. So, money initially left the US and the industrialised world looking for higher returns in emerging markets. But, in more recent years, money has come from abroad into the US and the industrialised world in search of returns in spite of or because of the US central bank efforts to engage in ultra easy monetary policy.[66]

The complaint in emerging markets is that they lose both ways, which is partly why their complaints are so easily dismissed by their detractors. Emerging markets could either raise interest rates or just let their currencies appreciate to solve the problem. But that would mean ending the export-led growth story that would ultimately mean accepting slower growth. No politician anywhere in the world can stand for that. So, they don't.

The impasse

The Fed takes the view that every country is responsible for its own monetary policy. They also believe there are no "spillovers" from the US or the industrialised world which carry over to emerging markets. Traders on the trading floors of the biggest recipients of the free money have a different view. They know their job is to take risk and make profits. So, when the central banks, like the Fed, give them record low interest rates and free money, the natural and obvious response is to use it. After all, the money is "free". If it does not cost you anything, you are, as a trader, almost obliged to find the riskiest thing you possibly can and use it to bet on that.

When the free money began to circulate, investors began to buy emerging market stocks, property, companies, debt and anything else they could find. After all, emerging markets seemed destined to outperform anything in the debt-impaired industrialised West. This is how the "wall of money" began to move into emerging markets. It was a "carry trade". This means you borrow free money here and invest it there for a substantial return.

Disagreement about the "carry trade"

Even if there were any spillovers of hot money, or a "carry trade", the emerging markets could have and should have taken

---

66 See "Ultra Easy Monetary Policy and the Law of Unintended Consequences", Federal Reserve Bank of Dallas Globalisation and Monetary Policy Institute, Working Paper No. 126 by William R. White, August 2012

responsibility for their own economies by raising interest rates and allowing their currencies to strengthen as a means of offsetting any unwanted "hot money". In other words, emerging markets should have made their own products and services more expensive and lowered their growth rate.

This is an outrageous suggestion as far as many emerging markets are concerned. Their leaders instead blame the US for having caused the financial crisis. Emerging-market officials say, "First of all, we are enduring a lot of pain, unemployment and loss of faith in the future due to your mistakes (it was *your* financial crisis and caused by your bad management). Now you want us to raise interest rates on an already impoverished, poor population?"

The Fed's view is this: by failing to take responsibility for their own economic situation, emerging markets have forfeited their right to complain. And, they are complaining, especially because the Fed started to nominally reverse its free money stance.[67] As the "hot money" began to leave the world economy (which is a result of the Fed reducing the liquidity by "tapering", or reducing, the pace at which they had been adding money to the system every month), emerging markets experienced record declines in the value of the stock markets and dramatic falls in the value of their currencies.

This is more than an argument. It is a fight. Every once in a while the players in this arena come to blows in public. In April of 2014, the Governor of the Reserve Bank of India, Raghuram Rajan, challenged the former Federal Reserve Chairman Ben Bernanke. Rajan accused Bernanke of having unleashed "Competitive Monetary Easing" which brings adverse consequences for economies everywhere. QE may have made sense in the immediate aftermath of the initial emergency but prolonged use of it creates even bigger distortions than those that warranted the need for it in the first place. Prolonged use brings unintended spillover effects. QE leads to QEE or "Quantitative External Easing" and this destabilises the entire world economy. If Bernanke thinks not, Rajan suggested,

---

67 I say "nominally" because the Federal Reserve is still adding record levels of liquidity to the financial markets. "Tapering" just means it is doing it less and less rapidly.

then there should be an "independent assessor" appointed to "assess whether some of these other policies have effects". Bernanke replied saying, "I think a lot of what you've been talking about today just reflects the fact that you are very skeptical about unconventional monetary policy."[68]

The domestic impasse

The real problem, as far as emerging markets are concerned is that the efforts to "reflate" or "inflate" or cause prices to start rising, are working. Prices are rising. This is a serious problem for the emerging markets and arguably even for the industrialised world. At this point, we now find ourselves at the centre of a heated debate: is the biggest problem in the world economy the problem of falling prices or rising prices?

At this juncture, I will indulge the forgiveness of those who understand the difference between inflation, disinflation and deflation, for the sake of those who don't.

Inflation is a sustained increase in the general price level of goods and services in an economy over time. Disinflation is when the average level of prices is falling. Central banks have somewhat arbitrarily concluded that an inflation rate of 2% is a kind of "magic number" that equals price stability. In other words, the conventional view is that a 2% inflation rate accounts for people changing jobs, shifting between full time and part time work, demographic changes and other factors to create a suitable level of inflation for a stable expanding economy. But, the choice of 2% remains controversial with some arguing it should be higher, like Janet Yellen, and some arguing that even a 2% inflation rate is eroding your money, like Paul Volker.

Deflation is a sustained decrease in the general price level of goods and services in an economy over time. Somehow if this happens above a 2% inflation rate we like to call it "disinflation", but if we think it is going to push the inflation rate sustainably below 2% we call it "deflation".

---

68 See The Brookings Institution, "Global Monetary Policy: A View From Emerging Markets. A Discussion With Raghuram, Governor Of The Reserve Bank Of India, Washington, DC, April 10, 2014", uncorrected transcript.

Disinflation is a happy condition. Deflation is a dangerous condition. The risk of deflation is what provoked central banks to pursue unconventional methods and adopt Quantitative Easing in their effort to get the inflation rate sustainably back above 2%.

Most would say deflation, or falling prices is the biggest risk. But the methods chosen to diminish deflation are designed to make prices rise. This is succeeding. After all, stock markets have consistently hit new record highs since the anti-deflation QE policies began. Property prices have hit record highs everywhere from Beijing to Mumbai to London to Sydney and New York. In fact, the Chinese authorities have had to introduce all kinds of controls to slow down the price rises in the property market. And even with those restraints prices rose by some 20% in the course of 2013.[69]

Price jumps have social consequences. Higher property prices usually signal higher rents and higher prices, generally speaking. This is because the cost of doing business rises for every firm that pays rent when rents rise. This is usually passed on to customers in the form of higher prices for goods and services. Families and individuals also feel it when property prices rise. They realise they can no longer afford to buy and can no longer afford to remain where they are. Rents rise for those who don't own. While some benefit from higher property prices, many are displaced by them.

Many food prices have also reached record new highs. The price of beef reached untold levels repeatedly in recent years and is now so high that even the price of the ammonia-treated leftover shreds and gristle (known as "pink slime") has risen dramatically. Dairy prices have risen too. The UN Food and Agriculture Organisation has a dairy price index that rose by 28% worldwide between January 2013 and January 2014. The prices of many important proteins from fish to lamb to poultry have all touched record highs, usually repeatedly, in recent years since QE began. Of course, rural agricultural farmland has also been reaching

---

69 The Wharton/NUS/Tsinghua Chinese Residential Land Price Indexes (CRLPI) "reports series on real constant quality land prices price across 35 major markets in China". In 2013 there was a period of sharp acceleration, according to this index.

record high prices during this period everywhere from the US to the UK and as far as Asia and Australia.

Emerging markets thus claim that inflation is indeed occurring. It is the result of the industrialised world's historic efforts to create it. As usual, inflation always hits the poorest first and the poorest today are found in emerging markets. No doubt the lack of lending to farmers plays a part. Also, the rising demand for food is a contributing factor as well. But, at the heart of it, it makes textbook sense that asset prices rise (stocks and property) when governments are trying to foment inflation. It also makes sense that hard asset prices rise. Food is considered a hard asset even though it is a "soft" commodity.

The central banks of industrialised countries say there is no inflation whatsoever. They are certainly not exporting it and there is none at home. Yet the rising cost of living has emerged as a major political theme even in the US and the UK. Rising grocery bills, transportation costs, electricity bills and property prices are causing the public everywhere to demand that wages rise. This has driven the demands for minimum wages or wage hikes everywhere from the US to the UK to Germany.

How do we measure inflation?

The Federal Reserve clearly explains, "Inflation occurs when the prices of goods and services increase over time. Inflation cannot be measured by an increase in the cost of one product or service, or even several products or services. Rather, inflation is a general increase in the overall price level of the goods and services in the economy." By that measure, overall, prices are still falling and thus warranting a discussion of more stimulus, more QE and slowing the pace at which QE is taken away. But, human beings are especially aware of some prices over others. The price of food causes real pain even if the price of say, insurance or a mobile phone is falling.

What about them onions?

So, there seems to be a widening gap between the actual rate of inflation and the fact that some prices are rising, especially prices that are important to local populations. The prices that matter most to emerging markets are not only food and energy, but specific foods and specific energy. In India, the most important core food staple is the onion. In India in 2013, the price of onions rose by more than 300%.

It rose triple digits the year before as well. In August 2013, the Indian Cabinet held crisis meetings to discuss the fast rising price of this single vegetable: onions. They may not sound like a big deal. But, a World Bank report by Mohammad Amin called "What is So Special About Onions in India?"[70] explains why a rise in their price can cause governments to fall in that country because it prompts social unrest and adverse electoral outcomes. By 2014, the Indian government had started to severely restrict the export of onions in order to contain the price pressure.[71]

Hot chilli peppers

It may not matter to those in the industrialised world that the price of, say, chillies has risen in Indonesia, India and elsewhere by 300% in the course of 2012. By early 2013 the price of chillies starting doubling across Asia in a single month and became equivalent to the cost of a pound of beef. For emerging-market workers chillies are as essential as milk is to a Westerner.

The point is that emerging-market workers aspired to move from two or three meals a week, which included meat protein to, say, four or five meals a week. The rise of food prices not only blocks their aspiration. It also threatens them with the prospect of returning to only two or three meals a week, which include meat protein. Food prices signal not only painful price pressure. They signal the end or at least postponement of a dream that had become rooted in entitlement.

These sensitive prices may seem random and unbalanced against other prices in the economy, which may well be falling and not relevant to Americans or Westerners. Emerging-market leaders

---

70 See "What is So Special about Onions in India", a blog by Mohammad Amin (a Senior Economist at the World Bank), 18 January 2011
71 Minimum Export Price (MEP)

know that nothing will propel the public into the streets faster than high or rising food and energy prices, especially the price of the items that are held most dear to that population. Whatever the West has to say about these price hikes, whether one concedes they are real or imagined, the Chinese and other emerging markets believe that it is real enough to be a genuine threat to social stability.

We've seen this movie before and know how it ends

As far as China, America's largest creditor, is concerned, the US has a long history of defaulting through inflation. There may be those who question this. But one view is that US "paid" for the American Revolution with inflation when the Continental Congress issued debt called "Continentals" to finance it. Individual states also issued their own debt. All these Continentals ultimately became worth less and less through money printing, inflation and devaluation, thus leading to the phrase, "not worth a Continental". America similarly "paid" for the Civil War with inflation. It defaulted on foreign investors when over-issuance of debt led to 9,000% inflation in the Confederacy, which rendered the currency, known as "Greenbacks", worthless. In the 1960s, the war in Vietnam and the Great Society programme, which encouraged the integration of African Americans into mainstream economic life, were also paid for through the inflation which began in 1965 and which was not choked off until 1979.

Goldfinger and silver bullets

From a Chinese and emerging-market point of view, it seems fairly obvious that America always defaults on its debts through inflation. Inflation is not a victimless crime. Not only do the debtors lose, but people feel the impact of a higher cost of living. I'm reminded of the moment that the villain Goldfinger turns to the mythic hero James Bond and says, "Mr. Bond, they have a saying in Chicago: 'Once is happenstance. Twice is coincidence. The third time it's enemy action.'" And enemy action it is, from their point of view. For China, and many other emerging-market governments, a default by the United States and other industrialised economies is not just an economic event. It is a national security issue. The problem is not simply that these investors are going to be paid back in pieces of paper that are worth less. Will China and others potentially lose money on the massive holdings of US Treasury bonds? Quite possibly. Wen Jibao, China's former Premier, is said to have regularly complained that the US was "stealing money from China's pocket every day". But this is the least of their worries. The bigger problem is that there are consequences when large economies face a massive debt burden and start stoking inflation.

Inflation or a rising cost of living (depending on how you choose to look at it) is happening. It just began to happen in the weakest, poorest part of a highly integrated world economy first: the emerging markets.

Now, before anybody reaches for a fire poker and begins to attack the logic behind this view, let's first try to understand what the world looks like if you hold this view. As the Chinese saying goes, "Wars are fought with silver bullets." The opening salvo in this new war has been fired, in their view, by the export of inflation from the US and other industrialised economies to emerging markets.

When emerging markets go up in the flames of protests and riots it is interesting to note that most people in the industrialised world attribute this to a sudden demand for democracy. But, do you really think everybody woke up one morning in Tunisia and across the Middle East and said, "Today is that day I have to have democracy"? Or, is it more likely that the vice of pain bears down on people and pushes them to protest?

Perhaps the re-appearance of protests over rising prices all the way from Sao Paolo to South Africa to Singapore is not happenstance or coincidence. Food and energy price fluctuations played a large part in the events that unfolded in the Crimea region of Ukraine in 2014. The public experienced fast rising food prices. They also realised that Russia might be prepared to raise and lower the price of energy depending on whether or not Ukraine complied with Russia's interests. This stimulated many Ukrainians to seek refuge under the umbrella of European Union membership. Or, it could be said that the EU, in its effort to grow and increase its influence, sought to expand by reaching out to Ukraine and offering it a position in the EU. The threat of both such alliances prompted the domestic Russian population in Crimea to seek their own, separate solution.

The same economic pressures played out across Latin America as well. In Argentina, the price of bread doubled in a single week in 2013, even though Argentina introduced price controls on all food items in 2012. In Brazil it seemed that small increases in bus fares of 10 cents were enough to provoke substantial street protests between May 2013 and early 2014. But, these energy/transportation price hikes have taken place against the backdrop of rising food prices. In Sao Paulo a pizza can cost USD $30 these days. In May 2014 the President elect in Panama campaigned on and immediately implemented price controls on 22 basic food items as soon as he came to power.

In the Middle East, price pressures were so strong that many countries including the Emirates have had to place price controls on at least 750 food items. A rising cost of living has precluded the region from being able to reduce the ever more expensive fuel subsidies. And, yet, as the price of energy rose or stayed high, the drain on government resources remained beyond the capacity to pay. The oil price has remained stubbornly above $100 for most of the post-QE period. Fuel subsidies are common in the emerging markets, which is another way of trying to protect the citizens from the pain of a higher cost of living. Countries that have tried to reduce or remove fuel subsidies, such as Jordan, have also seen unrest. In November 2012 in Jordan, King Abdullah II, who is generally popular and widely admired, was faced with calls for his departure when his government attempted to reduce the increasingly expensive fuel subsidies.

Crack cocaine

Whatever analogy one cares to use, the reality is that every intelligent investor could see that the industrialised world had little chance of growth in the aftermath of the crisis, while emerging markets had the possibility of growth. So, emerging markets became the favoured investment destination after the crisis. The fact that one could borrow US dollars for very little, given the low interest-rate environment, and invest them into riskier investments such as emerging markets, meant that such a view could be turbocharged with leverage. Emerging markets were not the only siren call. The very same sovereign debt[72] that had in large part caused the financial crisis to begin with, suddenly became attractive again. That too was subject to the same sort of capital inflow on a leveraged basis.[73] This "carry trade", wherever the funds ended up, underpinned the profits at most major banks in the years following the crisis.[74] In this way, the morphine (QE) morphed into crack cocaine. So, it is hard to argue that QE had no impact on emerging markets or other risk assets. The whole point of giving away money at low interest rates, or cheapening money, is to compel investors to buy risky assets.

Here is the trickiest problems the QE defenders have. They want some asset prices to rise. It is welcome if the stock market and property market rise in response to the low interest rates and free money. Pro-QE central bankers are delighted to take credit for pushing such asset prices up. Other outcomes are not so welcome, however, such as the prices of much riskier assets such as commodity prices, emerging-markets equities and debt. In fact,

---

72 Sovereign debt, to be clear, is the government's debt, whether national or local government. Recall that trouble began when the market realised that sovereign nations, such as Greece, might not be able to repay their debt. Since then it is generally recognised that many governments have less ability to repay than had been assumed and this is why we see austerity and inflation efforts even in large, seemingly strong economies like the US and the UK.

73 Leverage means betting more than the capital you have. This can easily be done. Instead of buying stock in, say, Coca Cola, you buy the right to buy the stock of Coca Cola. In other words, you buy an option on the stock, which pays if the stock price moves in the direction of your bet (up or down). If your bet is wrong, you lose the price you paid for the option, which is usually pretty small.

74 A "carry trade" is when you borrow cheaply in one place, usually a country, and put a bet on asset prices in another, usually another country. So if the US gives away "free money" in the form of QE, you can use it to buy in the Japanese stock market, for example. You do this because the cost of borrowing money is so cheap and the expected rate of return on the investment is so high, and you can pocket the difference.

the banks started to buy and deal in the complex derivative structures that played a part in starting the crisis on but this time at even lower prices, with even lower covenants (repayment terms) and in even riskier deals. Why not if the money is free? Why not, if the central banks practically guarantee to keep interest rates low for many months, if not years, to come, and even tell the finance industry that it will have advance warning of when they change their mind. The catchphrase for this policy is "Forward Guidance". Essentially, it means the central bank promises the market that there won't be any surprises. It is an extension of QE.

So, having created a feeding frenzy, it is interesting to hear the Fed and other central banks say, "Well, we like certain outcomes but not others. It's good if the stock market and property prices go up here at home, but bad if the banks start doing 'risky' derivative deals and leveraging-up emerging-market bets or if food prices get pushed up." Interestingly, in the last few years many banks have announced their intention to sell their commodity trading businesses or to reduce their trading activities, especially in foodstuffs. It has become increasingly obvious that trading in such sensitive commodities is potentially dangerous to a bank's reputation. The regulators, like the CFTC, began inquiries to see if banks should be permitted to remain active in commodities.

Let them eat iPads

This brings us to the now infamous exchange on the 11th of March 2011 between the President of the Federal Reserve Bank of New York, William Dudley, and an audience in Queens, New York, who came to hear him talk about apples and Apples. Mr. Dudley was explaining that the price of commodities might be rising, but that's okay because the price of an Apple iPad is falling. On average, prices are falling, he intimated. A member of the audience asked, "When was the last time, Sir, that you went grocery shopping?" Another chimed in with, "Yes, but I can't eat an iPad."[75]

75 See Reuters.com (11 March 2011): "iPad price remark gets Fed's Dudley an earful" by Kristina Cooke

Wage price spiral

Following Dudley's "Let them eat iPad" PR debacle, we have to wonder whether the price of an Apple iPad *will* keep falling. It is possible that it will not or at least not at the same pace as in the past. Chinese and emerging-market workers generally are now demanding much higher wages. The upward cost of living pressure is compelling them to demand more. They also no longer believe they will be rich before they get old. Therefore they want to be paid more right now. Therefore the difference between emerging-market wages and industrialised market wages is narrowing. The high oil price makes businesses consider moving production back to the industrialised world in order to save time and shipping costs. So, not only has Apple announced their intention to move back to the United States but Foxconn, the Chinese assembler of Apple and Dell products, the second largest employer in China, announced on the 22nd of November 2013 that it is building a new $30 million production facility in Harrisburg, Pennsylvania.

From a Chinese or emerging-market point of view it is easy to see why this is now a war.

A boycott?

The 2013 Jackson Hole conference became a crucible for this white-hot debate. As the conference theme, the Kansas City Federal Reserve chose "Global Consequences of Monetary Policy". Chairman Bernanke did not attend – the first time in some 38 years that a Chairman had not attended. His absence was perceived as a kind of boycott since it was fairly obvious to all that, as far as the Fed is concerned, US monetary policy has no consequences and causes no spillover, so why bother discussing it? Even if spillovers were real, the responsibility lies with the emerging markets themselves.

The emerging markets, in the Chairman's view, had forfeited the ability to complain about the adverse consequences that occur when the Fed reverses QE because of their inability to take responsibility for their own economies.

It was deeply ironic that several emerging markets experienced financial emergencies at the time of the 2013 Jackson Hole meeting. The Governor of the Central Bank of Brazil, Alexandre Tombini, cancelled his trip to Jackson in order to implement an emergency currency intervention as the Real, their currency, collapsed as a result of the Federal Reserve's announcement that they would soon begin to reduce the level of QE by "tapering" the purchase of assets (namely government debt and mortgages). When "tapering" began in early 2014, it triggered a torrential outflow of capital from the emerging markets. The currencies of these countries began to collapse. In India the new central bank Governor, Raghuram Rajan, stayed home to implement emergency capital controls as his currency collapsed to its lowest value since India's 1991 balance of payments crisis. The Turks had to raise interest rates by 425 basis points or 12% in one single announcement to staunch the bloody haemorrhage that caused the Turkish Lira to lose 14% of its value in a matter of days when tapering commenced.

What is causing higher prices?

Sir John Hicks, the Nobel Prize-winning economist, wrote a lovely little book called *Causality in Economics* back in 1979, five years after winning the Nobel Prize. In it, he systematically trounced most notions of causality in economics. There are "separable" and "non-separable" causal relationships and the latter are heavily influenced by time. In other words, events are sequential or contemporaneous, for example. Either way, it is tricky to discern what caused what. So, I am wary of insisting that certain explanations suffice. I am also well aware that for those who believe the current models, methods and algorithms used to calculate inflation are perfectly adequate and can be trusted, no amount of explanation will convince those supporters that they are wrong. Similarly, those who believe the models are without any merit at all are probably guilty of the same blind prejudice. All one can do is lay out some possibilities and leave it to the reader to decide which arguments and which signals they believe to have meaning.

Hard assets

Many emerging-market central bankers argue that when governments start printing money it is easy to appreciate that each piece of paper is going to be worth less at some point simply because there are more of them. It does not matter if the piece of paper is an IOU (which we call a bond) or a piece of currency, a banknote stamped with the words "In God We Trust" or a picture of the Queen or any other symbol that imbues it with authority. When faced with a currency debasement, or any effort to make each piece of paper worth less, smart investors and good economic historians know they need to do several things. First, the principal refuge against the depreciation and debasement of paper money is to be found in "hard assets". So, even if banks are not lending the money out, investors are starting to seek refuge from the fact that more money in the system at low interest rates is worth less and less.

Hard assets include property and productive farmland. "Soft" commodities are also seen as "hard assets" because there is persistent demand for them, no matter how expensive they become, such as food, energy and raw materials. Hard assets also include things that potentially substitute for fiat money (money issued by the sovereign), such as precious metals (gold, silver and platinum) or even diamonds and other precious stones.

Some investors are prepared to start betting that rare and irreplaceable items will become more valuable during inflation, such as art and antiques, stamps and coins, diamonds and platinum. The work of 20th-century artists such as Basquiat, Pollock, Modigliani, Rothko, Lichtenstein, Bacon and others have consistently broken records for the highest prices ever paid since the QE began. There are investors who have built near monopolies and practically cornered the market in antique violins. Only 600 or so of Antonio Stradivarius's 17th-century violins survive today. They are in great demand in Asia, where classical music lessons are popular and people pay to rent them. The value of a Stradivarius has risen from $2 million to $6 million since QE began. High-quality antique pianos have attracted a lot of investor attention too. The share price of Steinway, the piano company whose strap line is "Making the world's finest pianos for over 160 years", hit a record high on a bid made for the company in 2013.

The price of high-grade diamonds has also soared into the stratosphere. The Pink Star, a nearly 60-carat stone, sold for a record $83 million in 2013, smashing the previous record of $46 million for a comparable gem.[76] It is an old story. For some, diamonds have proved a compelling store of value, given that a massive amount of wealth can be stored in a relatively small item that cannot set off a metal detector. Rough diamond prices have increased by 75% since the crisis and very high quality, rare diamonds continue to reach record prices.

Diamonds, gold, beef, pork, fish, wheat, soy, platinum, property, agricultural farmland and other such "hard assets" have reached record prices since the financial crisis. Granted, these prices are hugely volatile, but, in general, they keep rising higher in spite of news that global demand is actually slowing.

Endless QE but no lending

This is true, in part, because these price movements have been driven by scarcity too. It is not just demand that pulls these prices upward. Most of these hard assets (food, energy and raw materials) require a good deal of working capital to extract them. Agriculture and mining have, in the main, enjoyed lots of new investment into the price of the assets since the financial crisis. Just because the share prices of mining and agribusiness ventures goes up does not mean money is made available for actual operations. Banks pulled all their credit lines and overdraft facilities from such businesses and will not make new loans.

This divergence has puzzled economists and policymakers. On the one hand, firms can raise money in the capital markets at

---

76 The buyer ended up defaulting on the purchase. Isaac Wolf, a diamond-cutting expert, announced his intention to pay for the stone with the backing of outside investors on YouTube. When he defaulted, Sotheby's was obliged to stump up $60 million for the seller under the terms of the agreement. So, a record price was still paid. But, such a default might be an important signal too.

almost no cost, given that interest rates are so low – especially if they are big, blue-chip companies. But these firms won't deploy the capital into new investment. Instead they buy back their own shares, thus pushing the stock market up. Or, they sit on the cash. Meanwhile, firms that are not blue chip cannot raise money from banks or from the capital markets at any price, in spite of the fact that interest rates are low.

Many of the marginal suppliers in these fields went bust as a result of the crisis, thus putting more pricing power into the hands of those firms left standing. The end result is that fewer producers and less production make prices rise.

All this makes the prices more volatile. But higher volatility also dissuades people from owning capital-intensive production facilities. An interesting signal is that there are a record number of mines around the world that are for sale for less than the value of the proven reserves. Gold mines, iron ore mines, and diamond mines all fit this description.

No one will touch them for fear that they won't have enough capital to operate the facilities, for fear that the assets will be expropriated by governments once they bring the valuable assets to the surface, or for fear that the price volatility will hurt them.

China trusts

There is also the fear that the economy of China, the biggest source of demand, is slowing, which it is. China is one place where the quantitative easing liquidity was translated directly into higher prices for mined assets. Financial Trusts were formed after American QE began, by which investors would put their money into a financial structure that was collateralised by metals and commodities like iron ore and copper. The idea was that an investor would get his money back plus interest and the underlying investment would be backed by hard assets for which there was a genuine demand. This seemed a clever idea. After all, the Chinese leadership had made it clear in various Party announcements that it fully intended to build a new China: new buildings, new cities, new ports, new airports and all with a view to creating a domestic demand-led economy. The plan was to reduce China's dependence on exports.

As usual, when too much money is available too cheaply, discipline breaks down. More and more trusts were established that relied on more and more collateral. Soon as much as 25% to 30% of the record stockpile of iron ore in China was not being used to build the real economy but instead sitting in a Chinese port where it served as collateral buttressing the financial value of an investment product.[77] The fact that more and more iron ore stopped at the port and never moved inland was a signal.

Dig deeper

Meanwhile the rest of the world was delighted to continue serving China's seemingly endless demand for iron ore and other such raw materials, never asking about the final destination of their exports. And so nobody noticed or cared that the cost of the technology, equipment and personnel needed to extract and harvest raw materials had itself been rising. For the last 25 years, engineers and anybody else with math skills headed towards Wall Street because it paid so well. So, now many companies complain that there is a shortage of experienced engineers. Add to this the simple fact that most of the easy, near-surface extraction in mining and energy has already happened. You have to go down much deeper these days.

Remember the 2010 Copiapó mining accident in Chile, which captured the attention of the world, when 33 miners were trapped some 2,300 feet (700 metres) underground? The reason "Los 33" were so very far below the surface and were so hard to rescue is because there is a premium on the people and equipment that can successfully engage in deep and lateral drilling; a premium on those who are willing to take the risks. The crisis in Chile was a signal about the complexities and costs involved in modern mining.

Farming is also becoming more expensive. The rising value of farms forces farmers to make their land more productive.

---

77 Bloomberg News, 17 February 2014: "China Ore Stockpiles Rise to Record on Financing Deals"

Otherwise it would make more sense to sell the land and take the cash. Technology is the key to productive farming now. Modern industrial pivot irrigation systems cost $1 or $2 million and large farms need several. Satellite-based systems are increasingly required to tell farmers whether they are irrigating or fertilising land evenly and judiciously. Satellite resurfacing of the land has become commonplace even if it is expensive. These days the most modern harvesting machines, which are required to maintain the lower costs that large-scale farming offers, now cost somewhere between $500,000 $750,000 each – that's often more than what a house costs. Farmers in industrialised countries are finding it hard to afford these huge costs, let alone emerging-market farmers who have even less developed access to working capital.

Across the industrialised world, from Canada to the US to Australia, dairies are closing at a record rate because the cost of producing milk and cheese, just like the cost of raising cattle, is now nearly commensurate with the price that can be charged. That means there is no profit margin. Furthermore, the size of cattle herds is falling worldwide, even in the US, where the cattle herd has fallen to its lowest level since 1953. The price of dairy items may have hit record highs in recent years, but so has the cost of production, crushing profit margins and helping to explain why there is little investment or lending.

From the air, one can plainly see that much of the arable land in New Zealand is covered with large green circles. These are fields of grass created by the new pivot irrigation systems that New Zealand has been able to afford due to its farm cooperative, Fonterra, which is now the largest producer of milk powder in the world. By banding together, New Zealand's farmers are able to raise record sums from the global capital markets to fund the purchase of the new irrigation systems. You won't find as many of those circles in other countries because individual farmers don't have that kind of money. They are being pushed out of the business. This means milk and cheese prices start to rise. Bloomberg reported in July 2014 that butter prices had risen 83% in a single year in the US. Milk prices hit record highs in 2014. Emerging-market observers smugly think, "Inflation is touching you too."

Supply-side shock

It can be argued that the events of the financial crisis have created the first serious supply-side shock in the world economy since the OPEC oil crisis of the early 1970s. This is counterintuitive to some. Surely new capacity in food, mined assets or energy can be created if there is new investment? If the prices rise enough, new capital will be deployed and new production will take place. However, new capital is unavailable until the banking system is clear of its massive losses and we become more comfortable engaging in calculated risk-taking again. The cost of extraction and cultivation is rising for many reasons, thus reducing the profit margins. Together with high volatility, this leads investors to avoid putting new capital to work. So, while most people think global demand is causing the prices of hard assets and soft commodities to rise, they miss the fact that reduced supply is also pushing prices up.

Consider another hard asset: mined materials. The plight of Rio Tinto, one of the world's largest mining firms, is clear. In 2013 it announced the largest loss in its history, which came from cost overruns in emerging markets. What caused these cost overruns? Now we come to the heart of the problem for emerging markets.

Quantitative Easing and Qualitative Squeezing

The social unrest around the world is prompted by price signals, and the social unrest itself signals that there is a common thread weaving itself through the fabric of the world economy. The free money and low interest rates may have held up asset prices and institutions in the industrialised world, but the success of the policy is causing socially meaningful asset prices to rise as well. These are increasingly squeezing the poor – initially in emerging markets but increasingly even in the industrialised world.

A Question

As food and energy prices rise, the workers in emerging markets find themselves caught in a painful vice. On the one side is the debt and deflation burden. They may not have a debt problem themselves, but the debt problem in the industrialised world means the emerging markets have lost their customer base and therefore their old source of income. They now know they will not be rich before they get old. These emerging-market workers spend 40% to 70% of their income on food and energy, so when these prices rise, they feel immense pain. The two pressures bear down on every person, every family, every company and every nation. The pressure escapes in the form of a political question: "Why is all the wealth in my society being distributed to someone else and not to me?" There are two broad responses to this important question. One is to change the system. People can turn to the ballot box or to the streets depending on whether the political infrastructure of the nation can be trusted or not. The other response is to innovate, in everything from changing the system to changing the government to changing one's own ability to generate more wealth.

When the two pressures of debt and rising costs bear down simultaneously, that simple question – "Why is all the wealth in my society being distributed to someone else and not to me?" – leads to clear outcomes. One of these is wage demands. Emerging-market workers today are demanding significant wage hikes. The good news is that the workers are receiving them. The bad news is that this simply means there is more cash chasing the same goods, so prices rise in response to wage hikes. In many emerging markets we see what economists call a "wage price spiral". The really bad news for emerging markets is that this gives them rising inflation and thus increasing social unrest and renders them less and less competitive. The good news for the industrialised world is that the higher costs and reduced political stability in emerging markets is causing manufacturing to return to the industrialised world.

Chinese workers at Foxconn, the Taiwanese multinational plants that produces Apple, Kindle and PlayStation products, are now demanding as much as 70% wage hikes each year. Apple has announced it is moving to full automation and bringing all production back to the US. In May 2013, Apple's CEO, Tim Cook, announced a new production facility in Texas.[78] In November 2013, Apple announced it would be building a manufacturing facility in Mesa, Arizona.[79]

Miners in South Africa were demanding more than 100% increase in their wages in 2012 and 2013. The response is that mining firms are closing and mothballing their mines. For me, an early signal of the wage-push problem came in 2010 when Bangladeshi workers went on strike for higher wages. Bangladesh is to textiles what China has been to manufacturing. When the government announced a doubling of the minimum wage, workers responded by engaging in riots that took several days to quell. Why would workers respond to wage hikes by rioting? Because the rise in the cost of living was so high that doubling wages still left the workers behind. Since then, wage demands have persisted even when further gains in wages have been achieved.

These pent-up wage demands have only accelerated across the emerging markets as the cost of living has risen. They will persist now that it is clear that the demands can sometimes be met. It won't do any good to tell China's workers that they are no longer competitive enough or productive enough to warrant such wage hikes. They will respond to any financial pain by seeking to unionise in order to achieve the wages they demand. This movement is already apparent.

With wages across the world standing at a record all-time low as a percentage of GDP, and corporate profits standing at a record all-time high, we have to expect that wage demands will persist, especially if the cost of living keeps rising. Frankly, it would be shocking if workers everywhere did not demand higher wages once the economy recovers. Already the debate in America about a "living wage" is under way. In the UK the rising cost of living has emerged as the central public policy issue that will dominate elections for some time to come.

---

78 See *The Wall Street Journal*, 6 December 2012: "Apple CEO Says Mac Production Coming to US" by Jessica E Lessin and James R Hagerty

79 See the press release of the Office of the Governor, State of Arizona, 4 November 2013: "Governor Jan Brewer Welcomes Apple to Arizona: New Manufacturing Operation to Create 700-plus Quality Jobs"

The simple truth is that the smartest people in the economy are already demanding higher pay, and receiving it. The less well paid are starting to make such demands as well. A week after the 2013 Jackson Hole meeting, fast-food workers around America shut down many of the restaurants across sixty cities in their effort to secure a 100% wage increase. Of course they won't get 100%, but they will no doubt get something more than the official inflation rate.

Is there inflation or deflation?

Supporters of Mr Bernanke, those who believe the mathematical models are entirely correct, would say, "Even if it were true that the US and others are exporting inflation (which they would not accept), then emerging-market central bank governors could easily manage this by raising interest rates." Emerging-market leaders would respond by saying, "We get unemployment due to your bad mistakes and now you want us to inflict more pain on our impoverished population?" America would then revert to its usual stance on the currency, which was beautifully expressed in the standpoint taken by the last Secretary of the US Treasury to preside over the start of inflation – John Connally, Treasury Secretary under President Nixon. In 1971 Connally faced a room full of European Finance Ministry officials who accused the US of exporting inflation with the same conviction as emerging-market leaders today. His reply was that the dollar "is our currency, but your problem".

Economists generally believe that the expectation of inflation, of higher prices in the future, is expressed by the bond market. As fear of inflation rises, people buy fewer bonds. The yield, or interest rate on the bonds, goes up, thus making it more expensive for governments to raise capital. Think of it this way. When we buy a government bond, or our pension fund or fund manager buys a bond, we are making a loan to the government. We are effectively "buying" a piece of paper that says "I owe you" in say, ten years time, the amount we are lending to the government plus some interest that reflects the risk that the government might not be able to pay us back on time and in full. We might say it is really risky lending to the government of an emerging-market country and charge a higher rate of interest than the amount we would charge the US, because we think the US is unlikely to default on its debt.

But now we find that the bond markets of the biggest economies in the world are dominated by governments themselves. In the US, the government will buy some three-quarters of all the Treasuries issued in the market in 2013 and 2014. In Britain the amount is less, but still at least one third. If governments are buying their own bonds then everyone else must follow their lead and buy as well, because governments are pushing up the price. That means the bond market cannot fulfill its traditional role as an early warning mechanism that alerts everyone to a rising risk of inflation. Governments have used QE to snap off the antenna. So, it's a kind of nonsense when central banks insist that bond markets are not signalling inflation when the very same central bank is ensuring, through its asset-buying activities, that it *can't* signal inflation. The central banks have cut the line as sure as a person can cut the line that connects the brakes with the wheels.

In other words, the point of quantitative easing is to hold interest rates down. This, governments believe, will protect citizens by keeping mortgage and borrowing rates very low. It also means that governments are seeking to generate inflation, however, which is a way of defaulting on citizens. Governments are prepared to hold up asset prices today at the risk that they reduce our standard of living in the future.

Another way to support the bond market in spite of a rising rate of inflation would be to compel pension funds to own more bonds. This is not hard. Governments can place regulatory pressure on pension funds, arguing that they should hold more "safe" assets. The definition of "safe" is the sovereign's bonds. In Australia for many years pension funds were subject to the 30/20 rule: 30% of the pension fund's assets had to be in Federal government bonds; 20% had to be in state or municipal bonds. If the state compels pensions to hold bonds we can be clear what this signals. It's a way of pushing interest rates down but it also pushes the loss onto pensioners and savers. This has also begun.

Fund managers are under increasing pressures from governments and regulators to deploy more capital in investments that support the government's interests, such as infrastructure. Moral suasion is real.

The Fed on steroids

Another argument is that the efforts to create inflation won't work. Some point to Japan. It tried to inflate for twenty years and yet deflation persisted. Efforts to inflate won't work in the modern context either. The losses in the global financial system are so large that inflation cannot offset the deflationary pressure, but this explanation does not really hold water. What is the point of jeopardising taxpayers by forcing us to bear the debt burden if it is believed this won't actually work? It is especially worth asking this question when Japan has announced its intention to try again by doubling the monetary base. As Gavyn Davies wrote in *The Financial Times*, "Bank of Japan Follows the Fed, on Steroids".[80] It is worth noting that Toyota announced the first raise of base pay in Japan in six years in March 2014. So, even in Japan wages are starting to rise. It is also a signal that the price of a burger rose by 35% in Japan in the few months following the announcement of its massive QE programme in April 2013.

Another reason QE defenders offer is that the effort to create inflation can't work. The heart of their argument is that "It can't work if the banks are not lending". The banks are still impaired by debt and also by the increased capital requirements that governments are placing on them to prevent excessive risk-taking in the future. Therefore, banks cannot lend. The lack of lending means there is no "velocity of money". That means the money is not making its way into the economy. It's just stuck in the bank, which is why bank profits are at an all-time high. Inflation cannot happen if there is no velocity of money. This is true only until the velocity picks up, which, throughout history, it always does – eventually. Markets are endlessly innovative and creative. It would be unusual for capital to always travel the same path. A financial

---

80 See *The Financial Times*, 4 April 2013

crisis is a storm that creates so much devastation that it also opens new pathways through which a recovery can take place.

Today we see an interesting set of signals on the horizon. Regional banks in the US and some parts of Europe are starting to lend again. Crowd sourcing is picking up the slack as internet-based businesses displace the banking system and connect lenders and borrowers without the need for a bank. Companies that cannot get any bank lending or credit are now able to post their details on-line and attract loans from private investors. Companies such as IndieGoGo and Kickstarter are able to raise tens of millions for businesses that no bank would have ever considered. Whoever offers the lowest interest rate or the best terms wins the deal.

Similarly, Rolls Royce, the British engineering firm that makes aircraft engines and luxury automobiles, concluded that it should become a lender to its 1,900 suppliers. After all, who knows the collateral better than Rolls Royce? If anything goes wrong, their engineers can redeploy all the assets in very short order. In Britain, credit to suppliers provided by the UK's top 35 listed manufacturers rose by almost 50% from 2009 to 2014.[81]

Traditional banks, such as California's Bank of the West, are back to doing what they always did – making old-fashioned collateralised loans to successful businesses. By these means the velocity of money begins to increase, even though it does not necessarily show up in any of the Federal Reserve's surveys. Some will say crowd sourcing and company-to-company lending is marginal and cannot replace bank lending. This is a signal that indicates that money is doing what it always does. It is innovating and finding its way to where the profits are.

There may be no inflation today by a central bank's measure, but it is worth noting that the White House has started to tie Federal Government benefits to something called the United States Chained CPI[82] Index (C-CPI-U). There are many measures of the cost of living. But "chained CPI" tends to be an even lower number

---

81 See *The Financial Times*, 16 February 2014: "UK manufacturer's lending to customers rises to record levels" by Tanya Powley
82 CPI or the Consumer Price Index

than Core CPI. By using this lower number, as *The Washington Post* explained, the Executive can save as much as $130 billion over the coming decade.[83] Or, put another way, chained CPI is a way of denying Federal workers $130 billion of benefits over the next decade. The only reason the White House would choose this lower number would be if they expected inflation.

In the UK, the Government much prefers to use the CPI measure instead of the old RPI[84] measure. Is it really just a coincidence that the RPI is usually lower than the CPI thus saving the government substantial payouts that would otherwise have occurred?

Shrinkflation is a Signal

There are signals that prices are starting to rise, or that inflation pressures are building, even in the industrialised world. Here are a few that strike me as notable: shrinkflation, zigzagging and changing the weight and aperture sizes.

Notice that things keep getting smaller. Cadbury's announced in 2010 that it was taking two squares of chocolate off its Dairy Milk Bar but keeping the price the same. In other words, the price per weight went up. The comments by a blogger called Carlos, who was reported on zerohedge.com in 2010, reflect "shrinkflation".[85] He wrote:

> I noted with interest that the Walmart I shop at had cleared the shelves of "Great Value" brand coffee in 39oz cans for about two weeks. Today the new can appeared, with the following differences: 1) Can is now 33.9oz, down from 39oz. Also conspicuously missing is the conversion of 2lb, 7oz therefore no comparison in pounds is easily made. 2) Price for this smaller can is up from $9.88 to $10.48, by my rustic math an

---

83 See *The Washington Post*, 10 April 2013: "The Ins and Outs of 'Chained CPI' Explained" by Sean Sullivan
84 RPI or the Retail Price (or Prices) Index
85 See www.zerohedge.com, 24 October 2010: "Here Is How Wal Mart Is Squeezing Every Last Ounce Of Decaffeinated Inflation" submitted by Tyler Durden

approximate 20% increase! 3) Contents of can are no longer "Premium Columbian" Decaffeinated. Now labelled "100% Classic Decaf."

There seems to be less cereal in the box and more air in the package. After all, compressed air has a weight, so technically there are still the same numbers of ounces inside the package. It's just that fewer of those ounces are cereal. Or, the amount of cereal in the box changes and is marked on the package but you don't notice it because the package is the same size or even larger. A box of shredded wheat in the United Kingdom, for example, was reduced from 525 grams to 470 grams in 2014, though the price remained the same.

The actual size of tins is also shrinking. Tunafish used to come in a 6oz tin and is now often found in a 4oz tin. There are fewer fish in a tin of sardines. Consider Coke, which is now sold in a 250ml can, far more slender and short than the old 330ml cans. What's more, the new cans cost more per ounce.

Some say that stores are describing ten items as the "new dozen". The British newspaper, *The Daily Mail* reported a story called "Food packet racket: The sizes are shrinking... but the price stays the same" in March 2013. The number of potato chips – or crisps as the British call them – in a bag of Walkers crisps had fallen to about 11. One fellow wrote in to complain that when was a kid, he remembers that packets of Walkers potato chips were always full, while now there is more compressed air.[86]

Shrinkflation affects property as well. In the US, the Census Bureau reports that the median size of apartments in new buildings fell in 2013 to 1,043 square feet. This is the smallest since 2002. What used to be called a cramped studio is now a "micro-unit". There is now an industry that builds "transformer apartments" where a 420 square foot micro-unit can be adapted to different uses during the day by providing sliding walls. New York City launched the "My Micro NY" program in 2013. It allows the

---

86 See *The Daily Mail*, 20 March 2013: "Food packet racket: The sizes are shrinking... but the price stays the same" by Sean Poulter

construction of buildings with apartments that range from 250 to 370 square feet.[87] The Actors Fund HD has supported these developments because, after all, actors, generally speaking, don't earn a lot and now the cost of living in New York is rising. Now you can fit more actors into smaller living spaces. No doubt this leads to many jokes about poor actors beginning to live rather like sardines in a tin can except the sardines now have more room since there are fewer in each can.

The point is that shrinking sizes may signal that the input costs are rising. It signals that companies are facing pressure on their margins and trying to compel the consumer to "eat" the difference in order to protect their profitability. Yes, this can be cleverly and legitimately disguised as portion control and concern over your health. But then why ask you to pay more per ounce? Shrinking the size of goods is exactly what happened in the early 1970s just before inflation proper set in. We would all be wise to find a friend who lived through the inflation of the early 1970s and ask them what they observed at that time.

Zigzagging is a Signal

Another way that producers try to pass on higher prices is "zigzagging". This means they raise the price of something, say sun lotion, and then reduce it and raise it and then offer it at "half price". But, if you compare the original price and the "half price" you can often find that the "half price" is the same or higher than the original price. Prices are meant to move in response to supply and demand. But fast changing prices can also permit producers to raise prices through a kind of "sleight of hand" that consumers can be easily duped by. Not all "discounts" are discounts, it seems.[88]

---

87 See *The Gothamist* 22 January 2013: "First Look Inside NYC's Tiny New "Microunit" Apartments, Creepy Old Man Ghost Included" by John del Signore

88 See *The Daily Mail*, 14 July 2014: "Uncovered…great sun cream swindle: Prices inflated then slashed to give the illusion of discounts"

Aperture inflation is a signal

Here is another signal that margin pressures are rising and inflation is creeping up on us: the apertures on bottles of powder and tubes of gel are becoming bigger. A friend noticed that she could no longer gently sprinkle cinnamon powder onto her porridge or talcum powder onto her baby without a deluge of dusty powder coming out. Somehow the size of the holes on the bottles was bigger and the contents less easy to control. This is not an accident. Larger apertures mean faster use of a product.

The companies that manufacture powder and gels know full well that anything that makes you use the product faster will result in more profits for them. I learned this from someone who had worked for one of the world's largest personal products firms. It is worthwhile making the top of the toothpaste tube wider. It is also worth putting less powder and gel in the bottle or tube and weighting the bottle so that it feels full even when there isn't as much inside. All are sly means of making the consumer pay more for less. Of course, over time we learn to handle the new packaging properly, but we have a right to be disgruntled at the thought process behind these size changes.

Rising Government Services Prices

Austerity may seem deflationary but it typically involves having the government push more costs onto the citizens. In the UK, for example, the price of rail transportation has risen by 50% over the last decade but the pace of this extraordinary price rise seems to be increasing. The price hikes are certainly above the inflation rate and three times faster than the pace of income since 2008.

Everyone knows that the cost of education has been rising dramatically worldwide. Perhaps this is another quirk that makes it hard to get a grip on inflation. Central banks are not as good at measuring services prices as real-economy goods prices.

The billion prices project

MIT launched its own inflation index in November 2010 – the Billion Prices Project (BPP) @MIT. It measures the prices of goods in a shopping basket that the project leaders believe more accurately reflect what people actually spend money on. So far its inflation rate is consistently higher than the Federal Reserve's Core CPI measure. The BPP team began by measuring the inflation rate in Argentina, which it found to be substantially higher than the government's reported inflation numbers. As we shall see later, Argentina introduced a new inflation measure in 2014 that confirmed that the government had been substantially low-balling prices for years.

The British economist John Williams makes a living calculating US inflation based on the old methodology that the US Government used before the decision was made to strip out food and energy and add in productivity adjustments, which economists call "hedonics". He argues that various changes to statistical methods since President Clinton arrived in office have systematically caused the inflation number to appear lower than it should be. He tries to prove his case by writing regularly on his website, Shadow Government Statistics at www.shadowstats.com.

Williams prefers not to adjust the data for hedonics, which were introduced in the early 1990s in part to allow inflation to be adjusted for productivity changes. For example, an Apple computer is becoming evermore powerful, but its price is falling. Therefore its value is rising. Hedonics, however, work only in one direction. Apple computers may be falling in price but real apples, the ones we eat, demonstrate the opposite problem. Everybody knows the apples that we eat these days are much prettier than they used to be. But they also have less or no taste and arguably less nutritional value, therefore their value is reduced. The one-way adjustment of hedonics reflects the falling price of an Apple computer but not the falling quality of the apple you eat. Obviously, this skews the outcome.

The perception gap

Another signal of inflation is when a gap appears between the actual rate of inflation we face in real life and the rate that the government claims to be true. This leads to surreal conversations at dinner parties and barbecues, where the main topic of conversation is the rising cost of living when the newspapers consistently report that inflation is benign because the central bank says so.

For example, in Australia it now costs AU$45 an hour to hire a bartender in Sydney or Melbourne and more than that in Perth. The teenagers at the back washing the dishes are getting AU$21 an hour. Yet none of this counts as an increase in wages. No, somehow these increased costs are officially designated as "triple time" and "penalty rates". Employers have to pay over the odds for people to work on weekends under the recent Australian employment rules.

Here is an interesting signal: Watch a man's jaw drop as he is rendered speechless at having to pay nearly AU$10 for a schooner of beer in a smart, downtown Sydney pub. Having paid the exorbitant price, we can then watch the same fellow down his beer with his friends and scoff at the idea that Australia has an inflation problem. Technically, the Reserve Bank of Australia is correct. Wages have not risen even though the cost of paying employees has.

Which is right? Are the algorithms and models used by policymakers to calculate Core CPI correct? Or, is the regular person, who feels the price pressures every day and bitterly claims that prices are rising, correct?

One thing seems sure. Even if the central bank models are right, the wider this perception gap grows, the more our trust in central banks will erode. This alone warrants attention by both central banks and the public.

Some governments will try to have it both ways. Consider the situation in Britain. On the one hand, Mark Carney, the new Governor of the Bank of England, says it is silly to abide by the inflation target that the Bank of England has been exceeding for several years now. Instead, he calls for a "nominal GDP target". In central banking language he is very clearly not calling for a "*real* GDP target", which means he is declaring his intention to stoke inflation. This is sufficiently obscure and obfuscated enough for the public not to notice the discussion or the decision. But the public do notice that property prices in London, and across other parts of the UK, keep hitting all-time record highs and are rising at least 10% per annum, which is at least four times faster than the national (declared) inflation rate. In 2013 the average price of a property in the UK rose for the first time in every single part of the country. In response to this price pressure the Bank of England then said that the UK should have price controls on property so that they can only rise by 5% each year.

This is exactly what China tried to do. It pushed money into the economy to keep it stimulated but then tried to control prices on property. But if you push the money in, it is not surprising that it pushes up asset prices. So we see the British actively adding QE, indeed aggressively choosing which assets and areas of the economy should receive relatively more or less stimulus and taking credit for the economy's "recovery". In the meantime, the British Prime Minister announces various summits and then the creation of a working group at the Treasury, which all aim to mitigate the rise in the cost of living. This would mean that even the politicians and the Bank of England staff know that the cost of living is indeed... rising. Otherwise, why would you need to set up government working groups to mitigate the rising costs?

Default signals

Whenever governments default, they deny, deny, deny and then announce they have defaulted. The usual sequence is something like this: The Finance Minister of the nation says, "We will never default." This is the first signal that a default is very likely to happen. He repeats his statement with increasing vigour until the Finance Ministry (not the Minister) then says something like, "Our nation has successfully extended the payments due to foreign creditors and is delighted to announce the new plan has been accepted by the creditors." This actually means, "Bring the defibrillator; we have defaulted and the creditors must now face substantial losses." In other words, "We will never pay back (on time or possibly at all)." Unlike most defaults, inflation is not announced at a press conference and clearly articulated as, "We will never pay you back in time or in full."

The wonderful thing about choosing inflation as a means of drawing down debt (or defaulting) is that no one feels the money slipping out of their back pocket. Central bankers today are gravely offended by the suggestion that they have chosen to inflate or that they have chosen to default on their own citizens. Jens O Parsson (the *nom de plume* of the American lawyer Ronald H Marcks) wrote in his 1974 book on economics, *Dying of Money*, that inflation comes to pass through the constant taking of the softest option.[89] It is not that governments choose inflation. They don't aim to default on their citizens. It is just that all the other options are so much worse. But, whether deliberate or not, such defaults will impact on the public and the public needs to be made alert to the process by which governments are breaking the social contract without declaring they are doing so.

The growing gap between actual inflation versus the government's assessment of inflation is a place where everyone will either make or lose a lot of money in the coming years, depending on whether inflation actually plays out. It is also where central banks will lose or retain the hard-won trust the public has held in them until now.

Inflation signals

Whether inflation is deliberate or inadvertent, citizens of emerging-markets are feeling the pinch of higher costs and higher prices. In Singapore, one of the most expensive cities in the world, the official inflation rate is about 5%, but everybody laughs openly at this number and knows that living in Singapore costs at least 10% or more each year just to sustain the old standard of living. Street protests have now begun, which is really something given the government's reputation of intolerance towards people who take to the streets. The authorities will now have a large dossier on every protestor.

London is the same. The official rate of inflation has been between 2% and 4.5% since the crisis began and yet everyone

---

89 This is probably the best book on inflation that I have ever read: *The Dying of Money: Lessons of the Great German and American Inflations* by Jens O Parsson (Wellspring Press, 1974)

knows that cost of housing, transport, food, energy, school fees and everything else that is essential to city life is rising far more forcefully than that. Of course, a prosperous city like London does not represent the entire nation's experience of price movements, although even secondary cities in the UK are now experiencing price rises. In general, though, large cities and megacities are arguably the hottest part of the economic crucible. The gap between the government's reading of the temperature and what people actually experience is what causes protests to begin – from complaints about definitions and methodology to marching in the streets.

Even if there is no gap between the actual rate of inflation and what the government declares it to be, there is a far more important gap: the one between real and nominal growth. The Swedish economist Knut Wicksell (1851-1926) explained that if we want to know where we stand, it is not enough to know what the growth rate is. We also need to know what the inflation rate is and to subtract that from the growth rate. This gives us the "real" rate of growth, as opposed to the "nominal" rate of growth. We also need to know what the actual inflation rate is rather than the government's definition of the inflation rate.

Just as we would warn a driver that there is a gaping, growing hole in the road, it seems only just to warn the public what will happen to them if, by some obscure possibility, the efforts by policymakers to stimulate and "reflate" the economy actually work. We need to think about what will happen to us if the gap widens between the actual rate of inflation and the official rate, or between real and nominal growth rates, or between the financial model's view of reality versus the reality that we have to live by.

Not one man in a million

Sadly, these gaps are not visible (until it is too late). In his book, *The Economic Consequences of the Peace*, the great British economist John Maynard Keynes (1883-1946) quoted Lenin, who pointed out that inflation is extremely difficult to identify. According to Keynes:

> "Lenin was certainly right. There is no subtler, nor surer means of overturning the existing basis of society than to debauch

the currency. The process engages all the hidden forces of economic law on the side of destruction, and it does so in a manner which not one man in a million is able to diagnose."[90]

This is exactly what makes inflation so very attractive to indebted governments – it is hard to spot. This is one reason why it is bound to be the preferred choice of every policymaker in the industrialised world today, in spite of our knowledge of history. If deflation must be avoided at all costs, then, by definition, policymakers are telling us they intend to take many risks with inflation.

But, the popular view is that there is no chance inflation will ensue. Today's rising prices, it is assumed, are temporary and will not translate into a more generalised price pressure. If anything, the central view is that "We should be so lucky as to get some inflation". The old saying, "Be careful what you wish for" springs to mind.

There are several confusing factors when it comes to inflation risks. One is that asset prices are rising but central banks don't include asset prices in their inflation calculation. When house prices go up, when stock markets hit record high prices, these factors are not well reflected in the core CPI calculation in most countries. Their impact is inevitably limited. Another tricky issue is that interest rates cannot rise because central banks are typically now the largest buyers of their own nation's debt. So, the usual signals of inflation have been absent. And yet, there is growing discomfort with the rising cost of living.

Meanwhile, in July 2014, Janet Yellen delivered testimony to the US Congress and declared that inflation was too low. She intimated that interest rates should not rise until there is a higher inflation rate. Within 24 hours, Hershey's, the most popular chocolate manufacturer in America, announced it would be raising the price of its candy by 8%.[91] The input costs for candy

---

90 From *The Economic Consequences of the Peace* by JM Keynes (1919), page 108
91 See *CNN Money* (15 July, 2014): "Hershey raises prices by 8%" by Katie Lobosco

175

had all risen dramatically. Farmland, cattle and cocoa had all hit record high prices by that time. Chocolate is being called "the new champagne" due to the price increases and the supply shortages. Candy bars and their sizes may seem a small and insignificant signal. But, it is a signal that tells us the input costs of daily life are accelerating whether the official data reflects this or not.

It is also a signal when the Federal Reserve and other central banks, like the bank of England start to raise interest rates and reduce liquidity. No doubt these institutions will argue that a single rate hike is the equivalent of killing inflation risk. But the reality is that it will take a lot of rate hikes to get the economy just back to neutral. Only from that point can a rate hike be considered a "tightening: of policy. Anything below neutral, however one chooses to define that, is just normalizing. Central banks will want it both ways. They will want to say they are not tightening and yet get credit for diminishing inflation risk. This itself is an important signal: if central banks feel the need to protect their reputations by being seen to be attempting to address inflation risks.

Hubris signals

What really worries many in the emerging markets and in the financial industry is the simple notion that the central banks of the industrialised world believe they can both control the markets and control the inflation outcome. It is also increasingly apparent that policymakers today believe they can control inflation. They think they are smarter, better equipped and more competent than any predecessors. It is this hubris that leads Janet Yellen to talk about "optimal control".

George F Will, the revered Pulitzer Prize-winning *Washington Post* columnist, wryly commented on a *Financial Times* description of Janet Yellen as "poised to take the tiller of the US economy". "Oh?" he wrote, "The economy has a tiller? And with it the Fed chairman can steer the economy? Who knew?"[92] Not only does the Chairman think she has control over inflation, she thinks it is a tool rather than a target. Her stance is clear: she will wait until

---

92 See *The Washington Post*, 28 September 2013: "The Fed has become a creature of politics" by George F Will

inflation starts to rise (in the official data) before she will act. This stands in sharp contrast to the normal practice in central banking. Usually central banks act some 18 months *before* prices change. Usually monetary policy takes some 18 months to take effect. Janet Yellen testified to Congress on the 15th of July, 2014 and confirmed that she intends to wait until inflation itself appears in the form of rising wages before she intends to act. By waiting so long, by believing the outcome can be controlled, by trying to use inflation as a tool, the Federal Reserve seems to be doing its level best to stoke a higher inflation rate. Signals of the stress arise from many quarters. Some FOMC members have begun to object. Esther George said, "Waiting too long may allow certain risks to build that if realized, could harm economic activity."[93] This was her measured way of saying, "this is a mistake". Another FOMC member, Richard Fisher has been more blunt. "Given that the inflation rate has been accelerating organically, I don't believe there is room for complacency." He made the same point more forcefully in a speech entitled "Monetary Policy and the Maginot Line" in July 2014.[94] He intimated that the economy is "drunk: on liquidity from the central banks. "Things look better when you have a lot of liquidity in your system."

I wonder whether an uninvited guest, a modern version of Gollum, has entered the house of modern government. Perhaps when governments moved the broken assets and balance sheet losses from the financial sector to the government's balance sheet, hubris leapt from the financial markets into the central banks.

What if it works?

Why should we care whether the efforts to reflate and inflate work? Surely it is better than facing a Japanese-style lost generation (or generations)?

---

93 See *The Wall Street Journal* (15 July 2014): "Fed's Yellen Hedges Her View on Rates" by Jon Hilsenrath

94 "Monetary Policy and the Maginot Line: with reference to Jonathan Swift, Neil Irwin, Shakespeare's Portia, Duck Hunting, and the Virtues of Nuissance and Paul Volcker " by Richard W Fisher, President and CEO, Federal Reserve Bank of Dallas, 16 July 2014

Here is the problem. Inflation usually ravages the very people policymakers are trying to protect: the poor, the middle class, the elderly and the savers. These are the people who, as Einstein said, "will pay". Those who pay more for less and who find they are called upon to shoulder the losses. Who will benefit? The wealthy, the financial institutions, the firms that have the power to pass on inflation to their customers and those who control the very commodities that people need to live. Lenin captured today's situation with his observation, "The way to crush the bourgeoisie is to grind them down between the millstones of taxation and inflation." The American hedge fund manager Stanley Druckenmiller has gone further, crying out that we are already experiencing the "largest transfer of wealth in history from the poor to the rich".[95] And this is before inflation has really even begun to get a foothold on the economy.

The signal is already apparent. In industrialised countries, especially the UK and the US, there is an increase in malnutrition. How can this be? The Trussell Trust in Britain found that in 2013 some 50% of British families had to reduce their spending on groceries due to rising costs for other bills. Visits to Trussell food banks rose by 170% from April 2012 to early 2014.[96] In America, *The New York Times* reported that the $10 to $20 reductions in food stamps, which was "the largest wholesale cut in the programme since Congress passed the first Food Stamps Act in 1964", meant the difference between being able to afford "one gallon of milk for the kids instead of two".[97] Basic food prices have also been rising in Germany in spite of its position inside the otherwise deflationary Eurozone. In early 2013 the price of food rose by 5.7%, which was a multiple of the national inflation rate. Potatoes had risen 44% in a year. UHT milk was up by 18% in a year. Butter was up 32% in a year. The US Department of

---

95 Stanley Druckenmiller made this remark on CNBC on 19 September 2013 in a live interview on the *Squawk Box* television programme

96 See the Trussell Trust press release, 4 April 2013: "Biggest ever increase in UK food bank use: 170% rise in numbers turning to food banks in last 12 months"

97 See *The New York Times*, 7 November 2013: "Cut in Food Stamps Forces Hard Choices on Poor" by Kim Severson and Winnie Hu

Agriculture issued a report called "Household Food Security in the United States in 2012" in which it stated that:

> ... 85.5% of US households were food secure throughout the year. The remaining 14.5% (17.6 million households) were food insecure. Food-insecure households (those with low and very low food security) had difficulty at some time during the year providing enough food for all their members due to a lack of resources. In 2012, 5.7% of US households (7.0 million households) had very low food security. In this more severe range of food insecurity, the food intake of some household members was reduced and normal eating patterns were disrupted at times during the year due to limited resources.[98]

Food prices are no longer an emerging-market issue. They are an issue for the poor worldwide, even in America. The problem is that the only cheap calories are empty calories. As the price of beef, dairy, lamb, fish and other proteins hit record highs, people are pushed into cheaper and emptier foods. Empty foods make a person fat but malnourished, hence obesity is emerging as a signal of deep rooted hunger.

We all need to ask ourselves, how long will we live? After all, we need to plan for retirement, for liabilities in pension plans, for insurance needs and to anticipate the level of social services that will be required in the future. The answer is that much depends on our personal income level. It may well be that even the early stages of shrinkflation and inflation are already pushing the poor into worse nutrition and shorter life spans while the rich can afford to keep up with the price hikes and ensure an even longer life than before.

We can dismiss the claims of emerging markets but we need to pay attention to the early signals that the acid of shrinkflation, of rising prices, is already eroding the incomes and the health of the poor, even in the industrialised world.

---

98 From "Household Food Security in the United States in 2012" by Alisha Coleman-Jensen, Mark Nord, and Anita Singh, Economic Research Report No. ERR-155, September 2013

If QE is an accelerant, then it is not so surprising that inflation in its various stages – reflation, shrinkflation, rising prices and the like – behaves like an acid. It burns. It damages and ultimately destroys the value of money. It erodes faith in institutions. The perception of new inflationary forces raises a problem of trust in the central bank. Is the problem, as Ben Bernanke sees it, that the public won't trust the government? Or is the problem that the public can't trust the government? This question hangs over us every day, especially as the gap between data and reality becomes wider.

The more the cost of living rises, the more likely the public is to call the social contract into question. Central banks are going to have to address this perception gap even as they forcefully defend their models. It does not matter whether the public is right or wrong in its assessment. If the public believes it is being lied to, it will cost central banks dearly.

I am reminded of the German economist and statesman Ludwig Erhard, the man who restored Germany's market economy after World War Two. After years of inflation, most prices in Germany were fully controlled and administered by the state. Germany had inadvertently become a centrally planned economy. Serving as Finance Minister, Erhard boldly decided to decontrol prices, allowing them to find their natural level. When reflecting on his experience, he wrote:

> To achieve increased prosperity, any policy which prefers apparent success to real progress must be abandoned. Whoever is serious in this must be prepared to energetically oppose all attacks on the stability of our currency. The social market economy is unthinkable without a parallel stability of the currency. Only a policy of this kind guarantees that individual sections of the population do not profit at the cost of others.[99]

We won't know for some years whether the bold experiment with stimulus and QE is going to work as planned, or whether the statements from the Federal Reserve and others about the

---

99 From *Prosperity Through Competition* by Ludwig Erhard (Frederich Praeger, 1958), pages 6-7

"costless" nature of the accommodative policy stance are genuine or mere public relations.

One hopes that the belief is real and grounded in reality, given Richard Feynman's wise observation. This world-class theoretical physicist was called upon to investigate the Space Shuttle *Challenger* disaster of 1986, when the shuttle blew up soon after take off, killing not only all seven of its astronauts but effectively killing the space programme as well. In his report, he wrote that, "Reality must take precedence over public relations, for nature cannot be fooled."[100]

Nature knows when it's in pain. Human beings know when we are in pain. We will inevitably respond to our pain when the economic vice tightens its grip upon us. This will be long before the data points that the central banks work with confirm that the bite into living standards has taken place; data points often being, by definition, lagging indicators. Therefore inflation may make an insidious reappearance on the landscape long before central banks see it. For example, eventually the size of things will become ludicrous. It won't be possible to offer just two potato chips in a bag. At some point the aperture of the toothpaste tube cannot get any wider. At that moment, the manufacturer will announce a price hike. When they do, central banks will find that their data changes and that inflation is coming to life. Some central bankers argue that they fully adjust the data for size and quality changes. Others say these efforts fall woefully short of accuracy. Either way, there is no need to be blindsided by this. The signals are clear and you can see them coming from a mile off.

People will start to question how central banks measure things long before data points move. For example, central banks believe that excess capacity and under-utilised factories will keep inflation under control. After all, such underused facilities can be put back to work, which would increase production of the volume of goods and thus bring prices down. But businesses in the US and elsewhere all say they are at maximum capacity because the old

---

100 From Appendix F of the Report of the Presidential Commission on the Space Shuttle *Challenger* Accident, "Personal observations on the reliability of the Shuttle" by RP Feynman, 6 June 1986

factories and facilities are so outmoded they can never be used again. Central banks don't make the distinction between under-utilised and obsolete very well. This may apply to their thinking about the risks associated with their actions too.

1951 versus 2015

The situation today is perhaps not so different from the financial landscape in 1951. During the Second World War, the Fed stepped in to buy US bonds to help finance the war effort and also to hold down interest rates during and long after the war. By 1951 one of the Federal Reserve Board Governors, Governor Eccles, was agitated about this loss of independence and the rising risk of inflation. Eccles, who later emerged as the Fed Chairman and after whom the Federal Reserve Building in Washington DC is now named, articulated the problem clearly. The Fed had become "an engine of inflation":

> As long as the Federal Reserve is required to buy government securities at the will of the market for the purpose of defending a fixed pattern of interest rates established by the Treasury, it must stand ready to create new bank reserves in unlimited amount. This policy makes the entire banking system, through the action of the Federal Reserve System, an engine of inflation.[101]

Today, the US Government, meaning the Treasury and the White House, is not specifically defining the acceptable level of interest rates. However, the Treasury and the White House are certainly pushing for a long-term commitment to ensure they are kept low and under control. This serves the interests of the White House, which would be under far greater pressure – regarding the budget and fiscal policy, let alone the recovery – if interest rates actually started to rise. This is why it will want to load the Board of Governors with like-minded folks. This is why the Federal Reserve finds it necessary to repeat the view that tapering and withdrawal

---

101 Cited in "The Treasury-Fed Accord, A New Narrative Account" by Robert L Hetzel and Robert F Leach, page 43, from US Congress 1951, page158

from asset purchases has nothing to do with interest-rate policy. This is a slightly awkward stance, since the purpose of the asset purchases was to hold down interest rates.

The important point is that it is not enough for the markets to be ready for tapering, let alone ready for interest rate hikes. The White House and Congress have to be ready too. Consider this exchange between Eccles and the Texan Congressman, Wright Patman:

PATMAN

Don't you think there is some obligation of the Federal Reserve System to protect the public against excessive interest rates?

ECCLES

I think there is a greater obligation to the American public to protect them against the deterioration of the dollar.

PATMAN

Who is master, the Federal Reserve or the Treasury? You know, the Treasury came here first.

ECCLES

How do you reconcile the Treasury's position of saying they want the interest rate low, with the Federal Reserve standing ready to peg the market, and at the same time expect to stop inflation?

PATMAN

Will the Federal Reserve System support the Secretary of the Treasury in that effort [to retain the 2.5% rate] or will it refuse? ...You are sabotaging the Treasury. I think it ought to be stopped.

ECCLES

Either the Federal Reserve should be recognised as having some independent status, or it should be considered as simply an agency or a bureau of the Treasury.[102]

102 In "The Treasury-Fed Accord, A New narrative Account", as above, pages 43-44, from US Congress 1951, pages 172-76.

Should the Fed simply be considered as an agency or Bureau of the White House? Have the Fed and other central banks – including the Bank of England, the Bank of Japan and the European Central bank – already lost their independence? This is a profoundly important question, given that so many governments in history have caused their own downfall by debasing their money and weakening trust in both the government and its currency.

In conclusion, let us consider whether the signals on the landscape support or detract from the arguments made by the Chairman of the Federal Reserve. Is it true that we can enter into and exit the largest experiment in monetary policy history without costs or adverse consequences because there are no spillover effects? But, the fact is that we live in a world economy that functions as a global market. It is very hard to see how we can make the following argument: The fall of the Berlin Wall brought in billions of new workers to the world economy who pushed down wages and prices and gave us the "great moderation of inflation" (which appeared in the form of stores like Walmart and Costco in the US or Aldi in the UK or more generally in the form of ever cheaper goods everywhere). But, now that emerging market workers are pushing up wages and prices it matters. Surely it matters that even a huge store like Walmart says it cannot hold back the price hikes that are coming from the emerging markets.[103] Your local shop cannot hold down prices either.

Is the Federal Reserve team really smarter and more skilled than ever before? Is it really comforting to know that the Federal Reserve and other central banks have entered into a historic release of liquidity into the world economy but we need not worry about the consequences because it will never work? That is what the "we should be so lucky as to get some inflation" argument assumes. Can central banks really micromanage the level of

---

103 Walmart and other huge stores buy in bulk so they can negotiate the very best discounts. They used to be able to say, "We will buy half a million pairs of shoes but at 20% less than the price at which China or Bangladesh offers them." These days the Chinese and Bangladeshis no longer agree to such discounts. Their message is, "Fine, good luck in finding somebody who can make them for less." Smaller stores have less negotiating power.

inflation so that we get just the small amount we need? Can we buy the argument that inflation is very easy to deal (while deflation is hard and truly menacing)? It assumes that central banks are good sharpshooters and will kill inflation when the time comes without damaging anybody. History tells us that somehow this is not very likely. What about the idea that the central banks can control the price of the Government's bond market? That may work for a while but in the end, central banks are not meant to underwrite government debt. That would render them an "engine of inflation" and completely crush any effort to introduce discipline on politicians and their fiscal expenditures. Do we really want a world where the government controls the price of money instead of leaving markets to determine it?

And so we circle back to George F Will's implicit point. Do we want a central bank that believes it can steer the economy and exercise Janet Yellen's "optimal control"?[104] Do we want inflation to succeed or should we be careful what we ask for? Does Quantitative Easing result in a qualitative squeezing of the poor? And, if the effort to reflate and inflate succeeds, have we just set the stage for another fifty or a hundred years of government intervention? Do we now live in a world where the interests of the industrialised world and those of the emerging markets are so painfully at odds that they cannot be reconciled? Is it possible that the same price pressures that are giving rise to social unrest in the emerging markets might also be eroding the income and health of the poor even in the industrialised world?

All this makes one ask that same question again: "Why is the wealth in my society being distributed to somebody else and not to me?"

---

104 Speech by Janet Yellen, "Perspectives on Monetary Policy", at the Boston Economic Club Dinner, Boston, Massachusetts, 6 June 2012

Can the Circle Be Unbroken?   8

China's Ministry of Foreign Affairs would not confirm this for days after the event, but on the 11th of January 2007 the Second Artillery Battalion of the People's Liberation Army launched an exo-atmospheric kinetic kill vehicle. The ground-launched object hurtled into space, bearing down on its target: China's own ageing weather satellite, which was orbiting some 535 miles above the earth. The satellite disintegrated on impact. Afterwards, the Russians and Americans complained about the dangerous debris China had left floating in space that now threatened other travelling satellites. Most of the international press focused on the technological feat. After all, China had just become only the third country, after the US and Russia, to aim at a target in space and actually hit it.

For many in the US defence and foreign policy establishment, the event was perceived as the "Sputnik" of our time. Sputnik was the first earth satellite and its launch from Kazakhstan in 1957 signaled that the Soviet Union, America's then rival, was ahead in the space race. The Chinese Anti-Satellite Test (ASAT) event signaled that the US defence stance could possibly be rendered useless by new technology. After all, if you destroy America's satellites you can potentially render the US Navy dead in the water. You can't easily pilot an aircraft carrier with a compass or a sextant. Without satellite guidance nothing happens: you can't navigate and weapons systems can't work. This has special meaning, given China's fears about America's endlessly increasing naval presence around its shores in the East and South China Seas and the Pacific. It is interesting that the Chinese military consistently train in conditions where they are deprived

186

of electricity, Wi-Fi, satellites and other high-tech support systems. This is also done elsewhere but perhaps not so consistently.

To informed observers, the event signaled something new: China's growing fear of its own economic vulnerabilities. It signaled China's realisation that the logistics of delivering food, energy and raw material at the right price to its population could easily be constrained by the US and its allies.

From a Chinese perspective the landscape is clear: It cannot feed itself. China's vastly depleted water tables and polluted water supply are a threat to the population. It also has limited arable land. The country lacks sufficient copper, iron ore, gas, oil and other raw materials to keep the Chinese housed, working and building. China is extremely dependent on bringing these things home from elsewhere.

As a result, China has become increasingly uneasy about the formidable presence of the US, which can potentially disrupt China's freedom to fulfill its basic needs. A glance across the South China Sea and the Pacific reveals the ever-increasing presence of the US Navy and those of America's allies. The US has steadily added to its forward capabilities in the Pacific since World War Two, but during the last decade the acceleration has been rapid.

As in China, American policies are often revealed slowly in a series of speeches and public comments. Secretary of State Clinton revealed that the US intended to redeploy military assets from the Middle East to the Pacific and around China instead. In an article in *Foreign Policy* magazine she wrote:

> One of the most important tasks of American statecraft over the next decade will therefore be to lock in a substantially increased investment – diplomatic, economic, strategic, and otherwise – in the Asia-Pacific region.[105]

---

105 See *Foreign Policy* magazine, 11 October 2011: "America's Pacific Century: The future of politics will be decided in Asia, not Afghanistan or Iraq, and the United States will be right at the centre of the action" by Hillary Rodham Clinton

Shortly afterwards in November 2011, President Obama gave a speech in Australia in which he said "As President, I have, therefore, made a deliberate and strategic decision... the United States has been, and always will be, a Pacific nation."[106]

Friction

The problem is that China does not necessarily view the US and its allies as friends. In fact, China fears that the purpose of placing more aircraft carriers and weapons systems closer to its shores is to make threats with, or actually use, them. The US Department of Defence Strategic Guidance issued in January 2012 made clear that the burden was on China to prove it was not a threat: "... the growth of China's military power must be accompanied by greater clarity of its strategic intentions in order to avoid causing friction in the region" it stated.

There *is* friction, however. It comes from the simple fact that the US and China have many competing interests. China wants security of supply and the US wants to remain close enough to China to disrupt that security if it feels it needs to. China wants to secure control over critical food and energy channels in the region, which the US and its allies contend do not belong to China. Philosophically, the US and China are also at odds. In the post-War period the US has championed a world in which the distribution of wealth and power in the global economy is determined by market mechanisms. China is committed to acquiring control over the supply of critical assets by any means necessary, including the use of state power. China's leadership finds it ironic to hear the US claim to support markets as the best means of managing economies, growth and power. Yet the debt burden that is owed to China is proving so onerous to pay that America is prepared to default on its debt through inflation, and to control market prices through QE and asset purchases. The question arises: "Who has more state control over the economy now, the US or China?" Which is a more "autarchic" economy:

---

106 From the White House Office of the Press Secretary, "Remarks By President Obama to the Australian Parliament", 17 November 2011

Russia or the US?[107] It can be argued that the US now has even more state intervention than China and Russia. As a result, the US has forfeited the ability to claim that China and others should be more "market oriented" and emerging market leaders are less inclined to answer America's questions about the way they use state power.

America's decision to bail out the financial system has consequences for China, as far as the Chinese are concerned, whether the US authorities concede this or not. So, not only is America trying hard to default on its debt to China, which means the Chinese public must incur a loss, but inflationary policies are driving up the price of food and energy, which jeopardises China's political stability. In this sense, some Chinese policymakers view US economic and defence policy as "enemy action". There are more than enough Chinese policymakers who understand that US economic policy is usually made without any consideration for its impact abroad. This subject can be argued over endlessly, and is. But it is impossible to argue about the purpose and presence of weapons that are within hitting distance. This requires a response, which China provides by focusing on dominance over space (the realm of satellites, GPS and communications); the high seas, where above-water capabilities (ships to satellites) can be challenged by China's focus on below-water capabilities (submarines to cables); and cyberspace, on which all military capabilities depend.

Meanwhile, most US and Western policymakers emphasise the commonality of US and Chinese interests, arguing that the two countries have far more in common than in opposition. But, there is a substantial group, especially in the US defence community, that see China's position as fundamentally hostile. There are those who fear that China will become more aggressive, given its

---

107 See "The post-Ukraine world order", the 50th Annual Lecture at the Ditchley Foundation by Professor Michael Ignatieff, 12 July 2014. He describes the differences between capitalism and capitalist autarchies, which are authoritarian in nature and involve a high degree of state control and intervention. Ignatieff calls them "capitalist in economics and nationalist in ideology".

increasingly precarious economic position, its rapidly ageing and predominantly male population, and the fact that the export-led business model is now damaged sufficiently that the Chinese public may not remain as quiet as in the past.

Shipping lanes

The only practical way that China can bring raw materials home is on ships travelling across the high seas and through the major shipping lanes that feed into its limited coastline. Some 90% of global commerce moves on ships, which is one of China's weak spots. It is dependent on shipping, lacking the infrastructure to rely on railways or airports, even though it fully intends to build some four hundred and fifty new airports over the next decade and roughly six times the railway infrastructure of Switzerland every single year over the same period. But, even then, air cargo and railways are expensive and logistically difficult. In the end, ships and shipping lanes are essential to China's survival and stability.

Anyone surveying the Chinese coastline can plainly see the overwhelming presence of the US Navy and the naval vessels of America's regional allies. Since World War Two, the US Navy has maintained a formidable physical presence, from Guam and Diego Garcia to Honolulu and Okinawa to Darwin in Australia. This presence has escalated in recent years. President Obama announced the "pivot strategy" in 2012, in which military assets will be diverted from the Middle East and Afghanistan to be redeployed in the Pacific. The strategy involves "strengthening bilateral security alliances; deepening our working relationships with emerging powers, including with China; engaging with regional multilateral institutions; expanding trade and investment; forging a broad-based military presence; and advancing democracy and human rights."[108]

All this is seen as potentially, or actually, hostile to China. It marks the continuation of an evermore aggressive US stance in

---

108 Reported in *Foreign Policy*, 11 October 2011: "America's Pacific Century" by Hillary Clinton

the region. The US has deployed its Navy in the Pacific under every US President since Japan bombed Pearl Harbour. After World War Two the US chose Qingdao in China, then Subic Bay in the Philippines, and later Asoka in Japan as the home of the Seventh Fleet, America's permanent forward-deployed naval capability in the region. All other carrier strike groups are based in the US. The purpose of having a forward presence in Asia has always been described by America as a means of protecting the region from anything that would disrupt the free movement of traffic along the many shipping lanes. In a statement to Congress by the Chief of Naval Operations in March 2012, Admiral Jonathan Greenert stated the position clearly: "Operating globally at the front line of our nation's efforts in war and peace, our Fleet protects the interconnected systems of trade, information, and security that underpin our own economy and those of our friends and allies."[109]

Who's protecting who?

The US and China are well aware that both countries share this common interest. But, while the Americans may say they are there to protect the shipping lanes for the benefit of all, including China, the suspicion is that the US is trying to protect the shipping lanes *from* China, not *for* China. Similarly, China may say it shares this common interest, but the US and its regional allies fear that China seeks to challenge America's presence on the high seas, space and cyberspace as a means of serving China's interests and not those of the broader community.

When the perfect circle was in play, common interests between the US and China were constantly reinforced by mutual benefits. Sales from China led to cash flows that the Chinese redeployed into the US bond market, thus lowering interest rates for Americans and further enabling American consumption of Chinese-made goods. In the perfect circle scenario, China had easy access to raw materials because it had the cash to pay whatever

109 See Chief of Naval Operations Admiral Jonathan Greenert's Statement before Congress on FY2013 Department of Navy Posture, March 2012

the market demanded. The US had no incentive to disrupt China's shipping because it served the interests of the US for the goods to arrive. The noise and pushback around job losses in the US was never enough to truly jeopardise the perfect circle, given the benefits that came to both countries.

Now that the perfect circle is broken, conflicting interests are far more apparent. China feels much more vulnerable to any possible disruption of the shipping lanes, especially in a post-Arab Spring world where it is clear that higher food and energy prices are a catalyst for social unrest. The fact that the US and its allies dominate space, cyberspace and the ocean waves creates the impression that the US could disrupt or interdict that traffic. This is a crucial practical problem when a lack of food stocks renders China highly sensitive to any supply disruption.

It also happens that natural gas finds in the South China Sea have ignited a new issue in the region. Modern technology now allows the profitable harvesting of the energy and mineral assets in the seabed underneath the seemingly insignificant rocks that form the territories that many Asian nations claim as their own. Oil and gas are now more valuable than ever to both energy-starved China and its energy-starved neighbours.

Further inflaming the disputes is the rise of nationalism and populism in the region. As Asian workers begin to realise they might not get rich before they get old, they start to question why the wealth in their societies is being distributed to someone else and not to them. Citizens are asking, "Why are the rich so rich and the poor so poor?"; "Why is corruption permitted?"; "Why should the current leaders be in charge if they are not serving my best interests?" These political pressures necessarily require the leadership in these countries to demonstrate that they can protect the national interest from a strategic security point of view. They have to show they can avoid food and energy-supply problems that would hurt the population.

These pressures also compel such countries to crack down on corruption. They must be seen to help the poor in their plight. Political survival depends on diminishing the widening gap between the rich and the poor. Different countries respond to these pressures in different ways: Singapore tries to restrict the number of Ferraris in its streets through onerous taxation. China puts corrupt officials on public display.

Fish

Let us not forget the fact that some 10% of the world's fish supply comes from these seas. In a world where the price of fish hit an all-time-record high in 2013, China and its neighbours are justifiably concerned about who controls that critical source of protein.[110] Arguments over fish are therefore intensifying, especially as the price of other proteins such as beef, pork, poultry and even soy keep rising. All fishing vessels in China now come under the auspices of the People's Liberation Army.[111] There have been an increasing number of confrontations between Chinese fishing and military vessels and those of neighbouring nations.

Cabbage Strategy

Fishing and fish are not the only drivers of conflict; physical presence is another. *The New York Times* described China's "Cabbage Strategy" in the South China Sea by quoting one of China's most senior Generals:

> "Since [the standoff], we have begun to take measures to seal and control the areas around the Huangyan Island," Major General Zhang Zhaozhong, of China's People's Liberation Army, said in a television interview in May, using the Chinese term for Scarborough. (That there are three different names for the same set of uninhabitable rocks tells you much of what you need to know about the region.) He described a "cabbage strategy" which entails surrounding a contested area with so many boats — fishermen, fishing administration ships, marine

---

110 See *The Financial Times*, 18 June 2013: "Global fish prices leap to an all-time high" by Emiko Terazono

111 See *The Asia Times*, 25 July 2013: "Fish the real hazard in South China Seas" by Lucio Blanco Pitlo III

surveillance ships, navy warships — that "the island is thus wrapped layer by layer like a cabbage".[112]

More recently China has become more willing to claim parts of the South and Near China seas as its own even though sovereignty of these areas is disputed by many governments. In a recent example, it seems at least 100 naval vessels from the People Liberation Army Navy (PLAN), which surrounded a gas rig which Vietnam claims is an illegal effort by China to claim their territory. Vietnamese and Chinese vessels faced off with water cannons and rammed each other. Ultimately China removed the drilling rig, but not before fully demonstrating how powerful the cabbage strategy is. In a more concerning development, Chinese workers and Chinese owned factories in Ho Chi Minh City in Vietnam have been attacked as a result of local anger about this dispute. Some 3000 Chinese were evacuated from Vietnam after several Chinese citizens were killed in the violent confrontations there in May 2014.

The South and East China Sea are now at the heart of a great contest. Countries are fighting for valuable assets: control of shipping lanes and food and energy supplies. These assets are worth fighting for. They represent real cash flows. The signals are compelling. On the surface of things, the US and America's allies are aligned with China by many common interests. Below the surface, however, the US and China are increasingly in conflict over these strategic assets.

Territorial claims

The most obvious territorial disagreements centre on the long-standing disputes over the many islands that lie within the 2.25 million square-kilometre radius of the South China Sea.[113]

---

112 See *The New York Times Magazine*, 27 October 2013: "A Game of Shark and Minnow" by Jeff Himmelman
113 See *Council on Foreign Relations* news brief, 11 January 2013: "South China Sea Tensions" by Beina Xu

The greatest and most obvious source of strain in Asia is the island of Taiwan, which is technically in the East China Sea and not part of the disputed island issue except that China claims that Taiwan *is* China. The American President is somewhat obliged by law to defend Taiwan under the terms of the Taiwan Relations Act of 1979, so, while there is a lot of noise in the arguments over Taiwan's status, China has used economic policy to calm the issues. China permits Taiwan's business community to become enriched by China's economy. China wins more support in Taiwan by deepening economic ties and encouraging wealth creation among the Taiwanese than by threatening military confrontation.

Taiwan, in large part, remains an important justification for America's forward presence in the region. The North Korean nuclear threat also justifies this presence, of course, but Taiwan is at the heart of America's rationale. It is also the many other, vastly smaller islands that drive the stress between China and the US. The South China Sea is riddled with island chains, craggy barren rocks that simply jut out of the sea. Most of them cannot be inhabited and yet their ownership is forcefully, and militarily, contested by China and most of its neighbours.

Follow the dotted lines

In 1948 a privately published map of the South China Sea showed eleven dashes that formed a line that indicates which islands were owned by China and which by Taiwan. Naturally the two governments still argue about where those dashes ought to be drawn. The complicating factor is that other regional governments claim those often obscure islands as well. In 2009, many nations formally protested against China's submission of a modified nine-dotted-line map to the UN. The line skirts close to the shores of every other nation in the region.

Protests were filed by Brunei; the Philippines; Vietnam and Malaysia, which filed jointly; and even Indonesia, even though it has no specific territorial claims. China responded by telling two senior US officials, the then US National Security Council Director Jeffrey Bader and Deputy Secretary of State James Steinberg, that this part of the world was now a "core interest" for China.[114] The phrase "core interest" has been used by China to indicate when an issue is non-negotiable. Initially it was applied to Taiwan. In 2008 it was applied for the first time to Tibet and to Xinjiang.[115] By 2010 it was being applied to the East and South China Seas.[116]

In other words, China has tried to declare the territorial disputes of the South and East China Seas "off limits" to outside parties. There is lively debate about President Xi Jinping's supposed use of the term "core interest" in June 2013 with regard to the Senkaku Islands, which Japan claims as their own.[117] General Martin Dempsey, then the chairman of the Joint Chiefs of Staff, was told in private meetings in Beijing in April 2013 that the term "core interest" was now applied to the Senkaku. This was quickly followed by a statement by Hua Chunying, a Chinese Foreign Ministry spokesman, who said, "The Diaoyudao Islands [China's name for the Senkaku] are about sovereignty and territorial integrity. Of course it's China's core interest."[118]

The US has escalated the issue as well. At a meeting of the Association of Southeast Asian Nations (ASEAN) in Hanoi in 2010, Secretary of State Hillary Clinton directly challenged China in front of this regional security group. China views ASEAN as a congregation of adversaries. Clinton said, "The United States, like every nation, has a national interest in freedom of navigation, open access to Asia's maritime commons, and

---

114 See *The New York Times*, 30 March 2011: "China Hedges Over Whether South China Sea Is a 'Core Interest' Worth War" by Edward Wong

115 See *The New York Times* "*Sunday Review*", 11 May 2013: "China's Evolving Core Interests"

116 See *The New York Times*, 28 August 2003: "Turnaround by China: Centre Stage at Talks on North Korea" by Joseph Kahn

117 See *The Asahi Shimbun*, Asia & Japan Watch, 12 June 2013: "In Summit With Obama, XI Declares Senkakus China's 'Core Interest'"

118 See *Japan Times*, April 27, 2013: "China officially labels Senkakus a 'core interest'"

respect for international law in the South China Sea."[119] This was the diplomatic equivalent of firing a machine gun into the air.[120] If you missed it, the relevant words were "has a national interest", which meant that the US and China now had directly opposing interests in the region.[121] Clinton significantly elevated the high seas issue by calling for "a resolution of the sovereignty dispute over the Spratly Islands and maritime borders in the South China Sea". She said this was a "leading diplomatic priority" and now "pivotal to regional security".[122]

Words were accompanied by actions, as reported by *Time* magazine. At the time of the speech,[123]

"A new class of US super weapon suddenly surfaced nearby (China), an Ohio-class submarine, which for decades carried nuclear missiles targeted against the Soviet Union, and then later Russia. This one was different: for nearly three years, the US Navy has been dispatching modified "boomers" [submarines] to who knows where (they do travel underwater, after all). Four of the 18 ballistic-missile subs no longer carry nuclear-tipped Trident missiles. Instead, they hold up to 154 Tomahawk cruise missiles each, capable of hitting anything within 1,000 miles with non-nuclear warheads."

The US also arranged for a number of aircraft carriers to arrive in the region that very same day. The *USS Michigan* appeared in South Korea and the *USS Florida* arrived in Diego Garcia, an island the Pentagon calls "Camp Justice" and the "Footprint of Freedom", which is central to America's capabilities across

---

119 Hillary Rodham Clinton, Secretary of State, National Convention Centre Hanoi, Vietnam, 23 July 2010
120 See "Secretary Clinton Delivers Remarks at ASEAN Ministerial" on Youtube.com
121 See Bloomberg.com, 23 July 2010: "Clinton Signals U.S. Role in China Territorial Disputes After Asean Talks" by Daniel Ten Kate and Nicole Gaouette
122 As reported in *The Financial Times*, 30 July 2010: "China blasts Clinton's Maritime Adventure" by Kathrin Hille
123 See *Time*, 8 July 2010: "US Missiles Deployed Near China Send a Message" by Mark Thompson

Eurasia. Diego Garcia has been the main base for staging bombing runs on Afghanistan and Iraq.

462 new Tomahawks

As *Time* put it, "In all, the Chinese military awoke to find as many as 462 new Tomahawks deployed by the US in its neighbourhood." These are subsonic, long-range, low-altitude "smart weapon" cruise missiles that are the most feared in modern warfare. No wonder it was rumoured that President Hu immediately summoned his security advisors. The spokesman at the Chinese Embassy in Washington DC soon said, "We hope the relevant US military activities will serve for the regional peace, stability and security, and not the contrary."

How could China respond to these developments? China has started trying to match the US and its allies by building a "blue water" navy with aircraft carriers and the like. But, it would probably be smarter, cheaper and more effective to simply disable the other side's logistical capabilities, hence the intense focus between the US and China on space (satellites) and cyberspace.

The White House launched the new "National Space Policy" in late June, 2010. This reinforced the high-tech ban the US maintains on China that, among other things, precludes all US and US company employees who work on satellites or space projects from entering China or having unreported contact with Chinese nationals. Overall, America's stance has been to maintain logistical dominance over China by denying it access to most high technology through America's control over space and satellites, which irks the Chinese terribly.

Is Google the CIA/NSA?

Similarly, China has always been suspicious that America's dominance of the Internet has a more nefarious side. *Wired* magazine's article, "Exclusive: Google, CIA Invest in 'Future' of Web Monitoring" only confirmed China's suspicion that Google *is* the CIA and the NSA (National Security Agency).[124] Ironically,

---

124 See *Wired*, 28 July 2010: "Exclusive: Google, CIA Invest in 'Future' of Web Monitoring" by Noah Schachtman

these fears were confirmed for them, and many Americans as well, the very week that President Obama and President Xi met in California in June 2013, when a young NSA officer called Edward Snowden took critical classified information from the NSA (on a thumb drive) on its systematic efforts to spy on China and on US citizens. It is perhaps no coincidence that Snowden went straight to a protectorate of China, Hong Kong, to reveal America's spying efforts to the world. This event further confirmed for China that the central target of America's cyberspace efforts is indeed China. In Snowden's words, "Thousands of technology, finance and manufacturing companies are working closely with US national security agencies, providing sensitive information and in return receiving benefits that include access to classified intelligence."[125]

These events made it hard for President Obama to continue in the American tirade against China's cyber warfare on American targets. But, the American left and right alike constantly complain about the extensive nature of China's hacking, whacking and espionage activities in cyberspace.

Meanwhile, the US side has upped the rhetoric about China's efforts to use cyberspace as a means of stealing Western technology and industrial intellectual property, from which China is currently banned by the US. Four Star General and military intelligence officer Michael Hayden, the twice-former head of the CIA and retired head of the NSA, was quoted by the *Financial Times* at the time. "As an intelligence professional, I stand back in absolute awe and wonder," he said of the Chinese campaign to wrest industrial and Defence secrets from major Western companies. "It is magnificent in its depth, its breadth and its persistence."[126]

Hackers and whackers

China's hackers (those who steal information) and whackers (those who damage systems) have repeatedly managed to get into the

125 See Bloomberg.com, 14 June 2013: "US Agencies Said to Swap Data With Thousands of Firms" by Michael Riley
126 See *The Financial Times*, 30 July 2010: "Ex CIA Chief Downplays Claims of China's 'Cyber War'" by Joseph Menn

Pentagon at all levels, including the personal laptops of various Secretaries of Defence, into the Patriot missile systems, the F-35 Joint Strike Bomber, the silent P-C3 submarine technology and many other critical defence systems. Given America's systematic spying programme, it would be a reasonable bet that the US has accomplished the same kind of penetration of targets in China. It is assumed that these targets go far beyond the military and include US banks, the Congress, America's power grids, technology firms, defence contractors, energy companies, human rights groups, law firms, private equity firms and any other entities that can provide useful information in China's search for critical hard assets.

Similarly, the Chinese are offended by America's repeated efforts to spy on them and potentially inhibit their internal systems. America does watch and listen to China in many ways. In 2006 the US started sending spy satellites over China, explaining that it wasn't its fault that it can't watch the nuclear threat from North Korea without catching a glimpse of China. China responded by "blinding" America's satellites with land-based lasers as they passed by. So, America shifted to higher-orbit satellites, only to find China's anti-satellite tests proved that it was only a matter of time before China could hit a US military satellite even in high altitude. The US then engaged in its own ASAT tests, but instead of destroying the whole satellite, they knocked off just a corner of it, thus proving the US has something China lacks, namely precision. The two countries remain locked in this competition as to who can throw further and more precisely.

Reconnaissance aircraft are permanently deployed by both countries against each other. This is what led to the accident over Hainan Island in April 2001. Hainan is said to be the base of China's submarine capability and where an American EP-3 spy plane from the "Worldwatchers" Squadron and a Chinese J-8 spy plane came within a few coats of paint of each other near the disputed Paracel Islands. The Chinese pilot, Wang Wei, was killed and the US crew forced to make an emergency landing on the very island they had been spying on. It took a week of tense diplomatic negotiations to get the US crew back home. The plane was returned months later in July 2001 fully disassembled.[127] China delivered it back to the US hollowed out, stripped of all its instruments and in pieces on Polet, the Russian Airline, no doubt to make a point. China's and America's spy planes continue to try and fly a few coats of paint apart but do so more carefully now.

Who's to say who is right? What is clear is that there is a new kind of Cold War and it is focused on ownership of commodities. If the old Cold War was the CIA in Langley versus the KGB in Moscow, perhaps the new war in cyberspace is the NSA in Fort Meade versus People's Liberation Army Unit 61398 on the Datong Road in Shanghai. Russia too is involved. It is believed that the Russian intelligence services use internal and outsourced cyberwar experts. It has been argued that the world's center of "denial of service" cyber attacks actually come from Ukraine. If this is true, that just provides yet another reason for Russia to care who has authority over the future of that nation.

Huggers and Sluggers

The Chinese understand very well that there are two broad camps in the US when it comes to China. There are "China Huggers" and "China Sluggers".[128] China Huggers want to embrace its efforts to reform and want to align the common interests between the two countries. China Sluggers focus on the competing and conflicting interests between the two countries. The Sluggers take every incident as justification for further enhancing America's military and technological dominance over a potentially hostile China. The end result has been something US officials call the "Hedge Strategy".

Ashton Carter and Jennifer Buckley explained America's dilemma with great clarity in Harvard's *Pacific Asia Review*:

> China's military future is not a secret it keeps from the world – it is a mystery even to those inside the country.

---

127 See *The New York Times*, 29 May 2001: "China Agrees to Return Partly Dismantled Spy Plane as Cargo" by Erik Eckholm
128 Sometimes called "Panda huggers" and "Panda sluggers"

Not even top leaders know whether China will become the United States' friend or foe in the decades ahead. Given this strategic uncertainty, the United States has no choice but to pursue a two-pronged policy toward China. One prong is to engage China and encourage it to become a "responsible stakeholder" in the international community. The second is to engage in "prudent hedging" against competitive or aggressive behaviour by China, pursuing continued engagement rather than treating the country as an enemy.[129]

Many forces render China unpredictable. First, there is the matter of the testosterone surplus. It is obvious that men outnumber women by a significant proportion in China and this has economic and security consequences. The ageing population costs more and more to support and provides less and less income to the rest of the population and less revenue to the state. Western militaries assume that when the ratio of men to women exceeds a certain percentage, wars tend to happen.[130] The testosterone surplus issue is offset only by the rapidity with which China's population is ageing. China has relaxed the one-child policy over time and formally committed to it in practice at the Third Party Plenum in 2013,[131] but it takes time to build a different demographic landscape.

What happens if circumstances remove purpose and meaning from this male-dominated, proud and poor population? One of the great social issues of our time will be managing to tell one billion Chinese workers, let alone all the other emerging-market workers, "We're terribly sorry, but you are no longer competitive in the world economy at the moment, so it's time to go back to the farm, reduce your expectations and we look forward to hearing from you when you invent a new business model now that

---

129 *Harvard Asia Pacific Review*, Winter 2007: "America's Strategic Response to China's Military Modernisation" by Dr Ashton B Carter And Jennifer C Bulkeley

130 Afghanistan and Iraq come to mind

131 See BBC News online, 15 November 2013: "China Reforms: One-child policy to be relaxed"

cheap labour is not working for you anymore." You know the old saying, "You can't keep 'em down on the farm once they've seen Paris". China's testosterone-rich and cash-poor workers will not "go quietly into that dark night"[132] and neither will all the emerging-market workers that compete with China. Huggers and Sluggers alike fear instability in China and across emerging markets as much as the leadership of these nations do.

In short, America hopes for the best and prepares for the worst when it comes to China. Similarly, China hopes for the best and prepares for the worst when it comes to the US. This is true whether the Republicans or the Democrats are in power and whether the Hardliners or the Reformers are in charge in Beijing.

The US and China alike prepare for the worst by placing more and more military assets in the region. These include ships, aircraft carriers, basing stations, communications, cyber capability, and deepened relationships with regional partners.

Another aspect of cat and mouse is apparent from the continuing intrusions by China and Japan into each other's airspace, thus forcing both sides to scramble their fighter jets. China's first incursion into Japanese airspace since 1958 took place in late 2012. That year, Japan scrambled a record 306 times in response to Chinese jets breaching Japanese airspace. More recently Japan has complained about Chinese submarines and ships using weapons-targeting and fire-control radar on Japanese vessels. Prime Minister Abe said, "This was a dangerous action that could lead to unforeseen circumstances... At a time when there were signs that there could be talks between China and Japan, it is extremely regrettable that China should carry out such a one-sided provocation."[133]

In addition, Chinese military vessels are now regularly seen moving around Japan in sea lanes as far north as the Soya Strait

---

132 A reference to Dylan Thomas' poem for his dying father, "Do Not Go Gentle Into That Good Night" (1951): "Do not go gentle into that good night/ Old age should burn and rave at close of day; / Rage, rage against the dying of the light" (Verse 1)

133 See Bloomberg news, 6 February 2013: "Abe Calls China Radar Targeting of Japan Vessel Provocative" by John Brinsley and Isabel Reynolds

north of Hokkaido and around the "first island chain" that Japan considers its first "Defence perimeter". This runs from Okinawa to Taiwan. Japan's "second island chain" runs from Japan's southern islands all the way to Guam. This is now the site for drills by Chinese military vessels. On the 11th of September 2012 the government of Japan purchased a number of small islands in the disputed Senkaku area from their "private Japanese owner", much to China's chagrin. Chinese ships apparently sent military vessels into the Senkakus "on 229 days and Japanese territorial waters around the islands on 54 days".[134]

Russia has also been buzzing around Japan with similar visits by Russian Bear Bombers, Fulcrum Fighter jets and nuclear submarines. Japan and Russia have never formally ended World War Two by signing a peace treaty. They remain in dispute over the Kuril Islands in north Japan. Of course, this is a long-standing issue. The two countries have been arguing over these islands since the Edo period.[135]

QE as defence policy

This increased strategic threat is in part what led Japanese Prime Minister Abe to announce the record quantitative easing in Japan. Japan doubled the monetary base in a single year. This was not just an economic policy decision. By stimulating the economy, Prime Minister Abe believes he can support his principal goal: the rearmament of Japan. Keynesian economic policy is expected to expand and support the economy, which also makes it easier to spend more on defence, which itself further stimulates economic activity.

Expanding economic policy is meant to allow Japan to strengthen its defence capabilities at a time of increasing threat perception. The Prime Minister has called for a change to the Constitution to permit Japan to be removed from the constraints imposed in the aftermath of World War Two. Until now it has

---

134 See the *Asahi Shimbun*: Asia and Japan Watch, 30 July 2013: "Insight: China puts Japan on notice that warship drills are now routine"
135 From 1603 until 1868

only been permitted to maintain a "Self Defence Force". This caused Japan to rely entirely on the US for its Defence. Now the Prime Minister wants to formally re-establish a Japanese Navy, a Japanese Army and a Japanese Air Force. Japan is also calling for the use of the old "Rising Sun" flag, which evokes images of past Japanese aggressions in the region and is renaming military vessels with evocative names that harken back to past conflicts. The first new Japanese warship is called the *Izumo*, which is remembered by the Chinese as the Imperial Navy's flagship vessel that defeated China in 1937 during the battle of Shanghai.

Japan is but one symptom of an ever-intensifying game of diplomatic chess between the US and China in the Pacific. China views Japan as an arm of the US in the region. The more the US and Japan collaborate on defence, the more it reinforces this notion. In February 2014, The Japanese Defence Minister, Fumio Kishida, began to hint that it would break with past policy and permit US nuclear weapons to be deployed inside Japanese territory if there were a "clear and present danger". Clearly this potentially significant change of policy is aimed at China.

The Americans rely on aircraft carriers and their battle groups in the region. The Chinese have decided to focus more on subsurface and cyberspace capabilities. On the 26th of October 2006 a Chinese Song-class submarine managed to surface inside the carrier battle group of the *USS Kittyhawk*, America's only forward deployed carrier. This meant the sub had arrived, completely undetected, well within missile distance, less than 9 kilometres off the carrier itself. It seems it was not spotted by any of the 5,500 personnel on board but by an American pilot who happened to be practicing training runs, by chance looked down at the ocean from his plane and realised the large object in the water was not a whale. Such "pop up" surprises are now standard.

Two years later, in 2008, China denied the *Kittyhawk* the right to berth in Hong Kong, thus depriving many personnel and their families the opportunity to participate in the annual Thanksgiving weekend that had been a fixture of the Pacific Fleet's timetable for many years. Having been turned away from Hong Kong without reason (China later said it was a "misunderstanding"), the *Kittyhawk* was confronted by a Chinese destroyer, the *Shenzen*, and Song-class submarines. The *Kittyhawk* went to full battle stations. The stand-off lasted a day. The US responded by stating that China would not be permitted to control American access in the Straights of Taiwan.

The military incidents around the South China Sea Islands have accelerated markedly as well. They seem to typically involve Chinese "fishing vessels" and "surveillance vessels" and the "fishing", "surveillance" or "research" vessels of those who contest China's territorial claims. These ships are often found firing at each other, ramming each other, sinking each other, running each other aground, warning each other off the area in question and having stand-offs.

These incidents fall onto later pages of the global press and are seemingly both unrelated and unimportant. But, the global economic conditions have now set the stage for a greater likelihood of conflict over these issues.

ADIZ

At the Third Party Plenum in November 2013, China announced the creation of a National Security Council. Its aim is to consolidate existing foreign policy and the defence structures underlying it and specifically cites the intention to counter "hostile anti-China forces from abroad."[136] On the 23rd of November the nation's first action after establishing a new Security Council structure was to announce the creation of an "East China Sea Air Defence Identification Zone" (ADIZ).[137]

If we look at a map (see *The Economist*'s version, below)[138] we notice that the ADIZ covers some of Japan and travels all the way to Taiwan's airspace. This also covers some of South Korea's airspace. Note that the Chunxiao/Shirakaba gas field falls right in

136 See the *Asia Times*, 21 November 2013: "Xi's Power Grab Dwarfs Market Reforms" by Willy Lam
137 See *The Diplomat*, 29 November 2013: "Five Questions on China's Air Defence Identification Zone" by Justin McDonnell
138 See *The Economist*, 30 November 2013: "Face-off: China's New Air Defence Zone Suggests a Worrying New Approach in the Region"

the middle of China's new ADIZ.[139] China and Japan have been sparring over these gas fields for several years. Apparently, a spokesperson at the Ministry of Foreign Affairs in China was quoted as saying, "China has complete sovereignty over the Chunxiao oil and gas field and administrative authority."[140] It cannot be a pure coincidence that, at about the same time, the Japanese announced the establishment of a National Security Council as well.[141] Japan responded to China's ADIZ by announcing its intention to substantially expand its mid-air refuelling capability.

The US responded to the ADIZ more aggressively: by immediately sending in two B52 bombers over the Senkaku/ Daioyu islands, unannounced. As *The Economist* described it, China declared that "all aircraft intending to enter the zone had to file flight plans with the Chinese authorities, maintain radio communications and follow the instructions of Chinese controllers – or face "defensive emergency measures". The B52s did not. Suddenly a stand-off loomed between the world's superpower and Asia's emerging great power."[142]

The South Koreans and the Japanese also began flying into the new without warning. South Korea announced the expansion of its own ADIZ in early December 2013 by 66,000 square kilometres. It now covers some of the territory that China claims.

There were reports that China's ADIZ announcement came just as the US was moving the *USS George Washington* carrier battle group to the Philippines in response to the damage caused by Typhoon Haiyan. That storm had been more than 482 kilometres wide at the time of impact and affected millions. It may

139 See *Turkish Weekly*, 25 July 2013: "China, Japan conflict on Chunxiao/ Shirakaba gas field"
140 See *The National Interest*, 21 November 2013: "Inside China's New Security Council" by Samantha Hoffman and Peter Mattis
141 See *Japan Daily Press*, 5 December 2013: "Japan launches National Security Council, discusses China and North Korea in first meeting" by Ida Torres
142 See *The Economist*, 28 November 2013: "Regional turbulence: China escalates a dispute, angering Japan and unnerving its neighbours"

also have been more than a coincidence that China's first aircraft carrier, the *Liaoning*, was docked, for its first public outing, at China's new "dedicated base" in the South China Sea at Sayang (also known as Sansha),[143] an island chain that is actively claimed by the Philippines.

Cowpens and the *Liaoning*

The noise level around these disputes and standoffs continues to rise. On the 28th of November 2013 the *Liaoning* and its battle group of two destroyers and two frigates sailed through the Straights of Taiwan. This set off alarm bells among many of those who have territorial disputes with China, from Taiwan and South Korea to the Philippines. Then, on the 5th of December 2013, the *Liaoning* and the new carrier's battle group and the battle group of the *USS Cowpens*, a Ticonderoga-class guided missile cruiser, nearly collided. According to public news reports, the Chinese view is that the Cowpens and its vessels were tailing and harassing the Liaoning within Chinese-controlled waters. The American view is that they were in international waters when one of the Liaoning's support vessels, a People's Liberation Navy Amphibious Dock Ship, veered directly into the path of the *Cowpens* and stopped leaving less than 500 metres between the two ships. Apparently the Cowpens was forced to take evasive action. Whoever started it, it is clear that both sides were taunting one another. Both battle groups were well within each other's "inner defence layer".[144] With so much at stake and with both sides provoking one another, the tensions and disagreements increasingly raise the spectre of conflicts that would take effort to defuse. In early 2014, Herbert "Hawk" Carlisle, the Executive Director of America's Pacific Air Combat Operations Staff, said, "If you look at some of the things that have been going on in the East China Sea, both militaries (US and China) have been conducting

---

143 See *The South China Morning Post*, 29 November 2013: "Chinese aircraft carrier Liaoning takes up role in South China Sea" by Minnie Chan

144 See NBCNews.com, 13 December 2013: "US, Chinese warships narrowly avoid collision in South China Sea" by David Alexander for Reuters

themselves very professionally. But the potential for something, a mistake to occur or miscalculation or misunderstanding to occur, is out there. There is significantly more activity from both nations around the disputed territorial claims, and that to me is a risk."[145]

In December 2013, the territorial disputes once again escalated when US Secretary of State John Kerry said:

"Today, I raised our deep concerns about China's announcement of an East China Sea Air Defence Identification Zone. I told the Foreign Secretary that the United States does not recognise that zone and does not accept it. The zone should not be implemented, and China should refrain from taking similar unilateral actions elsewhere in the region, and particularly over the South China Sea."[146]

Clearly the US believes that the extension of Air Defence Identification Zones by China remains possible, if not likely.

The string of pearls

While America tries to move its military assets closer to China and it keeps its intelligence capabilities further and further away. The US prefers higher altitudes for military satellites in space and keeps listening stations in Japan at Yakima, Australia in Pine Gap and Goonhilly, Diego Garcia, Ascension Island, Turkey in Dayarbakir, Menwith Hill in the UK, Fort Meade and elsewhere.[147] China is also moving a long away from home. In 2003 China embarked on a strategy that a team of Booz Allen consultants called a "String of Pearls".[148] China began to build ports outside

---

145 See *The Sydney Morning Herald*, 10 February 2014: "US general criticises Japan, Philippines' anti-China Views"
146 "Remarks with Philippine Foreign Secretary Albert del Rosario", by John Kerry, Secretary of State Department of Foreign Affairs, Manila, Philippines, 17 December 2013
147 Well chronicled in *Chatter: Dispatches from the Secret World of Global Eavesdropping*, by Patrick Radden Keefe (Random House 2005)
148 "Energy Futures in Asia" by Julie A MacDonald, Amy Donahue and Bethany Danyluk, for Booz Allen, 17 January 2005

China that would help it secure greater control of its ability to ship critical assets back home. According to the Booz Allen report, the string is created by a series of ports around the world that China "funds and effectively controls". The principal purpose of the string is to lessen China's dependence on the Malacca Straights, which run between Malaysia and Indonesia and end with America's ally, Singapore. Every year, some 80% to 90% of China's energy travels from the Middle East through this narrow channel as does some 40% of global trade. By China's reckoning, the Straights are effectively under US control, which makes its leaders understandably nervous.

One can have a long and heated debate about whether these infrastructure investments are from the Chinese state or private sector. It is not easy to compare the two sides of the Monopoly Board, to use a board game as an analogy, because the US has much clearer criteria with which to distinguish a commercial private-sector project from a military base. In China's case, the state controls both the military and the companies that are engaged in commercial ventures. But, from a defence point of view, it is usually assumed that the Chinese government and the People's Liberation Army are behind such initiatives. Similarly, the Chinese assume that the hand of the US Government lies behind the activities of many if not most US companies.

Either way, it is worth remembering the words of Lord Curzon, the British Viceroy of India, who said in 1898 that countries are "pieces on a chessboard upon which is being played out a great game for the domination of the world". He was making reference to a popular book by Peter Hopkirk from 1842 called *The Great Game*, which chronicled the exploits of the British, French, Germans, Russians, Chinese and many others to gain control over various territories and countries around the world. President Obama made a similar reference when he spoke about Syria in 2013:

"We are no longer in a Cold War. There's no Great Game to be won, nor does America have any interest in Syria beyond the wellbeing of its people, the stability of its neighbours, the elimination of chemical weapons, and ensuring it does not become a safe-haven for terrorists."

Instead, he said, "I believe that America is exceptional" in its ability to "stand up for the interests of all".[149]

It may be that the US chooses to believe the Great Game era is over and that it stands for the interests of all, but others may not agree. There is still a scramble for influence and assets.

Chinese-backed ports and infrastructure (such as roads and railway links to such ports) were initially located along the routes to Middle Eastern oil. After all, the US counts as its ally every single major energy supplier from the Middle East, with the sole exception of Iran. This explains why China has gone to great lengths to deepen its ties with Iran. That is China's "hedge" strategy in the Middle East.

China's String of Pearls begins in Hainan Island, which is said to be the centre of its efforts to build a blue-water navy, in other words a navy, like America's, which is positioned far from home, in blue water.

One view of China

China has the port in Sittwe, Myanmar and the Coco Islands, which also belong to Myanmar. The latter are reputed to be home to a listening station that is principally aimed at India, a country that China views as America's proxy in the region, certainly since the US-India Civil Nuclear Agreement of 2005. Under this framework the US shares all technology with India and establishes joint defence capabilities. Keep in mind that while the US is prepared to share nuclear technology with India, it maintains a severe country-specific ban on all tech transfer to China. President Obama also announced a ban on the purchase of all Chinese-made computer technology based on the concerns about the possibility of a Chinese cyber attack.

149 See *The Daily Beast* (www.thedailybeast.com), 24 September 2013: "Obama's American Exceptionalism" by Christopher Dickey

As a result of China's mistrust of India, it is building ports and infrastructure around India. China is developing the ports at Chittagong in Bangladesh and Hambantota in Sri Lanka. Pakistan gave China full operational control over the port in Gwador on 18 February 2013. Rumours abound that the Maldives has awarded the Chinese the contract to build its new airport in Malé. The Seychelles is allowing China to refuel its navy there, and there is talk of Chinese listening stations in Madagascar, the Seychelles and the Maldives.

The Middle East has been difficult for China, given that all Middle Eastern oil producers except Iran have been aligned with the US, at least until recently. America's unwillingness to assist more forcefully on the Iranian nuclear issue has alienated both Saudi and Israel, while America's support for the rebels in Libya further damaged relations with Saudi and most other ruling houses in the region. The rise of natural gas fracking in the US and increased talk of US energy independence further alienates the energy-producing countries of the Middle East, who realise the US may no longer need their assets. Indeed the US may now become a competitor in the energy markets rather than a reliable consumer. The tectonic shift in the relationship resulted in Saudi turning down a valuable seat on the UN Security Council in 2013, which meant the US lost a Security Council ally. Prince Bandar, the Saudi Ambassador to Washington from 1983-2005, said, "This was a message for the US, not the UN."[150]

This breakdown of the Saudi-American relationship has opened the door for China to deepen diplomatic ties with Middle Eastern oil producers, especially now that the US presence in the region is diminishing, given the committed withdrawal of troops from Iraq and Afghanistan. The fear that the US will abandon the region altogether once it has achieved domestic energy independence due to natural gas finds and fracking has also led to deepening ties between the Middle East and China.

---

150 See *The Wall Street Journal*, 21 October 2013, "Spy Chief Distances Saudis From US: Prince Bandar's Move Raises Tensions Over Policies in Syria, Iran and Egypt" by Ellen Knickmeyer

In the meantime, China has reached out to East Africa, where it is building or extending ports in Djibouti, at Port Sudan in Sudan, Lamu in Kenya and Bagamoyo in Tanzania. Chinese entities have invested in similar infrastructure in South Africa and West Africa – particularly in Nigeria.

Most recently, China has sought to take advantage of the "fire sale" in Western Europe. Greece, being cash poor and deeply indebted, sold its largest port, Piraeus, to Chinese investors and granted them shipping lane rights too. There is also a new port in Croatia at Rijeka. Portugal appears to have sold or leased the old Lajés Field NATO base on Terceira in the Azores to China.[151] The Azores, lying right in the middle of the Atlantic, are considered by some in the defence community to be as strategically important for China as Diego Garcia is for the US. A little island in the middle of the Indian Ocean, Diego Garcia has been the source of many of the bombing runs the US has conducted during the course of the conflicts in Afghanistan and Iraq.

Chinese developers are also trying to acquire territory in Greenland, which is suspected of being a potential naval base designed to assist in China's efforts to establish a foothold in the mineral-rich Arctic. The Chinese now have the fastest icebreakers in the world and a great interest in creating Arctic paths for ships to travel through, thus shortening the time for delivery of assets to and from Europe. It also happens that Greenland is the site of a massive new discovery of rare earth metals, which China now specialises in. Rare earth metals are essential in almost all defence equipment but also many commercial items, including mobile phones and magnets, batteries, solar panels, turbines and the like. A Toyota Prius alone uses some 20 pounds of rare earth metals. As it stands, China has the vast majority of refining capability in rare earth metals. This is partly because the traditional process for refining is so toxic to the environment that no one else wants to refine, but ultimately this means that the Chinese have a virtual

---

151 See the Centre for International Maritime Security, 8 February 2013: "Will China's Navy Soon Be Operating in the Atlantic?" by Felix Seidler

monopoly on refined rare earths, which leaves the defence communities elsewhere feeling remarkably vulnerable.[152]

In Latin America, Mexico and China continue to negotiate about establishing a commercial port in Punta Colonna that is potentially twice the size of Long Beach, California. In 2013 Nicaragua gave permission for a private Chinese developer, Wang Jing, to build a 273 kilometre, $50 billion that will allow a new access route to bypass the Panama Canal, which is now owned by the billionaire Hong Kong business magnate Li Ka-Shing who is assumed to be associated with Chinese state investors. Similarly, there remains talk of China's plans to back the construction of a 50-kilometre canal across Thailand at the narrow point of the Kra Isthmus, which would allow China to bypass the Straights of Malacca. These infrastructure efforts reflect, in part, the need to accommodate the much larger vessels that have come on the market, such as the Maersk Triple E Class, which is four times the size of the largest existing container ships. In addition, China has begun to conduct naval exercises with Latin American nations. For the first time in history, in 2013 the Chinese Navy joined the Chilean Navy to sail through the Straights of Magellan at the southern tip of the Continent, and Argentina and Brazil received Chinese naval destroyers.

China is also embracing a land-based strategy. China's greatest resources and most difficult provinces are all found in the far West, en route to Central Asia and the Middle East by land. China has been increasingly active in building up a military presence along the Indian border. India views China as a direct threat and assumes that the String of Pearls is actually an India encirclement policy. It is often said that China has never invaded another country, but India objects and reminds the world that China invaded India in 1962.

India's view is that China has also been testing this border. India claims that in April 2013 a unit of Chinese foot

---

152 See *Defence Acquisition*, 17 September 2013: "Rare Earth Elements in National Defence: Background, Oversight Issues, and Options for Congress" by Valerie Bailey Grasso

soldiers crossed the "line of control" near Ladakh in India by 19 kilometres. Others put the incident down to yak herders who inadvertently wandered off their land. Either way, the diplomatic stand-off between India and China lasted for three weeks, just before the Chinese premier Li Keqiang visited India, and had to be resolved at the highest levels between both countries.[153] India claims such border incursions happen all the time. The Chinese claim India is provoking them by building up a lot of manpower on the border. In 2013 India approved the deployment of a 50,000-strong new mountain corps, which is specifically designed to enter foreign territory. India is now building an all-weather airfield called Nyoma 23 kilometres from Ladakh at 4,000 metres. India claims the build up of personnel on the Chinese side required such a response. China is now building an airport at Daocheng Yading in the autonomous Prefecture of Sichuan, which has the second longest runway in the world.[154] Other airports include the Lhasa Gongar, Shigatse Peace, Ngari Gunsa, Chengdu and Bangda in Tibet. From China's perspective these are necessary for integrating the poor Western China into the richer Eastern China and for bringing back raw materials. From India's perspective this is an encirclement policy that allows China to deploy military assets to the Indian border with increasing volume and speed.

China continues to extend the Karakoram Highway to Pakistan and to link it to Gwador Port. India bridles at China's increased presence in Afghanistan, Iraq, Iran and throughout Central Asia. However, the most pressing issue for all of China's Western neighbours is its effort to control and divert the water supply from the Himalayas. After all, it is the water shortage in China that drives much of its need to reach across its borders for assets. India and China have failed to agree on terms for sharing the use of this water. Tibet supplies almost half the world's population with water, so it is no surprise that India,

---

153 Apparently at the Depsang Bulge area in the Daulat Beg Oldi (DBO) sector of Ladakh, according to *The Times of India*, 26 May, 2013: "India, China troop face-offs continue after Ladakh military stand-off" by Rajat Pandit
154 Today, Edwards Air Force Base in California has the longest runway

Pakistan, Bangladesh and others bridle at the thought that China is somehow diverting or blocking the flow. China is actively building new dams in Tibet – such as the new Zangmu, Dagu, Jiexu and Jiacha dams on the Brahmaputra – mainly for hydroelectric power but also for water supplies.

China's resource quest is beginning to attract broad attention even if most people are unaware of the events described here. For more on the new "Great Game" see Dambisa Moyo's book *Winner Take All: China's Race for Resources and What it Means for Us*[155] and *By All Means Necessary: How China's Resource Quest is Changing the World* by Elizabeth Economy and Michael Levi.[156]

The end of the peace dividend

It would be a mistake to think that China alone is an aggressive actor on the world stage, competing nose to nose with the US and its allies for control over various locations on the global landscape. Instead, the signals are clear. All nations must be able to supply food and energy to their populations at a reasonable price or risk anger and resentment, if not rejection and revolution. This is exactly what compels other emerging markets to join in the competition for control over valuable assets and supply chains. Emerging markets are even more vulnerable than China because they lack the size, the resources and the state power to pursue their goals. And yet they must. Failure to protect citizens from the world economy's vice of pain – the deflation and the inflation – can cause social unrest and governments' downfall.

This is how economic forces have now set the stage for geopolitics to move from the wings to centre stage across the world economy. It is not that anybody wants a confrontation. Neither China nor the US has anything to gain by coming into conflict. But economic forces are driving both nations into a more confrontational stance.

---

155 Allen Lane of Penguin Books 2013
156 Oxford University Press 2014

It would be folly to think that emerging market workers whether in China or anywhere else will accept a falling standard of living without a fight. I cannot imagine how we tell these workers that they must postpone their dreams of a better life, of more meals with meat, of becoming rich before they get old, until they become more productive. The loss of faith and hope in the future is going to provoke arguments and fights. It is going to provoke competition for scarce assets. It is going to generate conflicts. It is in these ways that the world economy transforms the peace dividend into a conflict premium.

Enter Geopolitics: Commodity Conflicts

D id the Cold War end with the fall of the Berlin Wall? Perhaps that war simply subsided for a period of time while billions of new workers entered the world economy and began to believe they would become rich before they became old. People were too busy making money to fight. The headlines about coups, juntas, assassinations and military events, which had dominated in the 1970s, all drifted away. Instead, headlines were full of stories about wealth creation, growth and prosperity. Previously "Third World" countries morphed into investable "Emerging Markets". Many came to believe that such countries would outgrow and displace the US and the West. Few devoted thought to the possibility that Russia would send tanks into Ukraine or that there would be coups and attempted coups everywhere from Egypt to Greece to Thailand. The idea that the US, China, Russia, Japan and others would launch their spy planes and fighter jets in the air and engage in incursions into each other's airspace, would have been laughable in the prosperous years. Today, though, economic forces have pushed geopolitics back to the center of the stage, where the drama is playing out more visibly every day as coups, juntas, protests and military events fill the headlines. The following events sound like something out of a John Le Carré spy novel from the Cold War. Except, they actually occurred.

Death 11 and Death 12

In early June 2014, two US B-2 Stealth bombers (with the call signals Death 11 and Death 12) and three B-52 Stratofortress aircraft arrived at the Fairford Royal Air Force Base in the United Kingdom just west of London. Amateur plane spotters were extremely excited because these aircraft are usually based in Missouri at Whiteman Air Force Base. It is extremely unusual for the US to send these strategic nuclear bombers outside the US. Strange events had started on the 30th of April, 2014 when the Federal Aviation Authority confirmed that the rare presence of an American U2 spy plane overhead had zapped and scrambled the computers and air traffic control systems at LAX Airport in Los Angeles, forcing the cancellation of 50 flights and the delay of another 455 flights.

In early June 2014, while President Obama was en route to Japan in Air Force One, a Russian Su-27 Flanker fighter jet flew within 100 feet of an American spy plane (an RC-135U Combat Sent electronic intelligence plane), somewhere over the Sea of Okhotsk according to Rear Admiral John Kirby, who made a statement about the event on behalf of the Pentagon at the time.

Russian military jets had been breaching and violating the airspace of its neighbours since April of 2002 when there were reports that the Bear Bombers had flown within 37 miles of Alaska. They were intercepted and waved off by two American F-15s. Then, in January 2004 a crewmember of the USS *Kitty Hawk*, a nuclear powered American aircraft carrier, filmed a Russian Bear Bomber as it buzzed the *Kitty Hawk* at 2,000 feet while the carrier was on manoeuvers in the Sea of Japan. In 2005 a Russian fighter jet actually crashed near the city of Kaunas in Lithuania. Lithuania, Latvia, Estonia and several other former members of the former Soviet Union had only recently joined NATO, the West's primary military alliance, much to Russia's displeasure. The North America Treaty Organiszation traditionally served as the principal military opponent to the Soviet Union. In 2006, NORAD, the North American Aerospace Defence Command, spotted Bear Bombers heading toward both Canadian and Alaskan airspace. NORAD, is based at Cheyenne Mountain in Colorado and serves as America's primary alert system for detecting Intercontinental Ballistic Missiles, or put more simply, nuclear missiles. NORAD scrambled Canadian and American jets to prevent the nuclear-capable Bear Bombers from getting any closer. On the 10th of May, 2007, two Russian Tupolev Tu-95s appeared to be heading into British airspace, forcing the Royal Air Force to scramble fighter jets from RAF Leuchars Fife, in Scotland. It later became clear that the Norwegian Air Force had also scrambled their jets that same day because the Bears passed over Norway en route to Britain. The Russians said that the flight was a training mission.

Occasional training missions have now given way to something more sustained and more serious. Japan has scrambled their fighter jets more times in recent years than ever since the end of the Cold War. According to official government statistics they did so 810 times between April 2013 and April 2014 in response to incursions. Chinese incursions occurred 415 times. Russian incursions occurred 359 times in 2014 and 248 times in 2013. Why are the Russians and Chinese doing this? In both cases they not only have disputed territory with Japan; the disputed territory is rich with assets. The Kurile Islands are reputed to have large natural gas deposits as well as the world's largest deposit of rhenium (which is essential for industrial engines). It also has minerals and metals. But perhaps most important for Russia is the fact that these islands are key to their ability to access to the Arctic. The Kurile Islands are also a significant supplier of fish protein to Russia.

Russian Forces have been expanding their reach in the air, on the sea and on land in a multitude of ways for some years, though increasingly aggressively since the US began to pursue QE. But, to cut across the nose of a plane at a time when the President's Air Force One entourage was in the country was a bold and provocative move. Then again, China and Russia and most other emerging markets view America's economic policies, and those of the industrialised world, as seriously provocative too. The local response to a rising cost of living and falling hope has been the rise of conflict as the public ask questions of their leaders and of each other. This creates the catalyst for geopolitics to reappear, as it did in Ukraine.

Ukraine and Crimea

By 2013 and 2014, it was obvious that Ukraine had an unpayable debt problem, with the debt-to-GDP ratio so large it was killing all prospects of growth. Food prices and energy prices in Ukraine had been rising for nearly three years in advance of the events in Crimea. It was long suspected that the then President of Ukraine, Viktor Yanukovych, a close ally of Russia, had been artificially suppressing the inflation data for some time, trying to mask the upward pressure in the cost of living. At the time it was estimated that Ukrainians were spending more than 50% of their income on food alone at that time. As a result of the squeeze, many Ukrainians began to ask that important question, "Why is the wealth in my society going to someone else and not to me?"

For some the answer lay in pushing the Russian backed President, Yanukovych, out of power and moving towards a closer alignment with the European Union. For others, such as the majority of citizens in Crimea, the solution lay in pushing for independence from Ukraine and closer alignment with Russia. Whatever longstanding allegiances had been in place, the economic pressures caused people to choose sides. By February 2014, the citizens of Ukraine, Crimea and Russia had calculated their geopolitical interests and concluded it was worth making changes. The Ukrainians pushed for EU membership. The Russian-speaking citizens in Crimea began a violent separatist movement. Russia began to support the breakaway separatists.

It is always difficult to pinpoint the start of a geopolitical event but when the EU invited Ukraine to join its membership, Russia's leadership felt confronted by a singularly important geopolitical issue. This was summed up for me when a Russian Ambassador asked me, "Have you Americans completely forgotten about the Cuban Missile Crisis?" My answer was "Yes. We have".[157] We have forgotten that America was threatened by Russia's attempt to place nuclear weapons in Cuba in 1962 and we, in the West, sometimes fail to appreciate (or even desire) that a Ukraine inside the EU would also likely be a Ukraine inside NATO. That would mean Russia facing NATO nuclear weapons

---

157 I say this with some confidence because my father was one of John F Kennedy's defence advisors at that time and worked on the Cuban Missile Crisis.

on its border, which would be as unacceptable for them as it was for America during the Cuban Missile Crisis.

Beyond preserving a buffer against NATO, I suspect that Russia's leaders also appreciated that most valuable assets in Crimea are food and energy. Ukraine is the breadbasket of the former Soviet Union and the one of the largest producers of food in the world. It has the highest concentration of black topsoil of any nation in the world, which amounts to some 30% of the world's supply. It is one of the world's largest fertilizer producers as well. All this has real value in a world where food prices are substantially rising and causing social unrest.

Ukraine is also the centre point of Russia's natural gas pipeline network, which is used to supply Western Europe. Russia artificially subsidised gas prices while Viktor Yanukovych was in power but threatened to raise prices if he were to be thrown out. This merely heightened the awareness of the dependency on Russia. At one point, as part of the protest against Russia, the "Maidan" government in Ukraine announced it was cancelling 85% of all the natural gas contracts with Russia. Of course, there was no alternative source of supply but the action heightened Russia's awareness of its vulnerability to whoever controls the land the pipelines pass through and to the prospect of Ukraine defaulting on the substantial debt it owed to Russia. And so we see another example of price pressures around commodities becoming a source of conflict in the world.

Other strategic interests and assets were also at stake. Sevastopol in Ukraine had been Russia's only or principal warm water port since the late 18th century, when it became the home of Russia's Black Sea Fleet. Ukraine had announced the lease to Russia would end in 2042. Re-securing Russia's only viable warm water port had even more meaning because of geopolitical events elsewhere, namely Syria. The civil war there, and use of chemical weapons there, had forced Russia to evacuate, or diminish the use of, the two warm water ports that had built there over the previous decade: Latakia and Tartus.[158] These had been intended

---

158 See *The Christian Science Monitor*, 27 June, 2013: "Why Russia evacuated its naval base in Syria" by Fred Weir

to replace Sevastopol. So, Sevastopol must have taken on new significance in light of the loss of the ports in Syria.

There is one further asset worth mentioning which is found in Ukraine. That country is reputed to be one of the world's greatest credit card hacking and cyber warfare capabilities. Perhaps this had no meaning or value to Russia or anyone else. But, to me it seems pretty obvious that some kind of control over such a valuable asset would be worth having in a world where cyber warfare is increasingly prevalent. There are those who accuse Russia of running these hacker networks and those who say that such networks operate independently of any government. I have no idea but someone in the local community is bound to place a value on this particular skill set which makes it worth considering.

When Viktor Yanukovych's government dismissed the effort to join the EU on the 21st of November 2013, some Ukrainians, the Maidan Movement began to protest and then revolt, slowly at first but with ever increasing force. By the 22nd of February, 2014 Yanukovych had taken flight, and by the 27th of February, 2014 gunmen had begun to take control of Crimea. Ultimately, between the 1st and 6th of March 2014, unmarked troops, (some claimed they were supposedly from Russia's 76th Shock Troops unit, but they may have been local paramilitary troops), took physical control over the ports, the airports and the regional Parliament in Crimea, the Verkhovna Rada. On the 6th March 2014 Crimea declared itself a new state. It is worth noting that Russia engaged in a surprise simulated "massive retaliatory nuclear strike" in mid April, just as things were heating up in Crimea. They launched weaponless ICBMs (which usually carry nuclear weapons) from two nuclear submarines from the Northern and Pacific Fleets and one RS-24 Yars from the Plesetsk Cosmodrome near Archangel which hit its target in Kamchatka.

What prompted these actions? I come back to a central tenet of this book. The loss of faith in the future of Ukraine by all sides was clear. The local ethnic Russian population wanted the separatist movement to succeed due to their loss of faith in their state, Ukraine, especially as the nation fell into overwhelming debt and lost the capacity to manage its internal affairs. The non-Russian population clearly preferred an alignment with the EU, but this was unacceptable to Russia and, ultimately, unaffordable to the EU itself. With all the debt trouble within the EU and especially within the Eurozone, no one had any cash to bail out Ukraine. The Russians were not prepared to be defaulted on by any part of Ukraine.

One other valuable asset was "in play" throughout these geopolitical events – pride. Supporters of Russia are quick to say that Nikita Krushchev, when he was the Premier in Russia, gave up Ukraine and Crimea in a drunken moment when the Soviet Union was briefly on the back foot in the 1950s. The restoration of Russia's pride and the reach of the former Soviet Union has proved to be immensely popular in Russia, lifting Vladimir Putin's popularity to levels that are almost unimaginable for any Western or even emerging market leader.

So, considering all this, it would be strange if other valuable assets, and Russia's interest in them, stopped with Crimea. For example, Kaliningrad, Russia's outpost on the edge of the Baltic Sea, is surrounded by Poland and Lithuania. Clearly it has a strategic value. In 2014 Russia announced it was abandoning the 2001 agreement that permitted Lithuania to inspect Kaliningrad for weapons, including nuclear weapons. At the same time, Russia announced flights between Sevastopol and Kaliningrad would be heavily subsidised, indicating that there would be increased traffic between the two locations.

The disputed territories of South Ossetia (officially part of Georgia), Abkhazia (formerly part of Georgia) and the breakaway state of Transnistria (part of Moldova) all have powerful separatist movements that threaten to mimic what occurred in Ukraine. All have heavily pro-Russian populations; all began to experience separatist movements that involved violence. In June 2014, the Edinaya Ossetia, the United Ossetia Party, won a 43% return in local elections based on a 60% voter turnout. That gave them an absolute majority and 20 out of 34 seats in the local parliament. Their central goal is to achieve independence and reunite with Russia. Neither the EU nor NATO recognised the election.

In June 2014 the pro-Russian leader of Abkhazia, Alexander Ankvab, had to flee his palace when he was overthrown in a "coup" led by public protestors. Public elections were quickly scheduled. Meanwhile Georgia announced its intention to sign a pact, along with Moldova, with the EU over Russia's strong objections.

Moldova's separatist movement is in the Transnistria region. The locals there have wanted to reunite with Russia since 2001 and voted in favour of it that year. Transnistria is on the border between Western Ukraine and Eastern Moldova. Clearly it would have immense strategic value if Russia wanted to apply further pressures to Ukraine. Also, Moldova has as its capital a very large warm water port: Odessa. Fighting between pro- and anti-Russian groups in the region has lead to violence and killings. In response, the EU and the US keep offering Georgia and Moldova promises of cash and investments.

But, Russia's efforts to build and retain valuable assets are not restricted to its borders. Like China, Russia's reach is expanding. It plays its own hand at the "Great Game". On the 26th of February 2014, Russia's Defence Minister, Sergei Shoigu, said that Russia was preparing to build military bases in Vietnam, Venezuela, Nicaragua, the Seychelles, Singapore, and Djibouti among other far-flung locales.

The Eastern Mediterranean

Russia's desire for a presence in the Mediterranean has intensified for the same reason as China's interest in the disputed islands of the South China Sea: the discovery of energy reserves. There is a real possibility that the natural gas and potential oil reserves in the Eastern Mediterranean are extremely large and accessible given new drilling technology.[159] Of course, ownership of the gas fields is bound to be contested by many countries in the region,

---

159 10 trillion cubic square feet (TCF) at the Tamar gas field and 19 trillion cubic feet (TCF) at Leviathan gas field, both off the Mediterranean coast of Israel. See *Haaretz*, 26 January 2014: "Is the Leviathan gas field a sure thing or a whale of a problem?" by Eran Azran

given that the value of the gas could make whoever owns it the wealthiest in the world, per capita.

Based on the energy discoveries, Israeli firms have acquired most of the drilling rights and Israel's government seems to believe that this will lead to its energy independence from the rest of the increasingly turbulent and hostile region. The licenses were granted by the owner, Cyprus, which is partly controlled by the Turkish Republic of Northern Cyprus, which will also want to find a way to benefit from the gas fields. Eventually, Greece will no doubt challenge their ancient rival Cyprus over ownership, as will Turkey, Gaza, Syria and Lebanon which all have coastlines that border these same gas fields. Their entry into the conversation will not be a surprise. Meanwhile, Russia has much at stake as well. If the gas fields are as extensive as the geological surveys imply, then Russia could lose the grip on Western Europe that it currently enjoys as the sole nearby external supplier of gas. One wonders whether Israel's neighbours really want to see that nation enjoying energy independence from the region.

The consequences for Qatar are significant too. Qatar invested enormous sums in its natural gas fields and the world's most sophisticated delivery vessels. The Qataris assumed they would be selling natural gas to the US and China. Now the US is set to not only set to consume what it produces, but now it will compete with Qatar to become an alternative natural gas exporter. If China's economy remains weak, then the demand from China will not be as strong as Qatar had hoped. Meanwhile, as the Syrian civil war spills over into Lebanon, many in the region believe that Hamas and perhaps Hezbollah will also seek to claim some of the gas fields and cash flows. Hamas and Israel are bound to ensure the other does not benefit from these riches. Perhaps it makes sense after all that in 2013 Russia announced its intention to maintain a permanent naval presence in the Mediterranean.[160]

If there really are 122 trillion cubic feet of natural gas in the Eastern Mediterranean, then we have to expect that this part of

---

160 See Reuters, 6 June 2013: "Russia Announces Permanent Mediterranean Naval Presence" by Alexei Anishchuk

the world will become geopolitically "noisy" as key players in the region vie for control over the energy and its cash flows.

Opportunities for Russia and China arise in part because of geopolitical events elsewhere. There is now a real possibility that Egypt might be willing to offer Russia a warm water port in exchange for wheat. After all, Russia had such a port in Alexandria until Egypt's President Anwar Sadat pushed Russia out in 1972 (when Egypt aligned with the US). Now the Egyptians are broke and unable to afford to buy or grow enough wheat to placate the needs of its population. Egypt is the world's largest importer of wheat and if there is one thing Russia can offer, it is wheat (especially if Ukraine and Crimea remain at their disposal). Meanwhile the IMF, the World Bank, the EU and others have all declined Egypt's pleas for wheat arguing that Egypt has no means of repaying loans.

No doubt Russia, China and others see historic opportunities unfolding in the Middle East as the US withdraws from the region. America's military retreat from Iraq opened the door for Iran to step in and take control of that hugely valuable asset. No doubt this is a benefit to China, which, to reiterate, has long aligned with Iran partly on the grounds that it was the only major oil producer in the Middle East that wasn't aligned with the US.

Russia and Japan continue to argue more aggressively over the disputed Kurile Islands, no doubt because the gas fields and mineral finds there are perceived to be so valuable by both sides. That explains why Russian and Japanese fighter jets keep appearing in the sky.

Middle East

Many Middle Eastern governments and citizens would agree with the idea that rising food prices and a higher cost of living played a significant part in driving the Arab Spring. There are those who object to this notion, of course. Some believe that one-day, without much warning and after decades of dictatorship, the citizens of Tunisia and other countries in the region woke up one morning and suddenly proclaimed, "Today is the day I have to have democracy!" But, this does not ring true. The populations of this region have long harbored grievances and had unmet aspirations, but why did such enormous political upheaval happen at this particular time?

Perhaps it is not a coincidence that the man who triggered the Arab Spring was a fruit and vegetable seller. Tarek al-Tayeb Mohamed Bouazizi decided on the 17th of December 2010, at the age of 26, to douse himself in petrol and set fire to himself in broad daylight in protest against the dictatorial leadership of Zine El Abidine Ben Ali, who had ruled Tunisia for 23 years. Bouazizi's complaint was not just that food prices were rising beyond the reach of his customers, though he would have noticed that no doubt. His main complaint was that members of the state, including the police, were harassing him for ever-larger informal and even illegal payments. These "taxes" for doing business are a staple in emerging markets. But the rise in his informal tax rate combined with the rise in the price of fruit and vegetables pushed him over the edge. He chose to protest by "exiting". His death inspired the citizens at large to take to the streets and overthrow the dictatorship.

Hosni Mubarak ruled Egypt for 30 years. He used to say he did it by ensuring "bread and circuses". He meant this literally, at least in the case of bread. Egypt's political construct has long rested on one simple foundation: the provision of highly subsidised, nearly free bread for the poor. Egypt is the world's largest importer of wheat. When the wheat price went up in 2010 and then again in 2011 due to failed harvests and droughts in both Russia and Australia, the rising bread price played a part in prompting people to take to the streets. Once there, traditional grievances quickly came to the surface. When wheat prices rose again in 2013, the Muslim Brotherhood, who had thrown out Mubarak found themselves turfed out by a military coup. Any government that cannot provide bread in Egypt at a reasonable price cannot stay.

Most countries in the Middle East have almost no capacity to feed themselves. They suffer not only from a shortage of water and arable land but also from a shortage of cash. Consider the situation in the Kingdom of Saudi Arabia, the richest nation in the region by far. There are deeply conflicting views about how much oil revenue Saudi can depend on in the future. The so-called "peak oil" crowd argue that even the Kingdom of Saudi is running out of oil resources and is set to become a net oil importer by 2030, according to Citigroup and other observers.[161] Their detractors may argue that Saudi has plentiful oil reserves, but even they admit that Saudi cannot afford to subsidise food in the way it has done in the past. Being the highest cost base in the world means that Saudi production is vulnerable to price jumps, which hits it exponentially hard.

For example, in November 2012 the price of poultry in Saudi suddenly jumped by 40% in a single week. In 2013 the price of eggs rose by 58%. Chicken and eggs are core staples in the region, which is heavily populated by Muslims who won't eat pork and by Indians who won't eat beef. Saudi immediately announced an export ban to protect its citizens from shortages and further price jumps. But that left the rest of the region with much higher poultry prices, since Saudi was the principal local supplier. No one else in the region can afford to try to raise poultry given the outrageous costs involved of doing so in the desert. Saudi Arabia can't afford it either. In 2013 it announced the end of its 30-year effort to grow wheat in the desert. It had become too expensive even for the Kingdom of Saudi.[162]

Buying the peace

Saudi Arabia arguably has greater pressures than other countries in the region because of the nature of its social contract. It can be argued that the ruling family, the House of Saud, is given the latitude to remain in power, despite the fact that much of the population feel that there are better guardians of Mecca, because the royal family has agreed to permit the ultra-orthodox Wahhabi religious leaders a good deal of freedom in exchange for their support. This deal increasingly requires the royal family to share

---

161 See Bloomberg, 4 September 2012: "Saudi Arabia may become oil importer by 2030, Citigroup says" by Ayesha Daya and Dana El Baltaji

162 See *Arab News*, 14 April 2013: "Kingdom to halt wheat production by 2016" by Diana Al-Jassem

more and more of its wealth with the general public. With an exceedingly young population, of whom some 50% are under the age of 18 and often exclusively educated in religious schools, the higher cost of living begs the old question, "Why is the wealth in my society being distributed to a few and not to me?" Saudi Arabia and similarly wealthy states such as Kuwait, Bahrain and Qatar, have sought to fend off an Arab Spring of their own by raising wages, employing more citizens on the government payroll, capping food prices and putting more money into public infrastructure to benefit the general population. Such a strategy is expensive. It is also inflationary.

Raising wages further exacerbates the problem. Increased wages means there is more money chasing the same goods in the market (because the wage gains are not generated by productivity increases). It therefore becomes necessary to cap food prices or limit food exports. If the oil price rises, then fuel subsidies cost the government even more.

All this goes some way to explaining why Saudi Arabia and other regional governments were so distraught with the United States in the aftermath of the Arab Spring. The US position was clear: it supported the rebels in Libya and the overthrow of Hosni Mubarak. This opened the door for the citizens of Saudi and other royal kingdoms to start asking more persistent questions. In their view, the US raised the cost of staying in power for these royal families. Now they would have to spend more to buy the peace.

In addition, the US began to tout its ability to achieve full energy independence from the region. Whether or not this is achievable, it has caused many in the region to start thinking about new relationships to generate new cash flow. Energy-hungry and cash-rich China is the obvious country to start talking to. In this way, the geopolitics of the Middle East has now begun to shift away from its former US orientation towards China. Collaboration with China may be a smarter path for the Middle East although it remains in competition with China for hard assets, including food and energy.

All this goes some way toward explaining Saudi's sudden and unilateral decision to flood the market with oil towards the end of 2014. The one thing that undermines their biggest opponents in the region is a lower oil price. This damages the cash flows for Iran at a time when their power is growing and appears a formidable threat to Saudi. President Obama has signaled that the US and Iran might reach an accommodation, while Russia and Iran have tightened their security and intelligence alliance. All these causes Saudi to want to undermine the cash flows of their biggest opponents. When the oil price goes down it hurts Iran the most. It hurts Russia a good deal. The lower oil price arguably slows energy investment even in the US. This, the Saudis believe, will let them secure cash flows without as much competition and deny cash to their opponents.

Arctic

The resource fight stretches from the deserts of the Middle East to the icy Arctic. It is estimated the Arctic holds as much as 13% of the world's undiscovered oil and more than 30% of the available natural gas. China and Russia vie for control over the Arctic, as is apparent from the race between the two to produce the worlds fastest icebreakers.

In August 2007 Russia sent a Mir submarine to go underneath the polar ice cap in the Arctic. From that vessel, Russia planted a titanium Russian flag on the seabed of the Lomonosov Ridge, which divides the Arctic Ocean, a perilous 14,000 feet from the surface to symbolise their claim that much of the Arctic belongs to Russia. Subsequently, President Putin gave a speech on the bow of a nuclear powered icebreaker. He said that he expected that some 20% to 25% of Russian GDP to come from the incredibly rich Arctic resources including oil, gas, minerals, gold, nickel and even diamonds. Russia subsequently established a new division of the Federal Security Service, which deploys Special Forces commandos who are specifically trained for Arctic fighting.

It is telling, a signal perhaps, that Norway too announced the creation of an Arctic corps of commando paratroopers, designed to protect and defend its Arctic interests. It has also moved its military command headquarters from Stavanger to Bodø, a location inside the Arctic Circle, which was originally built in the Cold War and designed to withstand a Russian nuclear attack. Norway actively opposes China's efforts to become an observer on the Arctic Council and supports Russia's efforts to create an "Arctic Group of Forces". Since 2006, Norway has held a military exercise called Cold Response in what it calls "the High North" since four of the five countries that claim Arctic territory are NATO members: the US, Canada, Norway and Denmark. Finland and Sweden join in as well. But, somehow, despite the extraordinary training and skill required to be an Arctic Commando, it does not seem likely that Norway will be able keep a strong enough foothold on the Arctic to prevent Russia and China from exploiting the territory first. This is why the Norwegians launched a $250 million Arctic spy boat, called the Marjata, in 2014. The Head of Norwegian Intelligence, Lt. Gen. Kjell Grandhagen, said, "There is a demand from our political leadership to describe what is going on in this region," and "military aspects in terms of being able to defend that."[163]

China's approach to the Arctic is more commercial. As mentioned previously, China has forged a working relationship with Greenland now that it has self-rule, and has been independent of Denmark since 2009.[164] Greenland is not only extremely resource-rich itself (rare earth metals in particular), but it also enjoys great proximity to the Arctic. If China can figure out how to use its icebreaker technology to open a shipping lane across the Arctic, it can bypass the tricky Middle East situation/relationship and deepen trade ties with Europe.

Devaluing the Dollar

China and Russia compete for assets but they have also seen their interests align as a result of the changing geopolitical landscape. Both countries want to "de-dollarise" the world economy and

---

163 "Cold War Spy Games Return to the Arctic" by Karl Ritter, Associated Press, June 12, 2014

164 See International and Security Relations Network, 10 May 2013: "Greenland's Dilemma and its 'Reluctant' Alliance with China" by Bhavna Singh

increase the amount of trade that occurs in Renmimbi and Rubles. As examples, in May of 2014, Russia and China's leaders signed a deal, The Agreement of Cooperation, which encouraged both countries to bypass the US dollar and transact increasingly in their own currencies. In June 2014 they signed The China-Russia Agreement, which was the biggest gas deal ever done in the world. Part of its purpose was to encourage the use of only Rubles and Renmimbi to pay for gas and for Russia and China to create their own natural gas benchmarks and pricing in their own currencies. Both countries increasingly encourage the issuance of debt in these two currencies rather than US Dollars. Meanwhile the US has used financial tools to try and punish both countries. After Visa and Mastercard both blocked a number of Russian banks in the aftermath of the events in Ukraine, Russia has vowed to build their own equivalent brands. Both China and Russia will keep pushing for their currencies to become both reserve currencies and more broadly used currencies in their effort to diminish the influence of the US.

So we see that the Great Monopoly Board Game of geopolitics that preoccupies China also preoccupies Russia and others. I do not emphasise these events to condone military actions or to judge whether a nation should or should not pursue its interests. I am saying that China and Russia and every other nation is now propelled into a fight for assets by economic forces. When there isn't enough cash to go around and the value of these assets is rising every day, it is not surprising to see nations pursue control over commodities and assets with ever more vigor.

Others are drawn into a fight for greater control over increasingly valuable assets by economic forces. Argentina has re-raised the Falkland Island issue again with Britain now that gas fields are more easily developed given technology advances. Britain had to send a destroyer to Spain to protect the fishing rights of their protectorate Gibraltar in 2013. Burma and Bangladesh also face off over who owns the gas fields off their coastlines. China and India are arguing ever more violently as to who can do what with the water that originates in the Himalayas. All this begs us to recall the open letter Ernest Hemingway wrote in September 1935 in which he warned of the risk of another war in Europe:

"The first panacea for a mismanaged nation is inflation of the currency; the second is war. Both bring a temporary prosperity; both bring a permanent ruin."[165]

More recently the historian Margaret Macmillan has warned of dangerous parallels between the situation today and the run-up to the Great War of 1914. In *Rhyme and Reason: Why 2014 Doesn't Have to be 1914*, she writes: "The 100th anniversary of 1914 should make us reflect anew on our vulnerabilities to human error, sudden catastrophe, and sheer accident." The difficult of managing such vulnerabilities may be even worse today because "the speed of communications puts greater than ever pressure on government to react to crises... before they have time to formulate a measured response."[166]

Marikana

South Africa provides a poignant but very different example of the conflagration of economics and geopolitics. In August 2012, the South African police fired into a crowd of miners in Marikana, a mining town in the Northwest. It was the most important civil unrest event since the end of Apartheid. Few could imagine that the democratically elected government would ever find it necessary to resort to firearms, let alone shoot as many as 34 citizens. It was a profound break in South Africa's social contract. These miners went on strike for a 25% to 100% wage hike. After all, the assets they were pulling out of the ground at great risk to their life were reaching record high prices: gold, platinum, palladium, thermal coal, diamonds. These are the very assets investors want to hold when they fear the devaluation and debasement of paper money. So, the markets had bid up the prices of these valuable assets. The

---

165 From "Notes on the Next War: A Serious Topical Letter", first published in *Esquire* magazine, September 1935
166 From *The Rhyme of History: Lessons of the Great War* by Margaret Macmillan (Brooking Institution), 14 December 2013

same economic forces were also causing the price of fuel and groceries to rise by as much or more. The workers felt the pain of a rising cost of living against unchanged wages and went on strike to demand higher pay from the world's largest mining companies, Anglo. The firm agreed to a 25% wage hike in the aftermath of the shootings, even though the mining companies made it clear that the new costs would force the closure of some of the mines because the companies claimed they would no longer be profitable. Margins in mining are often pretty thin. As it turned out, Rio Tinto announced its largest loss in history in 2013 due to "emerging-market cost overruns."[167]

The South African government has made veiled threats to nationalise the mining industry, which compelled Anglo, Rio and others to meet the wage demands but to begin the process of closing mines and reducing their presence. Subsequently the workers have demanded a further 60% wage increase and another 100% increase on top of what was granted. As a result, mines are being closed and mothballed.

With mining operations around the world becoming more costly and the prices of mined assets being highly volatile, it is logical that the supply of these assets will be constrained or reduced at least. Looking around the world it is clear that there are a record number of mines for sale that no one will touch even when the price is lower than the value of the proven reserves. This is because potential buyers fear expropriation. They fear volatility. They cannot raise the working capital needed to bring the assets to the surface. And, they cannot afford the increasingly costly high-tech equipment or engineers who can reach far enough and productively enough to generate reliable profits. So, supply-side problems have developed in mining just as they have in agriculture.

But, in the main, inflation pressures have been localised during this period of history, at least until now. Inflation has begun to creep back into the world economy, undermining the efforts of

---

167 See *The Financial Times*, 14 February 2013: "Rio Tinto vow after its biggest loss ever" by Neil Hume

emerging markets to deliver the aspirations of their people. No doubt domestic policy choices have contributed to bad economic outcomes, like inflation, in many places. But, the decision by the industrialised world to deal with its debt by engaging in ultra easy policy has proved to be bait to those in emerging markets who rightly or wrongly seek to pin all or part of the blame on this. It would be somewhat foolish to even attempt to deny that the industrialised world is seeking to raise the inflation rate when every possible step has been taken to secure this outcome. The only questions are whether it will work and whether it will create unwanted or unmanageable consequences at home or abroad. But, whatever the cause, rising asset prices is stimulating governments, indeed nations, everywhere to vie for greater control of the critical assets needed to keep their populations stable. The higher the prices and values go, the harder nations will fight for control of these valuable assets.

Markets or statecraft

Meanwhile, in the industrialised world, the debt burden bears down on the defense community, forcing the kind of budget cuts that compel a radical change of thinking rather than just marginal adjustments. This is not a simple matter of finding a 10% saving here and a 10% saving there. These budget cuts are potentially crippling the current defense infrastructure everywhere. Thus the defense community is going to be forced into rethinking very basic assumptions about how to execute resistance and protection against threats and how to pursue national interests even though the money for such endeavors is diminishing every day.

Yet the defense community, just like all other sectors of the economy, wants to believe it will be exempt from the full force of debt. It devotes relatively more time and energy towards protecting the existing infrastructure and framework than to innovating in the new environment. In the US, and across the industrialised world, the pressure of debt splinters militaries. They are increasingly forced to turn against their fellow comrades as each part of the security infrastructure argues that it should have access to more of the available defense dollars than its peers. In this way we see, for example, the Marines pitted against the Navy or the Army, and the military as a whole pitted against the rest of the government's interests. Can the US or any other military as a whole be effective when it spends so much time fighting against the other divisions of its own defense forces?

It may be useful to remember the words of Admiral Jacky Fisher, who served as the First British Sea Lord in 1904, and the man who scrapped a large chunk of the British Fleet because the ships were "too weak to fight and too slow to run away". He replaced them by building the HMS Dreadnought, the largest gunship ever constructed at the time. He is attributed with the observation that Winston Churchill also loved to use: "Gentlemen, now that the money has run out we must start to think!" Circumstances demand a new way of thinking.

A new dance partner

When there was enough cash to fund the defense needs of nations, these arguments receded. Now strategic security and economics are forced to dance together on a more challenging and uncertain geopolitical landscape, but the defense community does not easily recognise or accept its new dance partner: economics. Nor does the economics community easily accept its new dance partner: geopolitics. Of course the two have met before. In fact, they are usually found hand in hand, but the experience of recent years leads many to believe that a post-Berlin Wall world is normal and the events described here are an exception to the rule.

It is hard to believe that inflation is playing a major role when the robust stance of the industrialised world is to assert that there isn't any inflation at all and that there won't be any, in spite of the extraordinary efforts to create inflation. It is hard to believe that the world economy can redeploy capital and move prices so fast that nations cannot keep up with the pace. And yet, this is what is unfolding. The state is being outrun by the market and in response state tries to outrun the market. This makes for an uncomfortable dance with a partner that has not been seen in a while and the memory of whom is uncomfortable.

Time, inflation, war

It is sometimes said that there are only three ways to deal with a serious debt problem: time must pass, inflation or war. An example of the first option is Japan. It simply allowed time to pass when its debt problem overwhelmed the economy. The result was 25 years of deflation and low growth. This model, the "allow time to pass" and accept deflation approach, now seems to be the preferred solution for much of Europe. Accepting deflation means the government chooses to lose a few decades to slow growth or even recession. But, this option is politically and personally painful. It would not be available to leaders in many countries including the US.

Inflation is obviously the more politically attractive option, especially since inflation usually makes the stock market and property prices rise, at least initially. Clearly most industrialised countries are betting they can produce just enough inflation to fix the problem but not enough inflation to cause new problems.

War is obviously nobody's first or even last choice. No one wants war, but in a world where there is excess capacity and/or too much money, economic forces often conspire to destroy excess capacity and excess capital. Nothing is more efficient at this destruction than conflict and war. Today the stage is increasingly set for conflict. States are competing with each other over physical spaces for physical access to commodities, for the loyalty of their disillusioned and pained citizens. Accidents can happen. Mistakes can be made.

Commodity Conflicts

What I have described here is not as simple as a return of the Cold War. Although James Galbraith pointed out to me that the Cold War was all about resource competition too, as George Kennen explained this clearly in his famous "X" article in July 1947. So, perhaps the Cold War and the new era of Commodity Conflict have something in common. The players and the drivers are different. The face off is not between communists and capitalists. Nor is it between superpowers alone. The central philosophical arguments today are radically different from what they were during the Cold War. But, there is still a significant fight about resources and about philosophy.

In the post World War Two era, the US led the creation of the "Bretton Woods" system, which has underpinned the world economy ever since. In short, it stood for a world economy in which the markets determined who would get what (not states or governments) and almost every important asset, especially food and energy, would be priced in US Dollars and the supply lines of food and energy would be policed by the US and America's regional allies. No doubt that Bretton Woods system is very different today than it was when most nations signed up to it in 1944.[168] More countries adhere to the principles of free markets and free trade today than when it started. The US and others have dramatically changed the system at times such as when Richard Nixon abandoned the Gold standard in 1971. But at its heart, there is one thing everybody has remained committed to. It is the most valuable commodity of all: price stability.

The appearance of price instability has brought with it the spectre of conflict. Today many countries are not content to leave outcomes to markets. Nations cannot tell their public that the price of bread quadrupled due to "market forces" and expect to remain in power. No, leaders increasingly prefer to use state power to ensure the outcome they want. The cost of failing to supply food and energy at the right price is very high, as we now know from the Arab Spring and the many coups, social unrest incidents and protests that have unfolded worldwide. This is how we have now entered an era of Commodity Conflicts rather than another Cold War. It is not simply that nations seek to secure enough food and energy. They also seek to secure control over access to food and energy. This may mean taking control of fields that grow food far from home or it may mean securing control of shipping lanes or cyberspace or satellites. It may mean buying a controlling interest in public companies. And, it certainly means that nations are no longer content to let the US drive the rules of

---

168 See "A New Bretton Woods", Remarks by Paul Volcker at the Annual Meeting of the Bretton Woods Committee, Washington DC, May 21, 2014

the game and the pricing of valuable assets like food and energy. Many question whether the US remains a steadfast guardian of the most valuable commodity of all. It is the glue that underpins the world economy: price stability.

Price stability is the holy grail of all central banking theory. If the post war economic order is based above all else on a commitment to price stability, then it cannot be surprising that nations begin to object if they feel the US is abandoning price stability, or taking excessive risks with it, for their own benefit at the expense of the others.

Ultimately each nation must be responsible for their own price stability. But, it becomes much harder to do this if the largest economies in the world are believed to be taking gambles with it. The Federal Reserve may be right. Perhaps they are not creating inflation, nor are they undermining price stability in any way. But, the pain elsewhere is high enough that it has become worthwhile to try and pin the blame on someone or something else. The emerging markets may also be right in their assessment that the record low interest rates, the record high injections of capital into the world economy are together creating spillover effects, imbalances, inflation and causing the kind of pain that governments have no choice but to respond to.

I think todays' leaders in Russia, China and elsewhere increasingly find it easy to think this way: You steal money from my pocket? Then this (land, asset, gas field, island, nation, shipping lane, etc.) belongs to me. Many countries are beginning to fight for commodities and valuable assets in an effort to ward off the inevitable consequences of pain. The vice of economic pressure is tightening its grip on every person, every company, every community, and every country. Caught between loss of growth and loss of faith in the future on one side, and the rising cost of living, which means a falling standard of living, on the other. People are in pain. Whatever the degree of loss and pain, governments know that the public will remove its leadership from power if it cannot deliver relief one way or another. Sustained upward pressure on such hard-asset prices brings geopolitical consequences because failure to deliver these items at the right time and the right price can propel people toward the ballot box or into the streets. The risk of higher hard-asset prices (whether correctly attributed to inflationary policies in the West or as the result of policy in the emerging markets themselves) is leading to newfound competition among governments for access to necessary resources around the world. Now that the perfect circle is broken, politics and geopolitics have staged a comeback. The vice of pain is compelling people to ask that simple question: "Why is the wealth in my society being distributed to someone else and not to me?" Suddenly, governments have to start thinking about how to ensure the delivery of whatever is needed and expected. Competition for commodities and for GDP now forms the basis for potential conflict in the world economy.

Is it really pure coincidence that the headlines about record high prices for beef and pork, for oil and gas, for property and stock markets are accompanied by stories of Russian fighter jets and Chinese naval vessels sharply cutting across the path of American planes and ships? Is it really a coincidence that the price of food, diamonds, platinum and coal all rose dramatically and then the miners in South Africa are shot and the workers in Bangladesh, China and elsewhere take to the streets? The link here may be false. It may be tenuous. It may be sound and real. But, it is certainly worthy of a conversation.

The fact remains that the perception exists today that price instability is real and must be fought by any means. The US and Federal Reserve supporters would prefer nations fight price instability by pursuing the correct, if painful, monetary and fiscal policies at home. But, the reality is that human beings don't like pain and will use whatever means available to achieve their goals in ways that involve less pain. Military policy can become a substitute for, or a supplement to, monetary policy. Economic forces can compel military responses. As Carl von Clausewitz memorably said, "War is the continuation of Politik by other means". By "politik" he meant all "policy" and "politics". This is being played out here. Military conflict is a continuation of monetary policy by other means.

Innovation

It all sounds pretty tough. The pain of the debt burden and the pain of a rising cost of living are bearing down in varying proportions in different parts of the world. The Peace Dividend is rapidly becoming a Conflict Premium. All seems grim but all these pressures produce the one thing that is required for the economy to sustainably grow: innovation. If I stick to my belief that GDP is created in the human soul as people balance hubris with their fear of nemesis, then all these tough circumstances produce the soul searching that leads to innovation. Happily, I see many signals that people are innovating and building the economy of tomorrow today.

Signals about tomorrow's economy arise from individual action. The MBA finds she cannot become an employee because no one is hiring, so she reinvents herself as an entrepreneur. The retiree realises that she cannot survive on a fixed income when interest rates are at record low levels, so she starts to find ways to work part time. Companies drop the business lines that no longer generate positive cash flow and enter the business lines that do. Citizens ask questions about the social contract that's in place with their government and seeks to modify it or reinvent it. The process of innovation is the positive outcome of pain. Of course some are forced to innovate downward. The homeowner becomes a renter. The employed person becomes unemployed and goes on state benefits. The college student realises that the college degree carries no weight and brings insufficient income to pay off the student loans and turns to manual labour. While not always warranted, welcome or ideal, the world economy forces people to continuously adapt and

242

innovate. Luckily human beings adapt to change and innovate their way out of trouble pretty well.

This chapter is about the future. It is about hope. It is a tricky subject because many will say that we cannot possibly know what the economy of tomorrow will hold. This is true. On the other hand, it is important to remind that there is always an economy tomorrow. One of the greatest, most innovative minds of recent decades, Albert O Hirschman, wisely observed that, "Creativity always comes as a surprise to us; therefore we can never count on it and we dare not believe in it until it has happened."[169] Remember when Nicholas Negroponte, who founded the MIT Media Lab, predicted the need for an Amazon in 1995? Remember what Newsweek wrote in response in an article called "Why the Web Won't be Nirvana": "Nicholas Negroponte, director of the MIT Media Lab, predicts that we'll soon buy books and newspapers straight over the Internet. Uh, sure."[170] Now Negroponte predicts that we will soon be able to take a pill and know Shakespeare. Innovation always reaches beyond the imagination of most people. Jeff Bezos must have had a lot of people saying "are you out of your mind?" when he set off to launch Amazon. Maybe that's what is now required – to go out of one's current mind(set) and imagine.

So, while no one can prove that any of the stories that follow are going to be enduring successes, I can make the case that people everywhere are trying to build tomorrow's economy. Perhaps their calculated risk-taking, whether they succeed or they fail, will serve to encourage the rest of us to pursue our own vision. The purpose of this chapter is to try and tilt things toward hubris, so that more people will begin to make their own contribution to tomorrow's economy. Yes, hubris got us into this mess and

---

169 Quoted in *The New Yorker*, 24 June 2013: "The Gift of Doubt: Albert O Hirschman and the Power of Failure" by Malcolm Gladwell
170 *Newsweek*, Why the Web Won't be Nirvana" by Clifford Stoll, February 26, 1995

ironically hubris, if balanced by sensible calculation of the risk, is what gets us out as well.

Innovation is the one truly effective and desirable way out of the formidable pressures that are bearing down on the world economy and on social contracts today. Innovation stands in sharp contrast to the one truly ineffective and undesirable way out: the continued bickering about how to redistribute a stagnant or declining pool of GDP which goes on while governments find ever more clever ways to take more of their citizens' money. Arguing about the redistribution of wealth is a mug's game that causes the character of the economy and public debate to degenerate into nasty arguments in which all sides adopt intractable, ideological positions. Innovation, on the other hand, creates wealth, enhances productivity and facilitates the transition from past limitations to future opportunities in tomorrow's economy.

Too often it is assumed that innovation means technology or a new gadget. Yet innovation can also mean the act of *personal* reinvention, when we change career or come up with a new vision for our individual, corporate, community or national future.

It is sometimes said that life begins at the end of our comfort zone, which is where a lot of people, balance sheets and nations found themselves in recent years. There is both a reluctance to abandon old models, ventures, policies, and definitions, and a pressing need to explore new ones. Today individuals, families, communities, companies and countries are all changing the definition of who they are and what purpose they serve, and are figuring out how to make ends meet in new ways. All these are entrepreneurial endeavours.

It does not matter whether we consider ourselves entrepreneurs or intrapreneurs (expressing entrepreneurship in the context of a large organisation); whether we are government officials or just ordinary citizens. What matters is that now we are all being forced by extraordinary economic pressures to ask the question that Peter Drucker said we should ask ourselves every three years: "If we were not already doing this, would we be doing it now?" It is a shame it takes a crisis to compel us to consider this question, but at least we find ourselves unhappy with the status quo and thinking about alternatives.[171]

Some have already begun to build the economy we shall have tomorrow, even as the debris from yesterday's economy continues to be sifted through, sorted, explained, defended and perhaps eventually vilified. Throughout history a phoenix has always risen from the ashes of our efforts. The British social philosopher Charles Handy called this the "Sigmoid Curve"[172] Like a radio wave, the economy has ups and downs but the next upturn starts well before the last downturn is over, just as the next downturn will begin before the last upturn is over. Our job is to find the signals that allow us to manage both.

One Million Cups

Consider the story of 1MC, which is a grass-roots effort by the Kauffman Foundation, based in Kansas City. 1 Million Cups (1MC), which brings together investors and other interested parties (such as possible employees) with people who have new ideas for starting businesses.[173] Each business gets ten minutes to talk about its idea and a sponsor pays for the coffee, which, as it grows, will amount to a million cups or probably more. These events are full in every location they are held in across the United States. Hundreds of people come along to hear about ideas and to see if there is an opportunity for them to invest or find a job or work with these new ventures in some way. They are looking for signals about the future and hoping to be a signal to others.

Of course, many will say, "but there is no lending" lack of lending and capital constraints grow. I disagree on both counts: lack of lending and capital constraints create discipline and force people to pursue only those ideas that can generate returns quickly. Jeff Bezos believes that lack of access to capital is a great

---

171 From *Classic Drucker: Wisdom from Peter Drucker from the Pages of Harvard Business Review* by Peter Ferdinand Drucker, p 29

172 *The Age of Paradox* by Charles Handy (Harvard Business School Press, 1994)

173 I am grateful to Barbara Mowry, the Chairman of the Kansas City Federal Reserve Bank, for bringing this organisation to my attention.

discipline. He says the most successful business decisions at Amazon have usually made by the teams that were the most capital constrained and had to use imagination and ingenuity to solve problems. When you run out of money you have to think. You have to innovate.

Crowd sourcing

The banking system is surely innovating. One positive outcome of the financial crisis is that the world economy will never be so dependent on banks for lending again. The internet has enabled the people who want to invest with the people who need investment. "Crowd Sourced" financing has become a common every day phenomenon. When someone wants to float an idea for a product, they can turn to IndieGoGo, Kickstarter, or a wide array of internet platforms and raise money quickly. These platforms allow the purveyor to see if there is a market for their idea or product. In short, you can get your customers to pre-buy your product and thereby prefund you production. In addition, such crowd funding efforts, even if they don't raise much money, they provide pretty cheap advertising and marketing opportunities.

It is true that some ideas fail, but then again, banks did not lend to every person or every idea even in their heydey. It is also true that crowd sourced funding has only touched a tiny fraction of the world economy. The typical corner shop or small business still needs an overdraft, a line of credit and a bank manager who can cut them some slack when the funds have not yet arrived from an invoice. But, it is important that even big businesses now have begun to find ways to bypass the traditional lending system and sort out their own cash flows without the help of a bank.

Invoice factoring is thus one of the most exciting developments on the financial services horizon. Essentially, a company is now able to sell their invoices to investors who take a bet that the invoice will be paid and paid on time. The investor provides the business with cash in hand today and takes the risk that the invoice might not be paid in three months times. The business employs a lot of people and it is profitable but waiting three months for an invoice to be paid ties up a lot of cash flow.

An investor charges something for taking the risk the invoice won't be paid on time or at all. But to the business, it is a small price for cash in hand today. Invoice factoring now permits firms to negotiate harder with banks and forces the interest rates on loans down.

One of the strangest and most deplorable side effects of Quantitative Easing has been that very big companies like Rolls Royce, which makes large industrial engines for aircraft and the like, can raise money on the capital markets at the drop of a hat. Really big firms can "issue paper" (sell a price of paper that says "I owe you", which is known as debt) very easily and at very low interest rates. But, their suppliers have not been able to secure any bank lending and they are too small to go to the capital markets. If a bank was going to lend to them in the aftermath of the financial crisis, it was going to be a high interest rate. This, of course, is one way that the central bank can recapitalise the banks. It permits a bank to borrow at a super low interest rate but does not permit the business community to do so. As a result, businesses get charged for the losses the bank had made in the past.

But, many companies, like Rolls Royce, found that their suppliers were disrupted by their inability to manage their cash flows. The price a bank charged for a loan was too high. So, in addition to invoice factoring, big firms like Rolls Royce said, let's be a banker to the company. After all, who knows the business and the collateral better than the biggest customer? Rolls Royce is better placed than the very best banker to understand which suppliers would be fine and which would not. So, the very old fashioned lending model of the 1950s and 1960s has come back to life.

All of these new channels for capital prove one thing: there are profits in lending. This has drawn banks back into the lending game. Who started lending? Wealthy individuals, businesses and even hedge funds started to realise that the rates of return in lending are very high if banks are refusing to lend. So, new lenders began to displace the banks. In recent years the rates of return for investors have been very high. I have seen lenders make well over 15% each year making plain vanilla loans (every day simple loans) to real businesses on a highly collateralised basis (offering ownership of equipment or buildings, for example, if the loan was not repaid).

Not only did these returns induce banks to re-enter the lending market, they also put new pressure on banks and fund managers in other ways. After all, if plain lending on a highly collateralised basis makes over 15% per year then why is it that fund managers everywhere say we must get used to very low rates of return? What do you need a sophisticated fund management product like a hedge fund if plain old lending gets you such a big return? Such returns are a powerful signal for the asset management industry. This just goes to show that the innovation in the real economy is starting to displace old business models and old notions of how things should be done.

When I sent this chapter to a number of my peers in the economic community, I got a lot of pushback. Many said crowd-source funding is a red herring. It's too small and too new to depend on. It does not change the game. But, I think it is a game changer even if it is small. I decided to launch the book you are reading on such a platform. After all, I can hardly write about calculated risk taking and innovation and then not do it myself!

The traditional model for publishing an economics book is to take the manuscript to a literary agent, if you could get one, who then cuts a deal with a publisher and then, if you are lucky, you get an advance and the book actually appears in a bookstore some 18 months later, by which time the book is already out of date. But, people have been buying fewer books since the financial crisis and buying more of them in digital format and or online and via Amazon. As a result, publishers have seen their margins and cash flows compressed. So, now if they pay an advance it is not uncommon to see the publisher sue for return of the money if the book does not actually sell. The advance is effectively a loan on very bad terms. Most publishers are uncomfortable with digital formats (which allows the author to continue to update the story with new examples and observations, as I am doing with the digital version of this book) and have not yet figured out how to capitalise on social media. Many authors complain that a publishers effort at publicity often comes in the form a phone call where they ask "do you have any contacts"?

I had one publisher tell me they would publish the book if I paid them £20,000. Then I checked and found that a self-publishing platform like Lulu.com would only charge me £5,000 for the same job. Part of the problem is that publishers, generally speaking, believe no one is interested in economics as a subject. People joked that the book would only sell if I called it *Fifty Shades of Economics*, which I am using for a series of video/podcasts on economics signals. But, everywhere I go, I find people are very keen to know about the world economy and how it will affect them. They love the subject and hate the way it is delivered, which is usually in a dense language that leans heavily on mathematics and through a book that is in the business section. My conclusion, my hubris, was to deduce that there is an audience for a book that helps people navigate better in the world economy.

That's when I realised that the best thing was to do both: do a crowd-source launch and cut a deal with publisher. That way I could control my own cover design (something you lose once a publisher has control). I chose hot pink because I wanted economics to stop being grey, boring and highly mathematical when it is in fact cool, edgy and should be considered a sexy subject. I am telling the story my way and in my own voice (instead of having to submit to the very young junior editor who could make me rewrite the book from scratch). At least I could launch an early edition this way. But, it is risky. No one I know of has launched a serious, non-fiction book on economics on such a platform. Given my thesis: signals exist, they matter: what better way to make the point than by taking this particular calculated risk?

After all, the signal that crowd sourcing sends is of the utmost importance. It signals that money is available to the economy even if banks are not lending very much. In other words, innovations and risk taking are occurring. Money is making its way to where the profits are and the velocity of money is being restored. These are materially important developments. Keep in mind that the Federal Reserve and other central banks are heavily emphasising the fact that the velocity of money is so low that there is no risk that QE will create inflation. But if the money is flowing, then inflation is a risk. It is no use saying that the flow of money does not count unless it comes from the sources we are accustomed to measuring. It may not be banks that are lending, although they are more and more. It may be that the financial crisis has actually unleashed a whole new torrent of cash which is now bypassing the banking system altogether.

Insufficient skills

Here is another signal: some say that the economy of tomorrow cannot occur because we lack the skills to build it. But, already we see many signs that businesses are starting to hire high school students, bypassing the pool of university graduates and MBAs and opting instead to build their own talent with the skill set they actually require. Of course, this means that college graduates are compelled to change jobs, careers, aspirations because no one is hiring them for what they had hoped for. This is not always a bad thing.

A banker and sewage

I know one fellow who lost his job on Wall Street, where he had been an equity salesman for a major investment bank. He was cagey and reluctant to reveal his new life when I talked to him. He sheepishly conceded that he had been forced to join a friend who was running a small sewage company in New Jersey, to which I replied, "How fabulous. Now that's something with a genuine demand and a genuine cash flow!" Sewage treatment is an essential service that protects the population from untold horrors. Once given "permission" to have made such a leap, he enthusiastically explained how they intended to improve cash flows, buy out competitors and eventually take the company to an IPO.

Job losses in financial services are bound to continue. Society will no longer permit banks and the financial services sector to gamble away the nation's financial future. Slowly, as we realise that the reckless losses in financial services actually jeopardised the social contract, citizens will demand that financial services be constrained. As financial services shrink, the weaker players will be pushed out. They will return to the real economy, because it's the only place they can go and frankly, the real economy can benefit from their skills. The algorithm experts of Wall Street will slowly end up as algorithm experts in manufacturing operations in the Midwest and elsewhere. Think of it another way. What is the most interesting place to pursue algorithms today? It is no longer the ever-increasingly constrained trading floor at a major bank. It is in a manufacturing operation or in the world of "big data".[174] Of course, not everybody has the required skills, especially mathematics skills, to succeed in these areas. But, education is changing to accommodate this problem.

Lifelong education

Higher education and universities have gotten themselves into a financial mess in the same way as nations and other balance sheets. They built infrastructure that is expensive to maintain and now lack the revenue to cover those costs. Students cannot afford to pay or are having to borrow enormous sums only to find that when they graduate there is no possibility of the kind of job that would permit them to pay off the loan. The value of a degree seems to have diminished, especially now that there are so many graduates and because firms are prepared to train their own staff. Many graduates also don't have the mathematics and writing skills that the modern work place demands. We now worry that the Indians and Chinese now get better scores in mathematics, which means graduates cannot keep up with the higher standards being established abroad. In addition, many universities lost their endowments and fundraising collapsed in the aftermath of the crisis. So, there is a good deal of soul searching going on in the realm of education.

People are trying to build new business models. Luckily, many have concluded that education is a lifetime undertaking and there

---

174 For an excellent and comprehensive study of big data and its applications to politics see *The Signals and the Noise: The Art and Science of Prediction* by Nate Silver, Penguin Books, 2012

is more and more content for learning available for those who wish to upgrade their skills. Consider the story of MOOCS.

There is now access to free online education from some of the best universities in the world through Massive Open Online Courses (or MOOCs). A global audience can be reach through a laptop. With less cash for shoes, clothes, technology and other "stuff", people are instead spending more on opportunities to learn new skills. In the immediate aftermath of the financial crisis, the demand for online education jumped upwards. Common sense tells us we must reinvent ourselves if we are going to find a job or sustain our earning power in a world where growth is low and unemployment is high. Indeed, if we live longer we may have to reinvent ourselves several times in a lifetime.

The aptly named Phoenix University is a good example of the new increased demand for skills. In ancient Greek mythology, the Phoenix is a magical bird[175] that lives for 1,000 years, after which it builds its own funeral pyre, throws itself into the flames, burns and then rises from the ashes to live for another 1,000 years. Phoenix University was launched in 1986, in the midst of the Savings & Loan crisis, with one class of eight students. Today it has campuses in 40 states in America as well as in Europe, China and Mexico. (At its peak it had 200 campuses although it has closed the majority of them after the financial crisis.) The founders of Phoenix were early pioneers in a phenomenon that is now becoming extremely popular: online education.

Today it is suffering because competitors including Harvard, Stanford and MIT are copying their success with MOOCs. A newer, virtually unknown competitor has emerged that is further revolutionising the delivery of online education – Southern New Hampshire University (SNHU), which few have ever heard of but which *Business Week* named as one of the fifty most innovative companies in America in 2013.[176]

---

175 The Phoenix myth is found in many stories of transformation, most recently *Harry Potter and The Order of the Phoenix* by JK Rowling (2003)
176 See *Business Week*, 9 May 2013: "Southern New Hampshire, a Little College That's a Giant Online" by John Hechinger

The President of SNHU, Paul LeBlanc, has lifted the enrolment from 2,000 students to 22,000 and launched College for America – an online, competency-based degree programme that costs $2,500 per course and $38,000 for the degree. Instead of requiring credits or a certain number of hours in the classroom, the course allows students to proceed based on competency. This means smart and dedicated students can finish the programme in as little as six months instead of the usual two years. SNHU expected to have 500 students but some 5,000 signed up. As *Business Week* reported, LeBlanc says his goal is "to reach out to students whose next best educational option is nothing at all":

> The total price of Southern New Hampshire's online bachelor's degree, $38,000 isn't cheap, but it's far less than the $112,000 – not including housing or meals – the university charges undergrads for four years at the brick-and-mortar college. For the current academic year, the university is projecting a $29 million profit from the online college, which amounts to a 22% margin.

It is interesting that the economist and Harvard University President Larry Summers chose innovation in education as his next venture after losing the nomination for President Obama's first choice to replace Ben Bernanke as the Chairman of the Federal Reserve. Summers and a small team of highly experienced academics have joined the American entrepreneur Ben Nelson, who founded the online digital photo printing service Snapfish, to create a new university called Minerva. It aims to offer first-class teaching from real-world practitioners, without the overheads of a traditional campus, to capture the gap in the education market at the high end.[177] Students are chosen from those that can gain admission to, but cannot afford, the world's best universities. The recruitment and teaching will take place worldwide. Faculty will be brought in according to skills rather than the traditional academic tenure system.

---

177 See minervaproject.com

Meanwhile, the pressures on budgets have pushed students out of some universities and into others. I am on the advisory board at Indiana University's School of Public and Environmental Policy for one reason. I felt that the recovery in the US was more likely to happen in the Midwest than anywhere else. So, I wanted a connection, a reason to be there. As it turns out that U.S. News and World Report ranks SPEA as the second best school of public policy after Harvard's Kennedy School. But, it costs a fraction of the price. So, while Harvard's enrolment has been falling, SPEA's is increasing so fast that the University can hardly hire and build fast enough. These are all good examples of the kind of change that push the economy forward.

Secret Cinema

Spending on experiences rather than things is a powerful emerging trend. It makes sense. When people are cash constrained a thing does not last the way an experience does. Education is one experience. Entertainment is another. Sure enough, we see some fantastic innovations in the delivery of entertainment experiences.

Consider Secret Cinema. In 2012, 80,000 British film lovers spent £40 (some $70) on a ticket to a film-based entertainment event without having any idea what the event was. This is because Fabien Riggall, the founder of Secret Cinema, realised that films and concerts needed to be reinvented. Film lovers were becoming bored by much of what Hollywood was churning out and uninterested in paying a high price to visit a cinema where popcorn costs as much as the film ticket. The Hollywood studio system and the movie theaters alike are collapsing under the weight of their own hubris and being eroded by online film access from Netflix and iTunes as well as the illegal bootlegging that technology makes easier every day. Riggall came up with a new way of entertaining people with film.

Imagine receiving a text message that tells you the date but not the location of an unnamed film, but says you must bring long johns[178] to secure admission. Then another text arrives telling you

---

178 Long Johns are two-piece thermal underwear that cover the arms and the legs

the event is being held at an abandoned prison. You buy a ticket in advance and later find yourself being checked into prison like convict. Everyone agrees to give up their personal belongings, including their mobile phones. Initially no one realises that the prison insurrection, which soon breaks out, is led by actors, who are posing both as prisoners and prison guards. The film shown is *The Shawshank Redemption*, but this is preceded by time in the prison laundry and the prison workshop, where guests learn to make little metal chairs from beer cans. After the show, some guests elect to stay the night in the "hotel". The sound of prison doors locking down echoes through the old building as they lie in their cells. The lights go out. Everyone wonders, "Did I really pay to be locked up overnight without my mobile phone?" Suddenly, a spotlight goes on and a stunning woman in an elegant burlesque costume and high heels begins to walk through the dark prison, singing. It's many prisoners' dream. The event is a mini concert as well as a film screening. Secret Cinema has created a cult-like following, and its fans adhere to the company motto, which is an admonishment to "tell no one". You can't get Secret Cinema guests to tell you when or where or what. It's a secret club that anyone can join. That alone may be worth the ticket price.

Riggall launched his concert business, Secret Music, by holding a show with the folk musician Laura Marling at an abandoned Victorian Gothic building. Dubbed "The Grand Eagle Hotel" for the night, the interior was designed to reflect her dream state. It was designed as if returning to the early 1920s, with vinyl records scattered alongside photographs of the era and windswept autumn leaves on the floor as Marling drifted from room to room giving small private concerts to whoever happened to be there at the time.[179]

What Riggall is doing is reinventing the business model, the film experience, and the traditional film and music business models. He is redefining modern entertainment and is now in great demand to produce and franchise film and concert events around the world.

---

179 The concerts are recorded and available online from LauraMarling.com or SecretMusic.co.

He is tapping into a broader trend shaped by economic pressures. In a world where we are caught in a vice between debt deflation and rising cost of living, spending has to be curtailed. It seems that this makes us inclined to spend less money on things and more on experiences.

I once met Harvey Goldsmith, one of the world's greatest concert promoters. He has staged tours for everyone from the Rolling Stones, Elton John and Madonna to Muse. As I listened to him, I realised that music fans are less and less inclined to spend money on huge music tours where they hear old well known music in large venues and where the same show is played over and over again for high ticket prices. There is still a market for these events. Eric Clapton, The Eagles and the Rolling Stones can still fill stadiums. But, increasingly, audiences want to attend events that are cheaper and rarer. They prefer smaller venues where they are closer to the artist in a space that permits the artist to innovate. Smart singers and musicians are increasingly seeking out such one-off opportunities, which is why Riggall is now besieged with phone calls from famous musicians. This explains the immense success of music festivals around the world, from Burning Man in Nevada to Glastonbury in England. These used to be "cult" events for a small crowd of edgy people. Now they are more mainstream and generating revenues that were unimaginable even five years ago.

Spending on experiences

The same economic forces are changing the way we shop. More and more shopping malls and department stores are realizing that people are more prepared to spend money on experiences than on things. A cash constrained person has to choose. He can talk about an experience for along time whereas a thing starts getting old and becoming outmoded from the moment you acquire it. So, it is interesting to note how Westfield, one of the world's best shopping mall firms, is offering ever more "experience" content. They have offered experiences in their Australian malls for a long time, being an Australian firm, but now they bring this to the rest of the world. Their malls have all the usual sorts of shops but they also have places to have a massage or manicure, drive a race car, a place where kids bungee jump and romp on jungle gyms or even ice skate. Their malls have valet parking and offer a dry cleaning service while you shop. Westfield is truly redefining the "shopping" experience.

Pop-up restaurants, clubs and shops similarly reflect the desire for a unique experience. The phenomenon was made possible because property owners had to become creative in managing the declining cash flows associated with properties. In the immediate aftermath of the financial crisis property values fell as people stopped going out and stopped shopping. Suddenly it made sense to cadge income where you could. Meanwhile small businesses could not afford to commit to an annual rent in a fixed location when testing out a new restaurant idea. Restaurants go in and out of business notoriously quickly. The two sides came together in recent years and solved each other's business model problems. When old businesses went bust and defaulted on their rental contracts, landlords needed to compensate by becoming willing to accommodate short-term renters who might then share part of their profits rather than paying a predetermined rent alone. The Internet allowed the launch of a short-term "pop-up" restaurants, shops and clubs appeared. They could be advertised worldwide and often to sell-out audiences. The brevity of the experience compelled even more innovation because it must be fresh and different each time. Derelict and underperforming spaces suddenly became a perfect venue for an edgy innovative experience.

I spoke at the "Makegood Festival" in 2014 in London. It was held in the Old Selfridges Hotel, which is a stripped-out, unused building. The floors are concrete. The walls are uncovered and reveal exposed electrical wiring and pipes. The Makegood Festival used the space for three days to showcase small manufacturers from all over Britain. The purveyors came from every sector: people were making textiles, handbags, shoes, whiskies, champagne, chocolates, jams and many other things. The "pop-up" experience was a great success according to the companies that came. Selfridges got some revenue from an otherwise unusable space. The companies got a place to display their wares to the public. Everybody benefitted.

Malaria nets

Some acts of innovation are really acts of invention. Mikkel Vestergaard's father ran a clothing company in Denmark that supplied Scandinavians with hospital uniforms. Mikkel decided to go off to Africa instead. Once there, he realised there was a profound need for malaria netting and thought his family firm could start making medical textiles. He created a fabric that is impervious to malaria-carrying mosquitos. The number of people who sleep under Vestergaard malaria nets is larger than the number of people who use Facebook. But Mikkel did not stop there. He also realised that countries like India lose as much as half their crop each year to pestilence and disease. So, he invented a grain sack made from a textile that cannot be penetrated by disease or rodents.

In 2012, India announced it was prepared to allow foreign direct investment into grain storage for the first time. I remember looking at a project that involved upgrading India's grain silos and improving storage. No one could comprehend that today's new silos only need ten people to operate them. That would mean displacing the 2,000 people who place grain in sacks for every single new silo. Mikkel's idea addresses the problem without displacing the people.

3D Printing Food

Ferran Adria ran El Bulli in Spain for many years. It was consistently ranked the best restaurant in the world. He is world famous for his ability to extract flavour from food. His cooking was more like an alchemical process than cooking. He has now closed El Bulli and is spending some of his time developing 3D printed food and opening a cooking lab called the _El Bulli Foundation_. It sounds disgusting, but technology now permits the fusion of first class flavor and texture with formerly unpalatable proteins. Clearly, plain vegetables like cassava can be converted into something flavorful. More challenging is the idea that powdered and crushed insects (protein) can be too. But, the innovations in the 3D printing of food are likely to astonish us. They are also capable of reducing the supply shortages that, for now, plague the world economy. 3D printed food technology would also permit increased nutrition even for the poor and the sick. Hospitals can now anticipate 3D printers that allow doctors to adjust the nutritional content to fit an individual patient's needs. So people recovering from surgery will soon have identical meals with differing nutrition or, even better, whatever meal they want with exactly the nutrition the doctor "ordered".[180]

There is no doubt that many innovations are being brought to bear on farming and food production. Satellite based laser resurfacing can make land far more productive. The new mega tractors can tell the driver the exact value and weight of different grades of grain being harvested even as the driver has no need to even touch the steering wheel.

Caleb Harper runs City Farm at the MIT Media Lab. He aims to grow food inside urban areas, in and on urban buildings. His approach needs no soil, little water, no chemicals, very little fertilizers and a manageable amount of energy especially when compared to how much energy is used to bring in food from rural areas. His approach propagates plants three to four times faster than traditional methods. Urban food for urban consumption will diminish food vulnerabilities.

The innovations in the food sector are astonishing. The only question is how fast they actually happen. Can they happen fast enough to avoid more Arab Springs and more social unrest in the near coming years? Probably no. Can they be counted on to change the future we will face over time? Probably yes.

Starbucks and genetics

Stefan Roever is an entrepreneur who has backed several Silicon Valley ventures and is deeply interested in innovation. He has a strong personal interest in genetics and so noticed when the guy in

---

180 I am grateful to Egbert-Jan Sol who is the Director of Innovation for High Tech Systems and Materials at TNO in the Netherlands for this insight.

front of him at the Starbucks in Silicon Valley had a book on genetics. He struck up a conversation. It turned out this new acquaintance had dropped out of Berkeley University, where he had been studying the subject, in order to devote his time to building a machine that could identify genetic markers without requiring samples to be sent off to a lab. He was building this machine in his garage, without any funding, without any partners and without any certainty it would ever work. Stefan had a look at his project, concluded he was onto something, agreed to back it and became the CFO of what is now known as Genia. The company's goal is to reduce the cost of genetic testing to $100 from its current price of thousands of dollars and to provide an on-the-spot answer to almost any genetic question, rather than oblige the patient and doctor to wait for test results from a lab. Genia is on the path to revolutionising genetic medicine, and has now been acquired.

This kind of innovation has spurred another sort of innovation which militaries and defense departments are now alert to which is the possibility of bio warfare based on genetics. In November 2012 *The Atlantic* published an article called 'Hacking the President's DNA"[181] in which they suggested that governments everywhere are keeping the DNA of their own leaders safe (which seemingly involves asking the Secret Service to vacuum everything the President touches) and trying to get a hold of the DNA other leaders leave lying around. This is because, in theory, diseases can now be created that will attack the one single person who it has been designed to attack. This constitutes a sobering innovation in how modern warfare and even diplomacy may be conducted.

Today we can build things as complex as genetic testing systems and new kinds of drones in our garages because we have access to computing power and materials that used to be available only in a classified defence lab. I mention drones because I decided to demonstrate my own commitment to innovation by taking an ownership stake in a robotics firm that makes helpful drones. They can be used to help a paralysed person experience real time "flying"

---

181 "Hacking the President's DNA" by Andrew Hessel, Marc Goodman and Steven Kotle, The Atlantic, October 24, 2012.

and enable them to go "chat" with a neighbor. They can be used to survey buildings, agricultural farmland and pipelines. They can help athletes see themselves real time as they perform sports as diverse as skiing, rowing and running. And, they can help first responders find and have a conversation with accident victims faster. The manufacturing of the drones has taken place in my office in London. There are soldering irons, glue guns and bits of electrical wire everywhere. Once the orders started coming in and production really started, we intend to move to a larger premises. But, in the meantime, the noise my office produces is a signal that gives me great comfort that the economy of tomorrow is being built today.

Angels and Hailo

Many new businesses are launched from around a kitchen table. No mathematical skills or degrees are required for this kind of innovation. Consider the story of Hailo. Three London taxi drivers found themselves unable to generate sufficient income after the financial crisis. The rich bankers and fund managers in London stopped taking taxis as much. The taxi drivers schemed with some friends who were tech experts about how to better connect with possible customers and came up with a novel idea. What if the customer could "hail" a taxi by using a mobile phone? Surely GPS technology would make it easy for the driver to decide whether it was worth a short drive to collect a passenger and whether it was worth it to the passenger to wait a few minutes for a taxi that would come to the door. The idea took off. Nearly half of all London taxis signed up for Hailo, it has become hugely popular and expanded into cities across Europe, North America and Asia. Smart investors like Accel and the founders of Spotify and Skype backed it. It worked beautifully until they raised their minimum fare to £10 on a weekday and £15 on a weekend. At that point another taxi App came into fashion, Get Taxi. That company has now expanded into the US, Russia and Israel.

The American equivalent is a company called Uber. The limos that hover around airports often have downtime between jobs, so they log onto Uber, as do the customers who know they can get a nice limo fast for a ride that doesn't cost much more than a taxi.

Uber connects the drivers who have downtime and passengers who need a lift. By the summer of 2014, taxi strikes were called in London and other cities as traditional taxi drivers began to comprehend the meaning of Uber. But, they still don't "get" what Uber really means. In August 2013 Google acquired Uber for US$258 million, which was 86% of the fund that Google had set aside for interesting acquisitions. Google simultaneously announced the acquisition of the first fleet of driverless cars, which will, no doubt, be used by Uber. Soon after the acquisition, Mercedes announced that its first driverless cars will be available to the general public in 2015. So, driverless limo's are not far away. Apparently such driverless cars now have a collective 700,000 miles on the road and zero accidents. No human being could match that.

Speaking of cars, the founder of Paypal, Elon Musk, has revolutionised car design with his new company, Tesla Motors, and has created a hugely successful luxury car from scratch (the Tesla Model X and Model S). Yes, it has had problems. The lithium battery has a tendency to catch fire when it smashes into something. Then again, I have seen car engines in flames on the roadside and they have a lot less innovation and glamour behind them. Musk's design is immensely innovative. The engine is underneath the passenger seats, leaving the front of the car for storage and a highly effective crumple zone to protect passengers from any frontal impact. Overall, it has the look and feel of an overgrown iPad and even plugs into normal electricity mains.

In the meantime, 3D printing has enabled customers to "print" highly customised professional racing bikes, such as the titanium Empire Cycles MX-6 full suspension bike and the titanium Flying Machine. Even motorcycles can be 3D-printed these days. The Italian Energica Ego bike is just one example. The classic Indian Motorcycle brand has also been brought back to life through 3D printers that copy the original designs. Happily, 3D printing has also been used to reconstruct the face of a Welshman who came off his motorcycle. Surgeons simply 3D-printed the missing parts of his skull, including the eye socket. Printed body parts and organs are becoming closer to every day reality. Innovation is everywhere.

Couture

All sorts of businesses can spring to life from such small ventures. It would be a mistake to think that skills of a geneticist or a car manufacturer are necessary. It is also a mistake to believe that only "hard industry" that involves the manufacturing of metal and machinery matters. Clothing, textiles and fashion move the economy too. Consider the story of Ralph & Russo. This couture clothing company creates fabulous fashion, from stage costumes for Beyoncé to the wardrobes for official state visits by various royal families. A dress from Ralph & Russo can easily cost tens of thousands of dollars running into the hundreds of thousands. Everything is made by hand for its clients from an atelier in Sloane Street in the epicentre of one of the most expensive megacities in the world, London. Tamara Ralph and Michael Russo, both Australians, met walking down the street in London, became friends, eventually married and founded their couture label. For Tamara, sewing was a family craft, passed down from several generations. Michael was a young entrepreneur who had launched several ventures. They started the business in 2007, just before the financial crisis, with only one sewing machine and no contacts among high fashion customers. Their biggest problem has been a shortage of workers with sufficient haute couture sewing skills.

Tamara told me, "Everyone wants to be a 'designer', but nobody wants to sew." The fashion world is full of people who can draw or style but is exceptionally short of craftsmen who actually know how to sew, how to work with beading or leather, how to perform the detailed and highly skilled techniques associated with making haute couture gowns. For me, this signals something everybody knows about the modern educational system. It is preparing people for a white-collar world that no longer exists and has failed to provide people with the real-life skills that give rise to innovation in the real economy. Thankfully, education has begun to innovate to reflect these changes. Luckily, there are many signals of the kind of edgework and reinvention that leads to economic recovery, growth, the creation of wealth and GDP. Rather than waiting for economists to confirm that change in the economy or for historians to explain it, edgeworkers are assessing the landscape, looking for signals, balancing the drive of their hubris against their fear of nemesis and choosing to "be the change" in the world economy.

Knitting and quilting

This brings me to a curious story involving the wife of a guest at a meeting of central bankers. In 2012, I happened to sit next to a quiet lady at the open-air lunch. Everyone craned their heads to hear what the influential policymakers had to say. I started to chat to her instead. After some gentle prodding, she revealed that she had started a knitting shop that sold specialist wool and provided classes to people who are serious about the craft. This shop not only survived the financial crisis but made a profit. After all, there are always people who love knitting and who are always hunting for innovative yarns and designs. I believe the weakened economy began to create the forces that would support the business. The financial crisis began to impact on personal income, thereby increasing the need to knit your own sweaters instead of being obliged to buy one. Knitting is also a good example of spending less money on things and more money on experiences. Meanwhile, as Bangladeshi and Chinese factory workers began to clamour for higher wages, the cost of buying a manufactured sweater started to rise.

The presence of such an entrepreneur in the midst of policy-makers struck me as a signal itself. How strange to be sitting next to a real, live example of the market finding its own solution, while surrounded by people who don't believe that this person exists. Worse, policymakers have chosen to define "the market" as Wall Street rather than a place where one can find millions of people like this who are carefully pursuing business ventures. But people like this do exist. They quietly build interesting businesses all the time. Consider the "Queen of Quilting", Jenny Doan. According to the *Wall Street Journal*, more than a million people (a number that most music bands would envy) have watched her YouTube videos in which she shows you how to make quilts easily and quickly.[182] Her shop, the Missouri Star Quilt Company, in Hamilton employs around 80 people, and as many as 50 to 100 customers arrive every day to buy everything needed to make an imaginative quilt. Apparently the diner and the hardware store in the town are doing extremely well too as the spouses of the quilters entertain themselves elsewhere.

Be the change

Stuck in past perceptions of "right" and "wrong", unbelievers will say it cannot be done. They assert no new Silicon Valley or financial services sector or product can replace what has crashed and burned. But, luckily, nobody has to be ashamed to change careers or jobs because everyone is doing it these days,[183] and never before have we had so many tools to facilitate personal and organisational risk-taking in exploring new opportunities.

The only question is whether or not we choose to "be the change" or simply be residual consequence of change in our global economy. That was Mahatma Ghandi's advice: "If we could change ourselves, the tendencies in the world would also change. As a man changes his own nature, so does the attitude of the world change towards him ... We need not wait to see what others do."[184]

There are those who will not or cannot wait for economists to have enough data to declare that the recovery from the financial crisis is comfortably underway. They will not or cannot wait for historians to explain what went wrong early in this century or to explain what the right solutions should be. Instead, the sharp demands of reality draw forth strength of character and cause some of us to explore and exploit change without the conviction and clarity of vision that others need before they are willing to

---

182 See the *Wall Street Journal*, 31 January, 2014: "Entrepreneur Stitches Together a Quilting Business" by Jim Carlton Short
183 Just as Peter Drucker predicted in the 1980s in various books and articles
184 Often paraphrased to "Be the change you wish to see in the world". The original quote is in the *Collected Works of Mahatma Gandhi*, Vol. 13, Ch. 153 ("General Knowledge About Health"), p241

act. Some of us are compelled to change by the prospect of an empty refrigerator.

Whatever the cause, acts of risk-taking are signals, beacons in a fog that lead the way out of the storm and into the economy of tomorrow. It takes hubris to engage in such great leaps of imagination and edgework. It potentially takes one million cups of coffee and a willingness to break with conventional expectations about how we should behave, what we should believe, and what is expected from us.

Why are these stories important?

The whole point of the central banks' response to the crisis – the low interest rates, the unlimited liquidity, the asset purchases – is to hold up the market because if it were allowed to fall the economy would descend into oblivion. These policymakers believe that Jenny Doans, Tamara Ralph, Stefan Roever and the owners of knitting shops and drone ventures the like cannot be trusted to discern the signals for themselves, to see when rents fall to an all-time record low, to realise that the financial strains on families will result in people wanting to make their own quilts or sweaters instead of buying them. No, the Fed says, these people benefit from keeping interest rates at record lows because it holds up asset prices and encourages risk taking.

The Federal Reserve and other central banks believe that the failure of every large bank and many businesses in the economy at one moment in time could never be fixed or offset by even a million Jenny Doan's, Tamara Russo's and Elon Musk's. No doubt this is true in the moment of a financial market-and economy-wide emergency. Central banks should stand as the lender of last resort under such conditions, but when does the helping hand of central bank support in an emergency become the hand of government that crushes the entrepreneurial spirit? No econometric model can tell us where that line is drawn. It will be in a different place in every society depending on the prevailing social contract. It will take creative thinking to figure out where it is and where it could be, wherever you happen to live.

Animal spirits and hubris

Central bankers also fear that the entrepreneur or "mompreneur" and even the consumer cannot overcome their fear. They need encouragement to begin risk-taking and spending again. Their "animal spirits"[185] have to be enticed into action, (and then restrained later when all is going well). It will take shockingly low interest rates to compel them and other risk takers to take their cash out of their bank account and put it to work in the market.

It is possible that the failure of a major bank was enough to paralyse risk taking in the economy. After all, the failure of Lehman Brothers was a lighting flash that exposed the fact that almost every financial institution was potentially illiquid if not insolvent. "Panics," as John Stewart Mill observed long ago, "do not destroy capital; they merely reveal the extent to which it has been destroyed by its betrayal into hopelessly unproductive works."[186] The Lehman Brothers event, and the panic and crisis that ensued, revealed that almost every industrialised economy had a debt problem that could not be financed if the banking system failed.

Freshwater and saltwater thinkers alike were compelled to grab the steering wheel from a market that was punch drunk on its own hubris. Having taken control of that steering wheel and seemingly guided the economy back to a safer place, it is understandable that policymakers are reluctant to relinquish control back to the unpredictable market to a sea of unknown anonymous individuals engaging in seemingly small ventures from their kitchen tables and garages. That same sea is filled with the killer sharks from the financial markets who will take the free

185 This term was first used by JM Keynes in his book, *The General Theory of Employment, Interest and Money* (1936) and more recently revived by the Nobel laureates George Akerlof and Robert Schiller in their book, *Animal Spirits* (2009), in which they write: "The proper role of the government, like the proper role of the advice-book parent, is to set the stage. The stage should give full rein to the creativity of capitalism. But it should also countervail the excesses that occur because of our animal spirits."
186 John Mills, *On Credit Cycles and the Origin of Commercial Panics* (1867)

money and still savage their prey. This is an important signal of hubris itself. Perhaps when policymakers moved the losses from the banking system and placed them on the government's balance sheet (which means on the shoulders of the taxpayers), they also unwittingly allowed hubris to move from the financial market into the heart of government. Policymakers now trust their own capabilities more than those of the markets. They believe they have control over the outcomes.

The Great Depression

It is hard to know whether QE and other government efforts are prolonging the slowdown or quickening the recovery. The debate harks back to the Great Depression years. Saltwater types tend to love President Roosevelt. They believe his efforts to put the nation back to work with the building of the Hoover Dam, the Tennessee Valley Authority and the many "ditch digging" programmes saved the nation from an even worse outcome. However, there are others who believe that Roosevelt's ditch digging efforts actually prolonged the Great depression. I find myself in agreement with the author Amity Shlaes,[187] who believes that Roosevelt's efforts to control the price of milk and steel and other core goods, actually destroyed the market mechanism and doomed the economy to an unnecessarily prolonged recession. The economy would have revived but government intervention inhibited the recovery by interfering in prices. Today many governments from Latin America to the Middle East to Asia area once again seeking to control the price of food by restricting exports, taxing imports and setting prices instead of allowing markets to do this. But the most important development in the world economy today is that many governments are artificially suppressing the single most important price in any economy: the price of money.

While these two camps debate counter-factuals, the facts for today's financial crisis seem clear. In response to a historic loss that jeopardised the nation's citizens, governments gave the financial

---

187 *The Forgotten Man: A New History of the Great Depression* by Amity Shlaes (Harper Collins, 2007)

services sector a blank cheque. Far from being held to account for the losses, the financial services sector has been given access to so much cash that it no longer had to sell its broken assets. Meanwhile, the real economy has learned to manage without them. With seemingly unlimited support, banks can just wait for the economy to improve and sell when prices came back to normal levels. Some policymakers explained to me that their purpose in bailing out the banks was to buy time, to hold open the window of opportunity to sell. They fully expected banks to sell their broken assets so that the market could invest again and the banks could strengthen their balance sheets. This plan backfired. The free money from government allowed the banks to not only retain these assets but to double up on them.

Doubling up, thank you

As I write in 2014, many in the market observe that transactions are occurring at higher prices on less collateral and easier lending terms than even before the crisis began. Some argue that the risk in the banking system today is even higher than it was in 2007. Tom Hoenig is the Vice Chairman of the Federal Deposit Insurance Corporation (FDIC), the nation's bank insurance system. He spent eighteen years on the staff of the Federal Reserve and then served as President of the Kansas City Federal Reserve for another twenty years. This is a measured and knowledgeable man who is not inclined to hyperbole who says the excessive risk-taking combined with reduced capital buffers in the banking system is "ridiculous"[188] and that banks are "horribly undercapitalised". Such a dissenting voice is too important a signal to be ignored.

What matters now is whether the policy stance of government is stopping or slowing innovation and the building of the economy of tomorrow. In his book, *Competition as a Dynamic Process* (1961), the American economist John Maurice Clark wrote that competition "is the modern substitute for the medieval idea of a

---

188 See Reuters, 14 June 2013: "Exclusive: Deutsche Bank 'horribly undercapitalised' – US regulator" by Emily Stephenson and Douwe Miedema

'just price'."[189] It is competition that keeps prices down and fair, but there are "enabling" and "underlying conditions" for innovation.[190] These include "the character of the people" and whether the "problem-solving" population "should operate under a secular government and religious attitudes that are hospitable to its exercise".

Are policymakers and governments "hospitable" to risk takers and innovation? As it stands, most governments want to tighten rather than relax control of prices and markets to problem solvers. This issue stands at the heart of modern political economy. Yes, there is innovation as we have seen here, but can the innovations of the small business, the anonymous risk taker, outrun the innovations of the state? As I mentioned in chapter one, the world economy can be reduced to two fundamental forces: the power of the state to tax and the power of the individual to generate wealth. Both must balance hubris and nemesis within themselves to coexist with each other. This is why we now need to understand that the state is innovating too, which we will explore in the next chapter.

189 *Competition as a Dynamic Process* by JM Clark (Brookings Institution, 1961), page 65
190 Ibid, page 195

The State is Innovating Too

Some states and their governments are also innovating, endeavouring to align themselves with the interests of their citizens. Others are moving in a direction that pits the interests of the state against its citizens or sets its citizens against each other. It all comes back to the weakness of recent economies and the accumulation of debt incurred in trying to revive faltering economies. As states reach for revenue and default on their citizens in various ways, the pain level rises. This is reviving all sorts of historic arguments about the redistribution of wealth, who should pay, who should benefit, and by how much. The rising level of pain compels governments to become far more innovative in their effort to secure cash from their citizens: taxation, expropriation, and inflation are some methods; defaulting on promises, reducing benefits and slashing payments are others. Every such decision has consequences for every member of our society.

More signage

One method of government innovation is the introduction of more and more rules and regulations. Some of this activity is driven by the need to be seen by voters to be doing something to prevent another crisis, another fraud, another loss. Some of it is simply designed to raise revenue, with fees for reporting compliance and large penalties for breach of regulations.

The signals emanating from my hometown of Washington DC are quite striking. In 2012, the revenue from speed cameras in the District of Columbia jumped from $42.9 million to a record

$95.6 million.[191] The median price of a home in Washington DC hit an all-time high in 2012, while the rest of the nation recovered at a considerably slower pace, as people moved to the District to take part in the new regulatory crackdown by joining the government. Many government departments need new staff to enforce the existing rules and implement the new rules more aggressively. Others have moved there in ever-greater numbers to lobby for or against the new rules or to get paid a handsome fee simply for explaining what the new rules actually are. Washington DC is now jokingly referred to as the centre of the financial markets, not only because the Fed has become the biggest, most important price-maker in the market, but also because Washington is so aggressively redefining the rules of banking and other forms of lending, in effect redefining financial markets. In an effort to kill two birds with one stone, the regulators have applied record fines to the financial services sector for a multitude of infractions.[192] This helps shrink the risk-taking in the banking and finance arena and also encourages big banks to shrink and spin-off their more risky lines of business. The process of imposing greater compliance requirements and fines for breach of regulations has somewhat surprisingly also increased revenues flowing to regulatory agencies and the government as a whole.

Each new rule usually has an associated cost. It may be a tax or a levy or it may come in the form of a fine associated with failure to comply with new or existing rules. It may be that the new rule forces risk-takers and edgeworkers to hire more advisors or more manpower. This too is a cost. It may be that new rules just cost time, but, as everybody knows, in business time is indeed money. Moreover, demand for additional attorneys continues to

---

191 See *The Washington Times*, 10 January 2013: "DC's speed camera cash skyrocketed in 2012" by Jeffrey Anderson
192 For example on insider trading alone, John Nester, a spokesman for the Security and Exchange Commission (SEC), is reported to have said, "We have brought a record number of insider trading actions in the last four years and will continue to do so." (See *The Financial Times*, 5 January 2014: "Red alert over record year for insider dealing" by Madison Marriage)

grow, and as everyone knows, lawyers are paid by the hour, with a strong incentive to work slowly and delay the outcomes of disputes.

The premise behind new rules and regulations is that the state can protect the citizen from future losses. Of course no one can outlaw fraud or hubris. Both occur regardless of the law. We can make fraud illegal, but the Bernie Madoff's of this world will find a way to commit fraud if they want to (Madoff was arrested in 2008 and later indicted for a fraudulent "Ponzi" investment scheme). I can hardly imagine a law that would outlaw hubris. Such a strategy would not only be silly but would also deny citizens the opportunities that arise with the possibility of loss. After all, as Julius Caesar observed, "It's only hubris if I fail." More government protection implies less need for the citizen to assess the signals and the risks properly themselves.

The state would argue that losses and failure can be permitted, but very large losses and very large failures that pose risks to the entire financial structure (systemic risk) cannot. This lies at the heart of the "Too Big To Fail" and "Too Big to Jail" ideas that justify the propping-up of many banks with policies that bear consequences for the rest of the population. Of course, the purpose of a central bank is to act when the market fails. No doubt markets sometimes do fail, but the state, once involved, wants to stay involved. It feels as if the environment is safer when government is directing outcomes, protecting citizens from uncertainty and potentially unsafe results.

So, governments put up more and more street signs (rules) in the hope that it can protect citizens from accidents: fill out this form, report your results in this new complex way, and the like. This is one path we can take, and was described by Friedrich von Hayek many years ago as the consequence of an expanding role of government in society.

Von Hayek described how both the political left and right begin to offer state planning and redistribution as a means of relieving the citizen of the burden of figuring out how to manage the economy after a crisis. The moderates in the middle warm to the idea that a "little" state protection is warranted, given the damage that the "free market" has inflicted on the citizens. This is how we find ourselves stepping back onto what Hayek called "The Road to Serfdom": the road to less freedom, less choice, less productivity and less GDP.

Exhibition Road

Perhaps another road could be considered: Exhibition Road in the South Kensington neighbourhood of London, well known as the city's museum district. The striking quality of this road is that there are no street signs at all. There are no markings to distinguish the curb from the road itself. There are no parking lines on the ground, or any "street furniture" such as road signs, speed limit signs, traffic signals or anything else to indicate where to walk, park, drive or stop. The funny thing is that when you walk or drive into this street, the absence of signals and signage compels everyone to slow down and concentrate. The uncertainty about the environment slows pedestrians and drivers alike, who suddenly realise they have to take responsibility for themselves. When signals and signage are removed, the accident rate collapses.

The Dutch traffic engineer Hans Monderman pioneered the idea that removing signage makes streets safer. He was placed in charge of road safety for the district of Friesland in the Netherlands in 1982 and concluded that all the street signage and official signalling was so overwhelming and hard to process that it was actually increasing the accident rate. Central bankers have debated and usually dismissed the idea of removing or simplifying regulatory signage on the grounds that the risks of removing the signage would be too high. But perhaps this "innovation" ought to be considered.

Such innovation could equally apply to the complex system of taxation that exists in most industrialised countries and emerging markets. Tax is a central driver of behaviour in economics. How many people don't sell assets including property or stocks at the right time because they would then have to pay tax on the gains? Tax incentivises people to assume their profits are real when in fact nothing is real until the cash lands in your pocket. How many investment behaviours are driven by the tax code? Most, perhaps. How many people really understand the laws that govern taxation? In the US in 1913, when the Federal Income Tax was created, the tax laws were initially printed on 400 pages. One century later in 2013 the US tax code stood at 73,954 pages, according to the CCH *Standard Federal Tax Reporter*.[193] I wonder how the small entrepreneurs manage to build a business, sort home life and still find time to manage their taxes. It seems obvious that a big firm with huge resources can manage the complexities of the tax code and get their tax obligation down to nothing. Meanwhile, instead of modifying taxes to encourage more wealth creation, governments are trying to find more and more innovative ways to increase tax revenues so as to increase the share of private wealth governments get to keep. One question the government and the public alike must ask is this: what signals is that tax code sending?

Red hats

One interesting signal, a tax signal, has been the brief reappearance of the "Red Hats" in France. France is sometimes believed to be a country where there are no limits to taxation. France is often referred to as the most socialist of all industrialised nations. Some even say that Communism still exists in only one place: France. One can debate all that but it is interesting to see that the French Government under the leadership of François Hollande has sought to raise the rate for personal income tax to 75%. That's one way to innovate. The risk is that the citizens object, which they are doing in large numbers. Today many of the entrepreneurial French are leaving France. The Mayor of London, Boris Johnson, has joked that he is the Mayor of the 5th largest French city because London has attracted such a large pool of French émigrées.

---

193 See the CCH (Commercial Clearing House)/Wolters Kluwer's report, *Tax Law Pile Up* (2013)

Meanwhile, back in France, protestors have appeared wearing red Phyrgian Caps or *Bonnets rouges*.[194] There is a long tradition in France of citizens who put on these caps to protest government taxation. In the 17th century, the *Bonnets rouges* were insurgents from Brittany who wore the now-famous Phrygian caps that we associate with the peasant's revolt against Louis XIV's fiscal policy. These are still called "Liberty caps" (Bonnet de Liberté) because those wearing them flooded the streets of France in 1675. They protested the huge tax increases Louis XIV had imposed on tobacco and transactions involving any documents (stamp duties). This was how he hoped to pay down the debt he had incurred from his ongoing wars with the Dutch. Today the *Bonnets Rouges* are still based in Brittany. Now they protest against President Hollande's proposals to raise taxes in similarly painful ways.[195] The reappearance of these red hats, such highly emotive symbols of dissent, is a signal that even in socialist France the social contract is being stretched to its acceptable limits. Even in France the state cannot tax the citizens beyond a certain point without pushback.

Marijuana and tax revenues

There are ways in which governments can innovate without pitting the interest of the state so sharply against the interests of the citizens. In 2012, Colorado announced the legalisation of marijuana, as did Washington State. Why? Did public morals in Colorado suddenly change? No. The simple fact is that if you make something legal you can tax it. Colorado announced the opening tax rate on sales of cannabis would be 30%. On the 1st of January 2014, the first day of legal trading, the state-regulated pot industry produced a price of $250 per ounce and generated sales of over $1 million.[196] Colorado expects some $600 million in sales and nearly $70

---

194 Who are France's Red Caps? The Telegraph, 14 November 2013
195 See *The Financial Times*, 22 November, 2013: "France: The people see red" by Hugh Carnegy
196 See *The National Review*, 3 January 2014: "$1 Million in Pot Sold in Colorado on First Day of Legal Sales" by Alec Torres

million in revenue in 2014 alone. It turns out "Maui Wowie" can generate an awful lot of revenue for the state.

Washington State has also legalised it. California and New Hampshire are considering legalising the drug as well.[197] Washington DC is decriminalizing its use. Current and former Presidents of Mexico have said that Mexico is on the same path and will certainly legalise if California does. Columbia has also announced its intention to legalise marijuana. If this unfolds, not only will it add to the tax revenue in California, Columbia and Mexico, but it will also dramatically diminish the resources needed to enforce against its use. The Mexican Drug War has generated immense negative publicity. Some 100,000 people have died or gone missing and the continuous headlines about headless corpses frighten investors and tourists alike. So, any effort to change the focus of policy will probably work to the benefit of both sides of the border.

There will always be those who argue that legalising one drug will simply fuel the trade in illegal ones. That may be, but what matters is that these local and national governments are clearly trying to innovate their way out of a problem without killing the entrepreneurial efforts of the citizens.

Government can be a source of innovation. For those who want to explore this idea, they should read, "The Entrepreneurial State" by Dr Marianna Mazzucato.[198] But, in the main, governments are today, under the burden of debt, focussing more on taking wealth from its citizens than on investing in their future well being. It may be that the state plays a part in promoting innovation but it largely coincides with good times when tax revenues are high and government budgets are well funded. In bad times, government tend to concentrate their innovations on new ways to tax.

---

197 New York's Governor Cuomo has announced plans to loosen the terms under which seriously ill patients can be permitted to use it, but not to fully legalise it. New York will be the twenty-first state to pursue this idea. (See *The New York Times*, 4 January, 2014: "New York State is Set to Loosen Marijuana Laws" by Susanne Craig and Jesse McKinley)

198 America's Underappreciated Entrepreneur: The Federal Government New York Times Opinion page, March 23, 2014

Fines and penalties

Generating more fines is a favourite way for governments to raise revenues. Lowering the speed limit or increasing surveillance of the city are just a few of the ways in which governments can generate more cash, which is why fines for traffic offences are increasing. However, tax offices are also coming up with ingenious and innovative ways to increase the tax take. In Washington DC and across the EU, there are proposals that all cars should be fitted with a black box to permit governments to measure mileage accurately and thereby tax on the basis of usage of public roadways.[199]

Google and tax enforcement

Speaking of surveillance, Lithuania's tax office teamed up with Google Earth to launch a crackdown on property-related tax evasion.[200] Using Google images, the tax office was able to identify many cases of tax evasion relating to property deductions. The former Board Chairman of a major bank in Lithuania, Bank Snoras, was found to have built on his property. He apparently failed to declare his ownership of the buildings and was found to have underpaid his tax. Obviously a fine would have been applied as well as the back tax. The tax take on property-related violations increased substantially.

Fines for bankers

The financial services sector has been subject to an endless stream of fines related to tougher enforcement of existing rules and the introduction of new ones. JP Morgan has emerged as one of the most fined financial institutions. By the end of 2013 it had been subjected to a record $13 billion in fines in a single settlement with the US Government over allegations that it had misled investors

---

199 See abcnews.go.com, 1 January 2014: "Feds may required cars to talk to each other to avoid crashes"
200 See *The Wall Street Journal*, 30 May 2013: "In Lithuania, the Tax Man Cometh Right After the Google Car" by Marcin Sobczyk

over mortgages in the run up to the financial crisis.[201] It also paid another $1 billion in fines over trading losses associated with its Treasury function, the "Chief Investment Office".[202] The cumulative fines are hard to estimate because there have been so many in the aftermath of the crisis, ranging from claims of market abuse to misleading investors.[203] One thing is certain, however: every bank feels it is under far more rigid scrutiny than ever before and regulators want them to feel this pressure. The fact that such pressures generate revenue is an added bonus.

Governments are also attempting to innovate when it comes to the question of incentives in the financial services sector. There has been much talk of re-imposing the Glass-Steagall Act on the American banking system. Created in 1933 and repealed in 1999, this law was an emergency measure to counter the failure of almost 5,000 banks during the Great Depression. It compelled banks to separate commercial deposit-taking businesses from the more aggressive investment banking-based speculating businesses. At the heart of the matter lie incentives. Today, far from disincentivising extraordinary risk-taking, policymakers have actually encouraged it. After all, what happened to the banks that were taking so much risk that the losses in the banking system had to be moved onto the shoulder of the citizens? Well, first they were bailed out. Then they were given almost unlimited free money in the form of QE from multiple governments. Far from being punished for their faulty judgement, these actors have been given a blank cheque.

The so-called Volcker Rule is a modern effort to reimpose Glass-Steagall on the banks. It amounts to compelling banks to separate their commercial banking activities from their speculative activities. But, the Volcker Rule is embedded in a variety of diverse policies and pieces of legislation and does not yet form a

---

201 See Business News, bbc.co.uk, 20 November 2013: "JP Morgan in record $13bn settlement with US authorities"
202 The so-called "Whale" scandal
203 See TheDailyBeast.com, 20 September 2013: "JP Morgan Chase's Long List of Expensive Legal Settlements Grows Even Longer"

comprehensive solution to the problem at hand – the incentives to speculate from a bank's point of view. Some have suggested that the state should innovate by capping the bonuses and even salaries of those in financial services. Others suggest a tax on financial services transactions. Another proposal has been to force every bank to use the same accounting standards of capital and assets, and set a strict limit on the ratio of assets to capital. Banks fiercely oppose this idea as it would end their ability to bet against investors with their insider knowledge of all market participants. No one has yet figured out how to remove the incentive to over-speculate while simultaneously protecting the ability of the financial services sector to keep innovating.

The subject of incentives lie at the heart of today's economy: how can bad, overly risk-taking behaviours be disincentivised? Of course, it is quite awkward asking this question at the very moment that government policy in most industrialised countries involves a semi-permanent commitment to handing the financial services sector a blank cheque in the form of low interest rates and virtually unlimited free money. In one sense, QE is a sado-masochistic policy that involves giving free money to the financial services community and then punishing them for using it in any way other than the sort of old-fashioned lending that most banks are no longer designed for, not equipped for, and not willing or able to undertake.

The Dog and the Frisbee

The point of such government policy is to make the financial services sector "behave better". Andy Haldane, an Executive Director of Financial Stability at the Bank of England and a member of its Financial Policy Committee, suggests a simple analogy: you can't teach a dog to chase a Frisbee; they just do it.[204] Knowledge of physics and flight dynamics will not help a

---

204 See *The Dog and the Frisbee*, paper by Andrew G Haldane, Executive Director, Financial Stability and member of the Financial Policy Committee and Vasileios Madouros, Economist, Bank of England given at the Federal Reserve Bank of Kansas City's 36th economic policy symposium, "The

dog to catch a Frisbee any better. Similarly, excessive efforts by governments to direct the hounds of the financial markets toward the right outcomes are likely to fail.

Some will object to the financial market participants being referred to as dogs, but I was one of them for many years and here is what I know about them: they are very good at finding the juicy red meat that we call profit. Assuming we do not support Communism or Socialism as an economic model, profit is the lifeblood of the economic system. (If we do support these other systems, then we still need to figure out how to generate more income than the government is paying out or else face certain bankruptcy as a nation.) If the economy fails to generate profit, it will kill any business and any nation as well. The puzzle is therefore how best to do this while avoiding the disasters that can occur when the hounds of the financial market are left unleashed and savage the innocent public. Record fines are one innovation governments are imposing to achieve this goal, but they do not address the central driver of behaviour.

Sheep dogs and pit bulls

I recall the words of John Whitehead, whom I met when I served in the White House. As the Managing Partner at Goldman Sachs, he developed the Fourteen Principles that should guide the firm in its actions:

> Our assets are our people, capital and reputation. If any of these is ever diminished, the last is the most difficult to restore. We are dedicated to complying fully with the letter and spirit of the laws, rules and ethical principles that govern us. Our continued success depends upon unswerving adherence to this standard.[205]

Changing Policy Landscape", Jackson Hole, Wyoming, 31 August 2012 (www.bankofengland.co.uk)

205 Goldman Sach's 14 Business Principles can be read on the website, www.goldmansachs.com, under "Business Principles" in the "Who We Are" section

He wrote this in the 1970s, a time when Wall Street and the financial markets were dominated by partnerships in which each partner was liable for any losses the firm might incur. After Wall Street shifted to a limited liability model in which the company could go bust without impacting on the personal liability of the senior management, the incentives changed.[206]

John Whitehead was, in a sense, a sheepdog. He could perfectly well go after the profits but would always do so without savaging the innocent sheep in the pen (pensioners, savers and the man on the street). As banks began to have shareholders instead of partners, as unlimited liability gave way to limited liability, it started to make sense to test the "letter and spirit" of the law. After all, the greatest profits are often found at the edge of the law and regulation. The presence of shareholders and the incentive of a rising share price seem to encourage greater risk-taking than the old partnership structures. When unlimited liability gave way to limited liability, the signals changed in ways that encouraged the transformation of sheep dogs into pit bulls.

I have yet to see a government innovation that encourages better behaviours. Instead, the policy response has been similar to the punishment the ancient Greek gods inflicted on Tantalus. The word "tantalise" comes from the legend of a man who angered the gods by not only stealing their ambrosia and nectar and revealing their secrets, but also sacrificing his own child and serving him up at the gods' banquet. As punishment Tantalus was condemned to stand up to his neck in water, within easy reach of the low-hanging fruit on a tree, but whenever he reached for the fruit, the branches extended away from his grasp, and whenever he bent to take a drink, the water receded away from him. The markets are now subject to a similar torture. Yes, there may be endless liquidity, but most of the time market participants are punished for using it. If banks made plain vanilla loans, the Gods

---

206 I am grateful to Dr Ngaire Woods, Dean of the Blavatnik School of Government at Oxford University, for her work on the subject of incentives arising from the public listing of banks.

of Regulation would tolerate it, but the banks fired all the lending officers years ago and replaced them with algorithms that have been proven to not work. But for most other activities banks are faced with a range of regulatory obstacles, from investigations[207] to caps on pay outs, that effectively prevent them from using the free money in the system. The problem with the "Tantalus punishment", which lasts for eternity, is that it renders the banking system incapable of getting on with the work society wants and needs it to do. Profits need to be captured. We have to think about something John Coates writes about: the "hour between the dog and the wolf" which is when a testosterone surge or a biochemical change causes traders to focus on their prey (a profit).[208] We want a dog that hunts but not a massacre. The question is how to rightly balance the hubris and the nemesis.

The Round the World Race

Governments can innovate with their policy responses but markets typically outrun them. During my time in the financial markets I came to see them as something like the Round the World yacht race. Players in the financial market always have the best and most expensive boats and equipment, as well as the ability to push hard against the boundaries of physics. Meanwhile, the regulators are usually in the equivalent of a dinghy, unable to keep up with or even see the race as it takes place. They find out what happened well after the events have already occurred. And yet, market participants spend most of their time focused on what the government prohibits rather than looking at new rules, new regulations, new taxes, and new interventions as a foundation for positive innovation.

Consider the birth of the Eurobond market. Some $4 trillion a year is raised through Eurobonds, which permit firms to raise money from investors worldwide in the currency of their

---

207 Such as the Libor and Foreign Exchange abuse investigations
208 *The Hour Between the Dog and the Wolf: Risk-taking, Gut Feelings and the Biology of Boom and Bust* by John Coates, The Fourth Estate, May 2012

choice. This began in 1962 when John F Kennedy, then President of the United States, came to believe that the debt problem was so large it had to be addressed at once. Little did he know how large it could become. He announced the imposition of a financial services tax[209] that would be applied to the sale of all US Government bonds. In response, a young man named Stanislas "Stanley" Yassukovitch, who headed Merrill Lynch in London, realised that US Government bonds could easily be sold from London, where they would be exempt from that tax. Yassukovitch is said by some to be the godfather of the now massive Eurobond market because he pursued this innovative idea that, ever since, has permitted companies to raise some $4 trillion every year from investors outside the United States.[210]

Foreign firms can also raise funds in foreign currencies on the Eurobond market, hence Dim Sum Bonds (which are denominated in Chinese Renminbi), Samurai Bonds (denominated in Japanese Yen), Kangaroo Bonds (denominated in Australian Dollars) and even Pho Bonds (denominated in Vietnamese currency).

Inflation as innovation

There are many examples of government innovation and its intended and unintended consequences, but I'd like to come back to the idea that inflation is an innovative method of taxation. It is an innovation today in the sense that it has revived an old idea that most have forgotten. Milton Friedman wrote:

> Since time immemorial, the major source of inflation has been the sovereign's attempt to acquire resources to wage war, to construct monuments, or for other purposes. Inflation has been irresistibly attractive to sovereigns because it is a hidden tax that at first appears painless or even pleasant, and, above all, because it is a tax that can be imposed

---

209 The Interest Equalisation Tax, 1962
210 This story was related to me by Michael von Clemm, another "father of the Eurobond market" before his death in 1997.

without specific legislation. It is truly taxation without representation.[211]

In theory, the bond market should serve as the brakes on government efforts to inflate. If money is debased too much, if interest rates are kept too low for too long, if too much money is printed, then the bond market ought to sell off. This places a constraint on the ability of the government to persist with inflationary policies, but there are innovations that governments can make to prevent the bond market from responding or slowing the inflation pressure. For example, we can already recognise and anticipate the introduction of regulations that increasingly compel pension funds to own "safe" assets. The definition of "safe" is the one thing that an investor wants to sell when governments are inflating or debasing paper money but which the government wants them to own: government debt.

For years, Australia had a law that required pensions to own government debt: the 30/20 Rule.[212] The Australian government describes it as follows:

> Under the 30/20 Rule, life insurance companies and super-annuation schemes received tax concessions if they held at least 30% of their assets in public securities with at least 20% of their total assets in securities issued by the Commonwealth.

It is not so hard to imagine governments reaching for some sort of a 30/20 rule in the future, but perhaps they needn't be so blunt. Regulatory pressure and moral suasion may be sufficient to compel fund managers to place more and more of savers' assets into the one thing that performs badly in periods of inflation and recovery – government debt. We can easily expect that this is an

---

211 *Monetary Correction: A Proposal for Escalator Clauses to Reduce the Costs of Ending Inflation* by Milton Friedman (Institute of Economic Affairs, London, 1974: Occasional Paper, no.41)
212 In force from 1961 to 1984

effective way of forcing the losses away from the government's balance sheet and toward the citizens' pocket.

The story of Cyprus

There is another innovation that governments can and have pursued. It seems unthinkable in this day and age, though it has happened throughout history: direct removal of cash from citizens' bank accounts. This is known as expropriation, or to disgruntled citizens, theft! This is what happened inside the Eurozone in Cyprus on the 16th of March 2013. On that day the World Bank, the International Monetary Fund and the European Union together demanded that the Cypriot Government announce a "one-off 'stability levy' of 6.75% on all bank deposits of 100K or less and 9.9% for deposits over 100K, with the aim to raise €5.8 billion".[213] Cyprus was also required to tighten the national budget by about 4.5% of GDP and the central bank of Cyprus was asked to sell almost all of its 13.9 tonnes of gold for cash.

These were some of the conditions the EU had set for Cyprus to qualify for a €23 billion bailout from the EU, which had become essential once it became clear that the Greek default had exposed the fact that the Cypriot banks and government were no longer just illiquid, they were insolvent and in need of life support. In exchange for their cash, the depositors at the Bank of Cyprus were issued with stock in their banks, which was presumed to be nearly worthless. Depositors at Laiki Bank got nothing. Obviously, such an event would normally prompt depositors to transfer their money abroad, so capital controls were introduced simultaneously with the expropriation announcement. Daily withdrawals from cash machines were capped at €260 for individuals and €500 per day for companies. Ultimately, the expropriation came to roughly 47.5% of the cash in every bank account in The Bank of Cyprus and Laiki Bank that contained more than €100,000.[214] Upon

---

213 See Eurogroup Statement on Cyprus, 16 March 2013 at www.consilium. europa.eu/uedocs
214 See *USA Today*, 29 July 2013: "Bank of Cyprus depositors lose 47.5% of savings", by Menelaos Hadjicostis

reading this my editor emailed me: "My friend's 85-year-old aunt in Cyprus has been left destitute and in dire straits by this as she can no longer pay for her homecare providers and has to move to some hideous charitable home for elderly beggars and the insane... Can you believe it?" Sadly, yes I can.

There were further extenuating circumstances. Some policymakers felt that these actions were justified because so many of the deposits, they believed, were owned by Russians whom they associated with organised crime and tax evasion. Other policymakers felt the actions in Cyprus needed to be sufficiently severe to stand as a warning to other Eurozone countries that might be slack in their efforts to tighten their belts and sort out their debt problems. European policymakers initially declared the Cyprus "bail-in" was a unique event, and would not apply elsewhere in the Eurozone. However, it was soon recognised in Eurozone capitals that there were not enough resources available among EU members to "bail out" any other banks in such countries as Italy, Spain or Portugal, so the Cyprus solution soon came to be recognised as the template for future EU bank failures. The days of bailouts have given way to a new era of bail-ins has begun.

Expropriation and nationalisation

There are many ways a government can expropriate wealth from its citizens. It is implicit when governments nationalise an institution. Even if a nationalisation becomes profitable, the state has to use the capital the citizens provide – taxpayer's money – to acquire the firm and recapitalise it. Governments always claim such events are in the citizens' interest. Not only does it save citizens from a threatening loss, they say, but they will profit from the endeavour. Sometimes that is true; more often it is not.

Sometime in 2011 I sat next to a senior official from Citigroup on a plane I asked him what he thought about the fact that Citigroup had required some $45 billion of taxpayer funds to bail it out (in exchange for preferential stock). He said that Citigroup was not bailed out. In fact, he insisted, Citigroup had provided the taxpayer with "the best profit opportunity in history". I replied that the taxpayer and indeed the government were not in the business of looking for profit opportunities even if a healthy profit was made on that event. With that, we hit an insurmountable conversational impasse. The bailout of General Motors with nearly $50 billion of taxpayer funds was not profitable. The loss has been estimated at roughly $10 billion. Either way, the government has chosen to spend those taxpayer funds on the bailout rather than on something else. The loss, or potential loss, would certainly fall on the citizen's shoulder because the gap would have to be made up somehow.

This is one of the critical issues of controversy among Eurozone governments. Any effort to bail out the deeply indebted peripheral countries (and their banks) immediately puts taxpayers' funds at risk in the countries that have any surplus. Of course if the bailout works, everyone wins. But if it fails, who will be left holding the loss? Those who actually have savings: the Germans. This is precisely why Germany has objected the loudest to bailouts and any effort to inflate away the debt. As the principal savers in the Eurozone, they would be the victims of such choices. Of course there may be other benefits. Germany exports to these countries, so supporting them might serve Germany's broader interests. But the point is that expropriation and nationalisation are ways in which governments innovatively put the taxpayer at risk even if the purpose of the exercise is to save them from risk.

Arguments persist about where the line between the state and government should be drawn whenever a private sector entity is bailed out. People are still arguing whether banks are "nationalised" if the government provides them with enough cash. Were Citigroup and Bank of America nationalised? Was General Motors? Has the entire banking system in Spain and Greece been nationalised? Whatever the outcome of the debate, it is certainly an innovation when government decides to take ownership of a private entity, even if only temporarily. It is also an important innovation if the government tells the depositors, equity owners or bond holders that the traditional rules no longer apply and they are being expropriated of all or some of their ownership stake. Bailouts and bail-ins alike involve removing cash from citizens. They just remove the cash in different ways.

Capital controls

Capital controls are another innovation that governments have been known to pursue. They can just stop money from leaving the country. Cyprus announced that people could only take €3,000 out of the country at a time. More recently India and Brazil announced capital controls. *The Economist* reported on India:

> The limit on personal remittances has been cut to $75,000 per year from $200,000 per year. And companies are now barred from spending more than their own book value on direct investments abroad, unless they have specific approval from the central bank."[215]

A number of the world's most important central bankers met in London not long after these events in honour of Sir Mervyn King's departure as Governor of the Bank of England. The policymakers I spoke with at the time gave me the distinct impression that the events in Cyprus "proved" that depositors would always be protected. Of course, they meant that depositors who had less than €100,000 of cash in the bank would be protected and, presumably, if a depositor had more than that amount they "deserved" to be "bailed in" to the loss that the nation had incurred. But, the public reaction in the financial markets was the opposite. Investors understood that governments, even those in the democracies of the industrialised world, could simply take cash from you without warning if your bank fell into serious losses. It can work in the other direction too. In early 2014, Italy announced a 20% withholding tax on all inbound wire transfers. This too is a type of capital control combined with a stealth tax.

Whatever your opinion of these government interventions, they are all about innovating policy in order to secure certain outcomes. There is a remarkable tendency for people to believe

---

215 See *The Economist*, 16 August 2013: "Fight the flight" by PF

that governments would never undertake such aggressive expropriations. Perhaps that is because everyone assumes that the "perfect circle years" were normal, when governments politely stayed on the sidelines and did not need to "bail in" or expropriate very much. Maybe it's because the deep conviction in the concept of rule of law and property rights is so ingrained, it is impossible to imagine a government breaking that aspect of the social contract. And yet it happens.

Cyber currencies

Perhaps the very best example of today's ferocious battle between policymakers and citizens is best viewed through the crucible of cyber currencies. As the state engages in innovation with monetary policy, the citizens begin to react to the potential loss of value. The public is smart enough to realize that expanding the money supply, velocity or no velocity, means that each piece of paper could be worth less in future. So we see cyber currencies come to life as people seek another way to protect the value of their hard earned wealth. If the state is going to expropriate your assets, it is worthwhile to see if you can trust someone else: someone like Bitcoin. There are now many versions of cyber currency. Bitcoin has become the most famous. The idea is simple. Money can be created by anybody. The trick is getting the public to trust that you won't devalue the currency.

But, one has to wonder whether a cyber currency can really be secure in a world where it has been confirmed that the US and other governments use sophisticated spying programs to track the communications of its own citizens and those of other nations. The revelations about Prism and Echelon, both US government mechanisms for capturing virtually every email, text and phone call for virtually everyone, raise real privacy issues. The US IRS decided to tax Bitcoin and cyber currencies (retroactively) as "property" not as currency, which means capital gains taxes apply. Furthermore, it is likely that governments will find ways to retrieve tax payments by taking funds straight out of your cybercurrency account. The question is whether a password is really secure in light of government's desire to eliminate or diminish viable alternatives to their own currency.

Demographics and sex

There are those who will say that demographics is the key to economic success. No matter what innovations the government comes up with, demographics will define the outcome. There is a lot of truth to this. As mentioned earlier, the only debt burden that the US did not need an inflation to solve was the debt burden accumulated from World War Two. The baby boom more than compensated for debt and helped pay it down through wealth creation. I, for one, strongly support sex as an alternative to QE (on the assumption that more sex leads to more children, one way or another). You may laugh, but demographics underpins economies. More people create more opportunity for economic growth. If anyone wants to support the idea that sex is a politically attractive alternative to QE, they should come out of the closet.

Governments can innovate on this policy front, or not. Today Japan is buying more nappies for adults than for babies, as Gillian Tett of *The Financial Times* often points out. Had Japan created incentives for families to grow, this might not be the case.[216] Meanwhile, in 2014 Kimberly Clark announced that it is decreasing the number of diapers in its packages (adult and baby versions alike) by 7%, it will sell them at the same price. Is this a signal that inflation is causing the input costs for diapers to rise to the point that Kimberly Clark has to pass on the costs by engaging in "shrinkflation"? Yes. And who will pay more: the elderly in Japan and the young elsewhere. I suspect Japan's demographics would look very different today if sales of baby diapers outranked sales of adult diapers instead of the opposite.

Other countries have undertaken many innovations to encourage a higher birth rate. Singapore restricts the number of small one-bedroom flats to discourage people from remaining single for too long. South Korea signals its desire to increase the birth rate

---

216 See *The Financial Times*, 5 August 2013: "Falling fertility rates pose threat to government revenues" by Gillian Tett

by holding "Family Day" on the third Wednesday of every month, when the lights in offices must be turned off by 7pm (presumably so that people go home to engage in friendlier relations). Similarly, China has finally abandoned the one-child policy.

The bottom line is that more people, more babies equals more growth and more GDP. A baby boom could arguably do at least as much to stimulate growth as Quantitative Easing over times. However, The appetite for abandoning Quantitative Easing and substituting Quantitative Pleasing seems strangely small. Nevertheless, I place great faith in the decisions being made every day by anonymous individuals who take the calculated risks, even with sex, that will define their personal future and thereby define the character and demographics of the economy we will live in tomorrow.

Innovation of definitions

In Argentina we see a different aspect of this same idea that government can innovate from within. Argentina innovated in recent years by fining or even arresting anyone who challenges the nation's official inflation data. In 2011 the gap between the actual inflation rate and the government's official assessment of inflation began to diverge so widely that local economists began to question the government's estimates. According to *The Economist*, the government's data showed something like a 9.7% rate while specialist private institutions/firms put the number closer to "24.4% and cumulative inflation since the beginning of 2007 at 137%".[217] This situation persists elsewhere as well, but the economists began to accuse the Argentine Government of fudging the data, if not manipulating the inflation models altogether. In response, President Kirchner announced that economists who challenge official inflation data would be criminally prosecuted. Fines were also applied to any analysis or forecast that "lacked economic rigour".[218] In 2014,

---

217 See *The Economist*, 25 February 2012: "Argentina's inflation problem: The price of cooking the books"
218 See *The Wall Street Journal*, 12 April 2011: "Argentina Fines More Economists Over Inflation Estimates" by Taos Turner

Argentina announced a new inflation measure that was developed in conjunction with the IMF. According to the new index, the inflation rate in January 2014 was not even close to the 1.4% that the old index showed for the prior month. Instead, it jumped to 3.7%.

Any efforts to manipulate the inflation rate can be considered as innovations that governments undertake to serve their own interests. So, for example, when President Obama declares his desire to use "chained CPI" when calculating payouts to government workers, we can be sure that there is a reason he has chosen this particular method of calculating the rate. Typically, chained CPI produces a lower final number than Core CPI, for example. In 'Wonkbook', a blog published by *The Washington Post*, it was noted that:

> "Chaining CPI" saves money by switching the government to a slower measure of inflation. That slower measure of inflation means Social Security slows down the cost-of-living increases built into its benefits. It also increases taxes, albeit by less than it cuts spending, by moving people into higher brackets more quickly.[219]

The AFL-CIO, one of America's biggest unions, said, "It's unconscionable we're asking seniors, people with disabilities and veterans to be squeezed of every last penny."[220]

Keep in mind that a higher inflation rate is useful to governments because the higher asset prices that usually ensue permit taxation at higher valuations. Milton Friedman tried to draw attention to this when he wrote that:

> Inflation increases the yield of the personal and corporate income tax by pushing individuals and corporations into

---

219 See 'Wonkbook', *The Washington Post*, 8 April 2013: "The trick of chained-CPI", by Ezra Klein and Evan Soltas
220 See aflcio.org, 4 June 2013: "Bad Policy: President Obama's Budget Cuts Social Security and Medicare by Damon Silvers

higher income groups, generating artificial (paper) capital gains on which taxes must be paid, and rendering permitted depreciation allowances inadequate to replace capital, so taxing a return *of* capital to shareholders as if it were a return *on* capital.[221]

The attractions are so great that central banks may be willing to change in many ways to avoid other painful choices and to gently "back into" the policy choices that permit inflation to begin. They may become willing to change or abandon inflation targets. They may be willing to calculate the inflation rate in ways that create at least the appearance of a divergence between what people experience versus what the official data says. They may be willing to discard dissent by giving voice only to those who share the views of the leadership. All efforts in these directions are important signals for the public.

Central bank independence

Governments may even be willing to forego the long history of central bank independence. The premise is that politicians are inevitably drawn to the idea that they control the money supply and therefore can produce more money any time they want simply by printing it. However, this debasement of the currency makes prices unstable. Prices start to move (up, usually) in response to the fact that there is more cash chasing the same goods and services. This is why central banks came into being – they are, in theory, the guardians of "price stability" or "stable prices", meaning prices that don't swing around too erratically. Price stability is the Holy Grail of most of the economics profession. It is the most desired outcome and the most difficult to achieve.

Everyone in politics is susceptible to the attractions of money printing. Central bank independence has proved hard to earn and quick to lose throughout history. Moreover, even as central banks

---

221 See *Monetary Correction: A Proposal for Escalator Clauses to Reduce the Costs of Ending Inflation* by Milton Friedman (Institute of Economic Affairs, London, 1974: Occasional Paper, no41)

begin to do the bidding of governments by printing the money they need and pursuing the inflation that serves their interests, central bankers will deny, deny, deny that their independence is jeopardised even as they potentially preside over its loss.

Dissent

The debate today rages fiercely over this important question: Have central banks already forfeited their independence? Some would say yes. When the central bank becomes the largest buyer of a nation's government debt, it cannot reasonably be seen as independent anymore. Others might argue that this does nothing to change the fundamental fact that the central bank makes its own decisions and is not doing the government's bidding.

One aspect of central bank independence is that it allows and even encourages lively debate. If a central bank begins to stifle dissent and shun alternative views it is an important signal. After all, if the institutions of justice in a society, like the courts, become biased, everyone understands that justice will not be as fairly and impartially served. The central bank is also an institution of justice given that it has the ability to change the balance of power between the lenders and the creditors, between the state and the citizens. The decision to inflate is not a technical economic decision. It is also a political and social justice decision.

The original purpose of the regional Federal Reserve banks was to ensure the Federal Reserve would have access to the stories bubbling up from the real and local economy to supplement the top-down national data generated by the Federal Reserve staff in Washington DC. The dissents in the aftermath of the 2007/8 crisis have exclusively come from the regional bank presidents.

The Federal Reserve leadership in Washington has not been very comfortable with that dissent, but central banking is a land of subtleties. Instead of attacking the dissent directly, the Chairman's office has threatened, ever so gently, to remove the research capability from the regional Presidents by centralising all research in Washington in order to "save money". It would clearly be harder to arrive at the facts required to muster a dissent if there was no research capability independent from Washington.

Luckily, the institution is sufficiently strong that the inherent checks and balances between the centre versus the regions continues to allow for a diversity of opinion within the Federal Reserve system. But, there are a number of signals that the Chairman and the Washington-based staff do not appreciate the dissent and will even do whatever is necessary to undermine or eliminate it.

For example, in the week before the 2013 Jackson Hole meeting of central bankers, a column appeared in *The Wall Street Journal* that suggested that the next Federal Reserve Chairman needed to be strong enough to "quell the dissent". Whether it is true or not, the author, Jon Hilsenrath, has been viewed by some in the markets as a journalist that Chairmen Bernanke's and Yellen his team trusted most to convey their views accurately and sometimes subtly. This view, that dissent ought to be "quelled", seems to sum up nicely what I know of the atmosphere inside the Federal Reserve in recent years.

Perhaps it is no surprise that the Kansas City Federal Reserve chose to exclude all private sector delegates at the 2014 Jackson Hole meeting. As one of the disinvited, and having attended continuously for nearly a decade, I applaud the decision. After all, the bulk of the "private sector" guests have always been the Chief Economists of the largest banks. They are the biggest beneficiaries of the largesse the Washington DC Federal Reserve Bank provides. They typically, with few exceptions, tell a story to the media and their clients that supports and encourages the continuation of QE and the continuation of the Washington Federal Reserve's view at the expense of dissenting voices. Dissent is lost if the markets and the media dismiss it. So, hopefully, the media may start to pay more attention to the dissenters at Jackson Hole.

The point is that democracies should encourage a wide range of policy views and choices and continuously test whether policies are really working and whether they actually serve the best interests of the nation as a whole. When policymakers spend time and energy trying to be heard or trying to prevent others from being heard, it signals that the institution is increasingly divided over the policy stance. Inability or unwillingness to tolerate dissent is probably a signal that policymakers have innovated to the point that dissent is real and persistent. Efforts to ignore it or undermine the authority of the dissenters merely reveals that the central bank has already started to tilt in the direction that benefits some members of society against the interests of others.

Then again, growing dissent could simply reveal that policy has become so innovative, that nobody is exactly sure of what they are doing, which would make anyone less open to dissent and debate at the very moment that there is more need for dissent and debate. At the 2014 meeting of the American Economic Association, Bill Dudley, the President of the New York Fed, apparently said, "We don't understand fully how large-scale asset purchase programmes work to ease financial market conditions."[222] In other words, QE is so innovative no one actually knows how it works or whether it works at all. After all, its end result is not yet known. Those who claim it has worked without causing inflation ignore the reality of daily life, preferring to follow an algorithm that may or may not present a realistic view. Those who claim it will unleash inflation get bits of evidence but will have to wait and see whether it becomes a generalised phenomenon.

People in America, and elsewhere in the industrialised world, are finding that the fall in the price of a mobile phone and a computer or even energy is no longer entirely offsetting the price hikes in other categories. So many things seem to be rising. As David Stockman points out, since 2000 the price of a movie ticket is up by 95.20%. Eggs have risen by 106.20%. College tuition is up by 68%. A postage stamp costs 48.5% more. Basic staples have hit record high prices. The Congressional Budget Office estimates that generic drugs will cost 11% more in 2015 than in 2014. Specialty drugs will cost 18% more. What do we make of the fact that in 2014 fuel prices fell by 2.7%, but utilities rose by 5.8 %? Meanwhile, the cost of a roast rose by 19%. A steak costs 15.6% more. Pork chops cost 13.7% more. Milk and cheese keep

---

222 See "Economics at the Federal Reserve Banks", remarks by William Dudley, President and CEO Federal Reserve Bank of New York, at the American Economic Assocation 2014 Annual Meeting, Philadelphia, Pennsylvania, 4 January 2014

hitting record prices on the Chicago Mercantile Exchange. In London, where I live, house prices are up 49.9% since the crisis and up 19% in 2014 alone. Average rents have hit a record high of £761 a month. The cost of energy bills, electricity, healthcare, education, insurance and shipping are all rising much faster than the official inflation rate. In the UK rails fares for remote parts of the country rose by between 43% and as much as 162% in 2014 alone.[223] It is estimated that it now takes 13.7 hours of minimum wage work to earn a Metrocard in New York City.

Hotels and car rental firms are slugging people with all kinds of sneaky charges. There is now an 18% fee for restocking a mini-bar in a hotel room. Hotels charge "Daily fees" to cover the gym and the pool even if you don't use them. Car rental firms charge as much as $30 in "administrative fees" for a toll that only costs $5.

The data shows inflation is low, flat or only marginally rising. Meanwhile, people feel they are experiencing bi-flation. There is a sense that everything that is mandatory in life is rising and some things that are discretionary are falling.[224]

Meanwhile, the debt problem just keeps compounding. The Congressional Budget Office estimates that the interest payments on US debt will quadruple to become the single largest item in the US budget by 2024.

The combined pressure and conflicting signals given off by such a huge debt and so many price hikes is bound to make people confused and scared.

Lessons from Ludwig Erhard

I am reminded of the reflections of Ludwig Erhard, the former Chancellor of West Germany (1963-1966). He was the man tasked by the German public to oversee the transition of the German economy from virtually total government control back to a market economy. His mandate was to remove government-

---

223 See Fury as rail fares in the north rise by up to 162% from today, The Daily Mail, September 8, 2014
224 I am grateful to Karl Massey for this bi-flation idea.

imposed price controls and restore the free market. It was an extraordinary innovation in public policy. It is hard to imagine how frightening it must have been to announce the end of price controls on bread and milk and have to wait and see what price the market would produce. Basic food was in short supply. After all, price controls and government allocation of assets had destroyed any incentive for anyone to create a business to supply these essential items. The price might have jumped to $100 or even $1,000 for a loaf of bread. The Germans had a recent and visceral knowledge of how high prices could leap in a short space of time. Just 10 years before, a wheelbarrow of cash would not buy a loaf of bread. Letting prices go would have been terrifying. But the innovation worked. Prices normalised. The market economy sprang back to life once the government abandoned "apparent success to real progress".[225]

Today, it is an open question whether the policies being pursued by central banks "prefer apparent success to real progress". Is it real progress if the stock market goes up but the standard of living goes down? Is it real progress if holding down interest rates gives rise to an inflation, even a small one, that the rich can outrun but which traps the poor? Is it success if policies benefit Wall Street but continue to leave Main Street relatively unaided?

Innovation in public policy is to be welcomed as long as it aligns the interests of the state with its citizens. If governments innovate in ways that work against the interests of the citizens however, it is hardly surprising that trust fades, questions are raised and various forms of protest begin. This is another way in which state innovation can either lead the way out of the economic difficulties that still plague the landscape, or steer society down a path that diminishes the ability of citizens to build the future they would like to have. Distinguishing the good innovations from the bad ones is a knotty problem, especially when the social fabric has already been made vulnerable by negative economic forces.

225 *Prosperity Through Competition* by Ludwig Erhard (Thames & Hudson, 1958), pages 6-7

In such circumstances, any and all signals become worthy of consideration and discussion.

It is amusing now to note a signal that appeared in Sweden in the 1970s. It was the reason that the most popular rock band of the era, Abba, decided to wear the outlandish costumes that are as distinctive and renowned as their music. The tax code at the time permitted deductions of costume costs only if you could prove the costume could never be worn anywhere but on stage. Obviously the spangles, and exposed tummies, and massive flared pants trimmed with feathers rendered these clothes entirely ridiculous if worn on the street. One could say the Swedish state's innovation instigated Abba's innovative response.

Cutting the Gordian Knot

12 CHAPTER

Every day, in moments of quiet observation and reflection, one can discern a cacophony of economic signals. As I write, the price of beef has hit yet another record high in the US, and a crime long consigned to cowboy movies has returned: cattle rustling. Cows are disappearing in the middle of the night in California and Texas, because it's now worthwhile to steal them. What people try to steal is often a good signal.

In the UK, another signal sends a shiver down the spine: customers have been shocked by jumps of 10% and above in the cost of energy bills, water bills and transportation, and were appalled when the Prime Minister's spokesman suggested people should just cope with the cold weather by wearing "more jumpers" (sweaters).[226] This is not going to win many votes. In the US the cost of electricity per kilowatt hour has just hit a record high even adjusted for inflation. Energy costs are bearing down even in the industrialized world.

Meanwhile, the signals from geopolitics are rattling the economic cage evermore loudly. Bloomberg posted a story entitled "How to Prevent a War Between China and Japan",[227] thus acknowledging that the signals from both countries, Japan and China, are not positive. The Chinese Ambassador to the United Kingdom, Liu Xiaoming, wrote in the *Daily Telegraph*:

---

226 See *The Guardian*, 18 October 2013: "No10 says people should consider wearing jumpers to keep fuel bills down" by Patrick Wintour.

227 See Bloomberg.com, 29 December 2013: "How to Prevent a War Between China and Japan" by Kishore Mahbubani (Dean and Professor in the Practice of Public Policy of the Lee Kuan Yew School of Public Policy at the National University of Singapore)

In the *Harry Potter* story, the dark wizard Voldemort dies hard because the seven horcruxes, which contain parts of his soul, have been destroyed. If militarism is like the haunting Voldemort of Japan, the Yasukuni Shrine in Tokyo is a kind of horcrux, representing the darkest parts of that nation's soul.[228]

Japan's Ambassador to the United Kingdom responded to this just a few days later, also in *The Daily Telegraph*:

There are two paths open to China. One is to seek dialogue, and abide by the rule of law. The other is to play the role of Voldemort in the region by letting loose the evil of an arms race and escalation of tensions.[229]

A few weeks later, Daniel R Russel, the Assistant Secretary at the Bureau of East Asian and Pacific Affairs at the US State Department, announced in Congressional testimony that the US does not recognise China's "Nine-dash Line". He said, "Any use of the 'Nine-dash Line' by China to claim maritime rights not based on claimed land features would be inconsistent with international law."[230] Later, in May 2014 China then placed an oil rig inside waters that Vietnam perceived to be within their territory and proceeded to protect the rig with more than one hundred naval vessels and five fighter jets. US Secretary of State Hagel said, "China has undertaken destabilising, unilateral actions asserting its claims in the South China Sea".[231] In response, Zhu Chenghu, a two star general who is the Dean at China's National Defense University, said that America suffers from

---

228 See *The Daily Telegraph*, 1 January 2014: "Liu Xiaoming: China and Britain won the war together" by Liu Xiaoming
229 See *The Daily Telegraph*, 5 January 2014: "China risks becoming Asia's Voldemort" by Keiichi Hayashi
230 Testimony Before the House Committee on Foreign Affairs Subcommittee on Asia and the Pacific by Daniel R Russel, Assistant Secretary, Bureau of East Asian and Pacific Affairs, State Department. Washington, DC, 5 February 2014
231 See BBC.co.uk, 31 May 2014: "Chuck Hagel: Beijing 'destabilising' South China Sea

"extended deployment" which, he went on, "has become the male type of ED problem: erectile dysfunction".[232]

Leaving humour aside, it was in all seriousness that President Xi Jinping said in July 2014 that "Sino-US cooperation will achieve things that are beneficial to both countries and the world, while confrontation will be disastrous." Clearly it is worth paying attention to the signals emanating from this issue.

Meanwhile, President Putin warned the world he was going to challenge what he calls America's "Universal Diktat", by which he means the US Dollar-led world order. He feels America is now exporting "chaos" in multiple ways. The speech was given on October 24th, 2014 at the Valdai Discussion Club in Sochi where Putin owns a home. Within a few days of the speech, NATO was promptly compelled to respond to some twenty-six reported air incursions by Russian jets and bombers, which occurred over a forty-eight hour period. At about that time, an "unidentified for-eign" submarine was spotted practically in the middle of Stockholm soon after Russia held their largest naval exercises in the Baltic Sea since the Soviet era. It was widely assumed, rightly or wrongly, to be a Russian vessel. The Danish intelligence service (Forsvarets Efterretningstjeneste - DDIS) released a statement saying that they had intercepted encrypted communications from Russian vessels in the Baltic at that time, indicating that Russia had "simulated" an attack on the Danish Island of Bornholm at the very moment that all Danish politicians were gathered there for an annual conference. The intelligence communities of Europe had been very focused on Russia given that the Russians had seized an alleged Estonian spy and the Estonian's nabbed an alleged Russian spy. It should not have been any surprise when Norway, Poland, Lithuania all announced the hardening of their the borders with Russia as of late 2014, thus further confirming that Russia's pressure on European borders extends well beyond Ukraine. Of course, if one looks at the expansion of NATO eastward since the Fall of the Berlin Wall, one can understand why Russia's leaders feel the West has been

---

232 *The Wall Street Journal Asia*, 2 June 2, 2014: "Chinese General Says U.S. Foreign Policy Has 'Erectile Dysfunction' Problems" by William Kazer

overaggressive and provocative. Add to this picture a Russian economy that is suffering from substantially higher inflation and the devaluation of the Russian Ruble to record low levels.

Taken together, these many signals convey that we have re-entered a period of conflicting ideas and goals which may be resolved militarily. Putin put is clearly in his Valdai speech when he said, "First of all, changes in the world order – and what we are seeing today are events on this scale – have usually been accompanied by if not global war and conflict, then by chains of intensive local-level conflicts. Second, global politics is above all about economic leadership". "We did not start this," but, if the US continues on this path, states "would be subjected to extreme hardship, or perhaps even total destruction". By invoking a reference to nuclear weapons, Putin drew attention to Russia's increased testing of nuclear and hypersonic missiles in the recent past. That too is meant to serve as a signal.

Germany has deported the CIA station chief, ostensibly on spying charges, and arrested a double agent from Germany's own intelligence community who was allegedly working for the Americans. Why is the US spying on Germany? One could say the US is spying on everybody.[233] Nonetheless, the German Chancellor announced that the BND, Germany's intelligence service, would commence actively spying on the US and its closest intelligence partner, Britain.[234] In fact, the German leadership has required that senior officials prepare truly sensitive documents on typewriters instead of computers while music is played in offices in order to make it harder to eavesdrop. The reality is that Germanys' seeming alignment with Russia (perhaps driven by the dependence on energy) has caused the US to view Germany as an ally of Russia. This raises a profound geopolitical problem given that the whole purpose of the US military presence in Germany and across Europe is to defend Germany from Russia. Awkward. This is a geopolitical problem for the world.

---

233 To add some levity to the serious gravity of these developments, I find it quite funny that the NSA is now considered to be the only part of the government that listens.

234 July 2014

Meanwhile, Russia's announcement of a ban on food imports was designed to hit Europe and Germany hard. Banning food allowed Russia to drive a wedge between local political interests (farmers and those tied to land an agriculture) from the elite in Brussels. It drives a wedge between the EU and the US. The food ban signals that Russia and Germany are not aligned enough yet from Russia's perspective. This makes things even more awkward for Germany. It is also driving up the price of food in Russia and weakening the Ruble very dramatically.

But signals from closer to home are also important. Signals need not be so big and dramatic as fighter jets and military movements. Some signals are very small. One signal that really energised a lively Twitter exchange I participated in was just before Christmas 2013, when the news that big-brand chocolate companies – including Mars, Cadbury's and Rowntree's – would be selling their Christmas collection chocolates for the same price as the previous year but with somewhere between two to eleven fewer pieces in the box.[235] By Christmas 2014, candy companies were shrinking their products again. Nestle's box of Black Magic chocolates were reduced from 376g to 348g but the price remained £6. Bassetts Jelly Babies were reduced from 540g to 460g but still cost £4 a box. Strategies like this generate outrage and affect the public's willingness to swallow what policymakers say. The credibility of official inflation statistics is therefore not only widely questioned in China and the emerging markets, but is also being called to question by citizens across the industrialised world. I write this eyeing the Hershey's Kiss on my desk, which will cost 8% more going forward, as I said earlier in the book.

The Grinch

Central banks are strongly signalling their desire to "do whatever it takes" to strive for "optimal control"[236] in an effort to protect

---

235 See *The Daily Mail*, 13 November 2013: "Manufacturers Reduce Size of Festive Boxes of Chocolates (But The Price Stays the Same)"

236 From a speech by Janet Yellen at the Boston Economic Club Dinner, Boston, Massachusetts, 6 June 2012. Read the transcript of her speech at www.federalreserve.gov: "Perspectives on Monetary Policy"

the poor, the weak and the innocent from the damage of debt and deflation. But, by continuing to pump liquidity into the system, the seeming superhero has morphed into the Grinch who stole Christmas, robbing the very people whom policymakers sought to protect and often further enriching the very people and institutions that caused the problem. Fed Chairmen Bernanke and Yellen extolled the virtues of the "wealth effect" of QE but, increasingly, ordinary people are asking whose wealth has been enhanced, exactly? Holders of portfolios of stocks and commodities have gained (the rich) but those who have no such portfolios find their cost of living rising (the poor). QE is gradually becoming recognised as a mechanism for redistribution of wealth from the poor to the rich. Now that Fed officials are gradually admitting that they are not sure how QE operates, their credibility is being challenged. All this takes place in a world where wages as a percentage of GDP stand at a record low and profits at a record high, thus foretelling sense of social injustice that will further undermine the social contract.

The demand for higher wages continues apace in the emerging markets. Bangladeshi textile workers were awarded a 77% wage increase in December 2013 on top of a number of double-digit wage hikes. They promptly announced their intention to strike in an effort to achieve even higher pay. These sorts of wage demands echo around the emerging markets, from Indonesia to Brazil to Africa to China. The demands in the industrialised world are also picking up. In the US, UK, Germany, and Japan workers are pushing for a "living wage" because the "killing wage" they are being paid is being eroded by a higher cost of living every day. Some claim there can be no wage hikes without union movements even though the signal is clear: workers can organise themselves faster than ever with a mobile phone and an app.

The tangle of signals seems impossible to disassemble. Unemployment in every economy remains uncomfortably high while wages remain at record lows as a percentage of GDP, even though profits have risen to record levels. Borrowing money is nearly free but hardly anyone can actually borrow through conventional channels. The efforts by policymakers to "save us" from economic disaster have made asset prices scream upwards but also cause the standard of living for most to fall. Yes, the stock markets are back at all-time inflation-adjusted highs, but nurses, firemen and shop staff can't keep up with their rent, have no hope of ever owning property, given what is happening to property prices, and will find themselves financially and physically stretched as they are forced to live further and further away from their place of work. Quantitative easing has come with a dark side: quantitative squeezing.

No doubt a falling standard of living is usually required in order to render an economy more productive. Many will argue that prices have not risen. Incomes have fallen. This may make the public even more sensitive to any price rise. But, the real question is, whatever the cause, how much pain can the public bear before they choose to exit, thus undermining the power of both the state and the citizen to resolve the debt problem?

Some exits are dead ends, literally. You can try to escape the high cost of food but the move to cheap and empty calories is already killing nutritional standards. You can escape economic circumstances by hopping on a plane, but this kills the economy left behind. You can raises taxes, but this kills entrepreneurial incentive. Some will choose suicide. Others will choose suicide of the ego and become someone quite different to whom they were before, accepting menial work and/or part-time employment or by completely changing their life plans (which involves the death of the ego).

For those that don't have or won't take the exit option, we can expect more "voice". The billions of emerging-market workers who already have a paltry standard of living are not going to take a cut quietly. Even in the industrialised world there is bound to be more push-back after years of belt-tightening. There are politically unquantifiable pain limits in every society. Social unrest is not going to be confined to emerging markets.

A knotty problem

The world economy finds itself twisted into a Gordian Knot, a problem that becomes more intractable as you push and pull at the individual strings and threads that constitute the many conflicting and commonly held views about what should be done. Central bankers use this very metaphor to describe one of the most tenacious strands of the problem. They worry that more liquidity can be pushed into the system, but this seems to amount to what central bankers call, "pushing on a string".[237] Once interest rates fall to zero, and we hit their so-called "zero bound",[238] there isn't much more a central bank can do than to start buying assets. But, government intervention in asset prices such as stocks and bonds destroys the most powerful signals the economy generates and instead creates artificial mis-signals, thus distorting incentives. Once governments start buying and controlling prices in the stock market and the bond market, it becomes hard for them to stop. A false sense of complacency permeates markets as central banks prop up asset prices.

Killing deflation seems to require giving life to at least a little inflation, which certainly benefits some at the expense of others. I mentioned Christine Lagarde's comment earlier: "If inflation is the genie, then deflation is the ogre that must be fought decisively."[239] Deep divisions exist over whether it is really possible to conjure forth the genie of just the right amount of inflation and put it back in the bottle before it hurts anybody. And, if a deal is going to be made, shouldn't we at least get a wish or two (or three) in exchange? As Larry Lindsey, a former Governor of the Federal Reserve and Economic Advisor to the

---

237 The origins of this phrase are often attributed to JM Keynes and also to Congressman T Alan Goldsborough during the Congressional hearings on the Banking Act of 1935. When the Federal Reserve Chairman Marriner Eccles stated, "Under present circumstances, there is very little, if any, that can be done," Goldsborough replied, "You mean you cannot push on a string." Eccles responded: "That is a very good way to put it, one cannot push on a string. We are in the depths of a depression and... beyond creating an easy money situation through reduction of discount rates, there is very little, if anything, that the reserve organisation can do to bring about recovery."

238 The "zero bound" is when interest rates have fallen to zero or nearly zero.

239 See Bloomberg.com, 15 January, 2014: "Lagarde Warns Officials to Fight Deflation 'Ogre' Decisively" by Sandrine Rastello

President, wisely observes, even in deals with the devil you usually get something in exchange for selling your soul. So far, none of the obvious three wishes has been granted. Unemployment remains too high, lending remains too low and the debt problem continues to grow.

Meanwhile, the signs of life in the world economy, though welcome, further fuel the demands for a fairer distribution of wealth, which means no one can be sure how much of their hard work will be kept by the state or redistributed to someone else. While the public finds ways to fish for profits, the government finds ways to fish those very profits back to its own pocket through taxation, if not expropriation, in order to meet its voracious need for cash. In the cold early months of 2014 in Washington, a common joke about the weather was, "It's so cold, members of Congress can be seen walking around the Capitol with their hands in their own pockets."

Taxes could be reduced, thus freeing the risk taker, but then the credit rating of the nation might be jeopardised, thus raising uncertainty and the cost of finance for everyone. Taxes could be increased, which would, in theory, raise revenue, but in fact might well incentivise economic risk takers to stop their activities, or move more of their economic activities to the black market, or to exit the country that is taxing them. All these ultimately reduce wealth creation and the tax take.

Each camp has become so entrenched in its own argument that it can barely tolerate any dissent or opposition. The freshwater and saltwater groups either ferociously argue or icily refuse to argue about the problems and the solutions: Is QE the culprit or the cure? Is government? Is spending? Is taxation? Is debt?

The world is now divided between industrialised countries that seek to foment enough inflation (or take risks with inflation) to save themselves from debt, and those, including Germany and the emerging markets, who view these efforts as an act of aggression designed to export inflation and instability at their expense. Each country is as divided as the arguments, while economic pressures pit the citizens of every nation against each other and pit the state against the populace. Throughout the

309

world, the social contract is coming under growing political pressure as the debt burden bears down on each and every citizen, company, community and country.

Alexander the Great

There is only one thing you can do with a Gordian Knot, as Alexander the Great demonstrated so many millennia ago.[240] The legend begins with his epic hubris. Alexander exhibited ego and arrogance on a scale that has rarely been matched in history. As a brilliant military commander, he led his armies though Europe, India, Central Asia and the Middle East, capturing and forcing into submission various kingdoms into what became a vast empire – and all of this well before age 33, when he died from food poisoning.

When he arrived in the small city of Telmissus, he discovered that a simple commoner, a very old fellow named Gordias, had become the King through sheer dumb luck. Apparently the local oracle had seen a signal: an eagle landed on Gordias's oxcart. The oracle declared that anyone entering the city on that oxcart would become King. Naturally, Gordias tried to tie the cart as securely as possible for fear of losing his newfound power. He tied it to a tree using an especially complex knot that could not be undone or unravelled and which actually became tighter the more one attempted to undo it – the fabled Gordian Knot. Of course, Alexander the Great assumed that it would be child's play to wrest control of a "magical" oxcart from a little old man. He tried to untie the knot, but, the more he tried, the tighter it became. So, he pulled out his sword and sliced the knot through the middle. Alexander entered Telmissus on the oxcart, was proclaimed King and promptly moved on to his next conquest.

It takes enormous personal courage, indeed hubris, to slice through a Gordian Knot. Preoccupation with the past and fear of the future sometimes preclude a clear vision of the similarly clear acts of hubris in the present. The sharp demands of reality draw forth strength of character and cause some to proceed with

---

240 Alexander the Great lived between 356 and 323 BC

nothing more than conviction and a clarity of vision that others don't yet share. These efforts are signals – even beacons – in an economic fog, and lead the way into the economy of tomorrow.

I heard Steve Furber, the ICL Professor of Computer Engineering at the University of Manchester, say something interesting when he accepted his prize at *The Economist*'s Innovation Awards ceremony in 2013.[241] He and his colleague Sophie Wilson invented ARM chips, which now "dominate the processor chips inside smart phones, digital cameras and other mobile devices". Some 40 billion units have been sold, which lie "at the heart of more than 35% of all consumer devices worldwide". Furber said, "The young have a distinct advantage when it comes to innovation. They do not yet know what is impossible."

Impossible things are happening in the world economy all the time. Innovation is everywhere once you begin to look for it. I have written about Stephanie Izard, who founded The Girl and the Goat restaurant and transformed a run-down district of Chicago, and Daniel Rose, who created Spring in Paris. But I am grateful to Zerohedge.com for bringing Damon Baehrel's extraordinary innovation to my attention. His restaurant in Earlton, upstate New York, has twelve tables and no staff, no business manager, no advertising, a 29 out of 30 rating by Zagat for his food and a 28 rating for service. He has a five-year waiting list. Based on that he takes home about $700 grand a year. He started the venture in 2006, just before the financial crisis, and has thrived in spite of it. He says, "I'm the chef, the waiter, the grower, the forager, the gardener, the cheese-maker, the cured-meat maker, and... everything comes from this 12-acre property."[242]

Some will say such examples of innovation are not useful because they are small one-off cases or because restaurants are notoriously difficult businesses to run. For every restaurant that

---

241 See *The Economist Innovation* Awards 2013 at www.economist.com. The ceremony was held at the British Academy of Film and Television Arts (BAFTA)

242 See www.damonbaehrel.com

succeeds there are many that fail, mostly within three years. Also, the barriers to entry in the restaurant business are remarkably low, making it susceptible to high turnover. Yet this fact is what permits a former Motocross champion like Baehrel to enter the playing field. It does not seem right that Motocross is a good training ground for a chef, but the expected never happens; it is the unexpected always.

One thing is obvious: Innovation rarely comes from doing things the way they have always been done or from people who are playing it safe. It often comes from people who have no choice but to take a risk, like Saeed Pourkay. He opened a one-man soup stand in the corner of a New York City restaurant where he makes and serves a complex soup called *Asheh Reshteh*, which is Iranian comfort food. His career in the soup business is a story of our times:

> "I ate my investments, I ate all my savings. I ended up leaving my wife, and when I separated, I have no place, no money. I got depressed a little bit, and it was difficult for me to find out what my passion is at the age of 55. What else can I do that I don't make a mistake again?"[243]

Even if just one person can figure out how to make a living from selling food, that is wealth, growth and GDP being conjured forth from nothing. What these people are doing requires hubris but on a scale they can manage with their skills. In a world overcome by the pressures I have described, such efforts are to be celebrated.

Follow the leader (but who?)

So, whose lead should we follow? Janet Yellen, the new Federal Reserve chairman, who pushes for "optimal control" and believes that inflation is a risk worth taking? Or should we follow Esther George, the Federal Reserve President from Kansas City, who pushes hard to save the market from policies that tilt the playing

---

243 See www.pri.org, 11 December 2013: "This chef serves Persian comfort food from the corner of a pizza joint in New York City" by Alex Gallafent

field toward the banking establishment instead of toward the interests of real-economy risk-takers? Perhaps we should follow the woman who is quietly running the profitable hobbyist quilting shop, or the man selling Iranian soup? These innovators are everywhere. They may be entrepreneurs who build something from nothing. They may be intrapreneurs who affect radical change from inside large institutions. They may be regular people who are changing their own consumption and spending habits, reinventing themselves, redefining the kind of work they can and will do in the future. The impossible dreams of regular people are at the heart of the economy we will have tomorrow. When each one of us balances hubris against the risk of nemesis, we all play a part in defining the quality of the future.

Wait or create?

While writing this book, I was often asked, "How does your book end? What is the solution?" The answer, dear reader, depends on you. You are also a signal in the world economy. What do you see? What do you think it means? Will you wait or create?

When confronted by someone who has the hubris to engage in a great leap of imagination, what will you say? What would you have said to Miles Davis and Charlie Parker as they abandoned perfectly successful styles of music in order to create something new? "Whatever for? Why change anything, you're a huge success as it is!" Or, "Wow! How exciting! You have a vision for something unheard of." What kind of signal will you be when someone you know decides to take a risk? Will you, as a friend or a colleague, welcome and encourage the act of reinvention, the pursuit of new ideas? Perhaps you will feel better advising them to wait until the economic recovery path is confirmed by the data and blessed by economists who won't sound the all clear until the recovery is well under way? How will you calibrate the decision with the specific skills and character of the person undertaking the risk?

Be the change

These many examples serve as a signal that people are doing the kind of edgework that leads to economic growth and wealth creation. Rather than waiting, these edgeworkers are choosing to "be the change" in the world economy. They are following Mahatma Ghandi's advice: "If we could change ourselves, the tendencies in the world would also change. As a man changes his own nature, so does the attitude of the world change towards him... We need not wait to see what others do."

It is a shame that it takes a financial crisis to compel us to reinvent ourselves, our companies, our communities, our social contracts and our economy. Perhaps the fact that there have been so many economic and financial crises in modern times is actually a blessing, at least for some, a gift wrapped in sandpaper. These events certainly force us to evolve and to face the underlying problems that government and growth alone won't fix.

It is not enough to reflect on the economic forces that drive change, however. At its heart, innovation involves abandoning the ego and reinventing the definition of who we are. Such personal innovation is a bloody business. The investment banker is dragged kicking and screaming to his knees by the losses he has incurred, by the limits placed on his ability to earn by politicians and regulators, and by a public that treats the profession and its participants with an approbation usually reserved for violent criminals. His emergence as something new is a blessing to the world economy, whether he is now transformed into a more innovative banker or whether he ends up bringing his energy and skills to some new part of the economy. All of us are subject to the same demand now. The question is what will you do?

Genuflect toward the future

Others are pushed to their knees through no fault of their own: the young who cannot find work; the college graduates who cannot understand why the degree that defined their purpose and meaning now has no value in the workplace; the youth of Europe, who are slowly realising that their leader's decision to stay in the Eurozone has potentially precluded any possibility of jobs for years to come; the Chinese and Bangladeshi workers who left only to find greater discomforts in city life. They have realised now they may not get rich before they get old. Everyone is being pushed to their knees in confusion, trying to understand not just what happened but how they are going to make a living going forward. We all need to ask ourselves, "Who will I be?" "What will I do to define myself?" If we reinvent ourselves, we can reinvent the world economy. We need to genuflect toward the future.

Lao Tze

There is a deceptively simple answer to the seemingly simple question, "What will happen next in the world economy?" It depends on us. Everyone is trying to balance the risks and the opportunities, attempting to navigate the uncertain and unprecedented economic pressures that surround us. The following beautiful saying is attributed to the ancient Chinese philosopher Lao Tze (and sometimes also to Henry David Thoreau): "Watch your thoughts; they become words. Watch your words; they become actions. Watch your actions; they become habits. Watch your habits; they become character. Watch your character; it becomes your destiny."

One choice we have is to continue arguing about how to divide and redistribute the existing economy. The left and the right, the freshwater and saltwater, the haves and have-nots, can continue to tussle over who should "pay" for the debt. They can keep arguing about whether the debt is a problem at all. These arguments will continue to dominate the news and the agendas of policy meetings. But the reality is that historic decisions have already been made that will define the economic landscape for years to come. There is an epic battle underway between those who fight for greater government control and intervention and see this as the solution, and those who keep their faith in innovation and risks taken in a million different and as yet invisible ways by unsung, unknown ordinary people.

Princess Amidala

I am reminded of the famous scene in *Star Wars: Episode III - The Revenge of the Sith*, where the Emperor has just declared himself a dictator, justifying this as necessary to successfully fight the impending war against the evil enemy Sith. Far from protesting their loss of power, the Senators rise to their feet to applaud him, in the firm belief that everything must be done to protect the public from this evil foreign attacker. Princess Amidala says, "So this is how liberty dies... with thunderous applause." In the same way, many now greet the government's efforts to ward off dangerous deflation with such applause. It is argues that there was no other choice. It was an emergency. Well, the emergency is over for now. If anything the current stance risks the creation of a new emergency. We become tolerant of having governments control prices, pursue risks with inflation, tax someone else and not us. There are fewer and fewer who remain faithful to the notion that the people who take calculated risks can be trusted to innovate and reinvigorate the economy to where it needs to be.

The media can try to dismiss Esther George and other dissenters on the Board of the Federal Reserve and other central banks as eccentrics and outliers, but it is worth thinking about what they are fighting for and whether it is in the best interest of those who are building the economy we want to have tomorrow. Both Esther George and Janet Yellen are fighting for innovation in public policy. The question is, which camp will *you* support?

Do you want an economy that depends on government largesse and government control over the most important prices in the economy, or one in which markets serve as a mechanism for allocating capital and risk without bias? If you feel markets are inherently biased by the current set of rules, regulations and tax incentives, then you need to join the debate about what would need to be done to "untilt" the market. Are you for changing the road signs that regulate the markets? Are you for removing or simplifying the road signs or for increasing their number and complexity? If you don't want to be on the road to a better-quality capitalism, then you need to get off the road and stand in front of the government agency that you wish to further empower by giving them more of your own money.

"Like a Hawk"

Do we want a government whose economic data does not match up to our day-to-day reality? If we judge there is a gap between the data and the truth, then there is an obligation to explore and explain why and to reconcile the two. The central banker who trusts the inflation models must explain the reality gap better or risk losing the trust and faith of the public. The public needs to judge whether its view is right and, if so, decide if there really is a gap between the official inflation rate and the actual rate we face in real life. If there is, then the question is how to change this and manage it.

My own view is that the Federal Reserve and many other central banks are going to do whatever is necessary to push the inflation rate from say 2% to 3%. This may seem immaterial, but it will raise the price of daily necessities significantly. I, for one, need to increase my earning power by investing in myself and my businesses, knowing that the best inflation hedge is yourself. I need to save more for all the things that matter to me because the prices are going to keep rising. More will need to be set aside for groceries, for buying a home, for transportation costs for energy bills and the like. If I am wrong and the world economy falls into another Great Depression, will this strategy prove costly or wrong? I think not.

Ultimately, the responsibility for the economic future lies in only one place: with ourselves. This is exactly the sentiment expressed with great clarity in a Goldie Hawn film from 1984, *Protocol*. Her character, Sunny Davis, an out-of-luck waitress who through a series of misadventures ends up with a job in the Office of the Chief of Protocol, gives many memorable and, in retrospect, prescient speeches.

"You know what my dad says? If you let a guy sell you a diamond ring for ten cents, chances are you own a ring not worth a dime. Well, I bought the whole mine... If I don't know what you're up to and if I don't holler and scream when I think you're doing it wrong and I just mind my own business and don't vote or care, then I just get what I deserve."

Simple questions stand before us. Do we want a world where the state protects competition or competitors? Are we for big government or big business? Are we for small government and small business? The lines between the power of the state and the power of the individual are being redrawn by economic circumstances. There is little use in complaining about the outcome if we fail to influence it.

What would be the cost of admitting that the current model, the current plan, the current idea, the current policy is wrong? Who would lose their power, their influence, their tchotchkes, their jobs? The spirit of Gollum looms large precisely because so much is at stake. The financial crisis and the threat of a weak economy have raised the call of duty. Now everyone has a responsibility to make their voice heard, either at the ballot box or in the streets or through innovation and reinvention. Those who prefer to side with convention will eventually find out whether that decision permits them to sleep at night.

The question of how to approach the Gordian Knot is profound. Niall Ferguson says, "If we do not embark on a wholesale reform of government finance, then…Western Democracies… [will] follow Greece into the fiscal death spiral". On the other hand, he continues, we can choose "some combination of default and inflation", which means "we all end up as Argentina".[244] I have tried to argue in these pages that the decisions that lead us down these roads have already been taken. Different countries have made different choices and will experience different consequences. I think that the default plus inflation outcome is more likely than any other. But, I also have great faith and belief that we can get in front of these powerful economic forces. We can prepare for the outcome and thereby mitigate the impact. Even better, we can build the economy of tomorrow, create new wealth and GDP that will permit us to outrun these economic pressures, at least to some degree. But all depends on whether governments can be constrained in their efforts to extract cash at the expense of their citizens – and whether citizens can be made to prepare for the vicissitudes of the world economy.

How will the public read the signals and how will they respond? Will we enter this next phase of the world economy

---

244 See *The Great Degeneration: How Institutions Decay and Economies Die* (Penguin, 2013), by Niall Ferguson, page 47

blind and deaf, hankering for a past that no longer exists? Will we willfully ignore signals and refuse to acknowledge and discuss them? It would be human nature to do so. Henry James had to implore his readers, "Try to be one of the people on whom nothing is lost!" We must take notice of the signals around us, taking care not to misread them because too much is at stake. The danger is that, "Most people, sometime in their lives, stumble across truth. Most jump up, brush themselves off, and hurry on about their business as if nothing had happened," as Winston Churchill observed. How inclined or disinclined are you to acknowledge signals?

Then, presuming we see the many signals in the world economy, the next question is, "What are we going to do now?" Our answer depends in part on our self-assessment. How are we balancing our hubris and the risk of nemesis? Does our hubris make us inclined to confuse luck with skill? Does the fear of nemesis make us hang back from taking calculated risks?

Sheila Bair, the outspoken former regulator and former head of the Federal Deposit Insurance Corporation, has admonished all CEOs to ask themselves, "Is it me or is it the Fed?[245] How much of my company's share price reflects our work versus government stimulus policy [QE]?" Indeed, each one of us needs to ask ourselves this question. "How much of my life is a result of my own hard work and how much is the result of government stimulus that, in the end, is my own money?"

Do we suffer from self-delusion? The American author Upton Sinclair (1878-1968) wisely noted that, "It's difficult to get a man to understand something when his salary depends on him not understanding it." Or consider the 19th-century political thinker, Alexis de Tocqueville, who came to America in 1831 at the age of 25, and went on to write the seminal work, *Democracy in America*. He is often attributed with the observation that, "The American Republic will endure until the day Congress discovers

---

245 As reported in *The National Journal*, 22 November 2013: "Bair: Economic Reform Requires Taking the Long View" by Jordan Carney

that it can bribe the public with the public's money." Whether he said it or not, it is a sobering thought.

Being bribed with your own money

Governments today are finding ways to bribe the public with their own money and many do not want to understand why. QE is an inducement, an encouragement, a bribery. Keeping interest rates low and offering "free money" to the banking system, money that was yours to begin with as the taxpayer, is a way of provoking your "animal spirits" and encouraging you back into taking risks that a rational person might not otherwise undertake.

But, it is also "intaxication" and "cashtration". These nonsense made-up words are clever innovations that sum up the process beautifully. Years ago, *The Washington Post* invited its readers to take any word from the dictionary and alter it by adding, subtracting, or changing one single letter, and then supply a new definition.[246] "Intaxication" was one such word. It is "The feeling of euphoria at getting a refund or stimulus from the government, which lasts until one realises it was one's own money to start with."[247] "Cashtration" was another. The original *Washington Post* definition was, "The act of buying a house, which renders the subject financially impotent for an indefinite period." Today, I'd say cashtration is what happens when government policy seems designed to give you more cash in theory but, in fact, involves stealing your income from your back pocket through higher taxation and a higher cost of living. Or, more specifically, it explains the regulatory approach to the banking system: give the banks free money but excoriate and fine them for both using it too aggressively and for failing to deploy it in the form of lending that the government would like to see. Cashtration is what happens when a big bank is given record access to cheap funding but finds this accompanied by record fines and prohibitions on many business activities that would normally deploy that free money, such as proprietary trading.

---

246 See "The Style Invitational" at www.washingtonpost.com
247 As above

The bozone layer

As an aside, other relevant and funny words *The Washington Post* readers came up with include "bozone" (n.): "The substance surrounding stupid people that stops bright ideas from penetrating. The bozone layer, unfortunately, shows little sign of breaking down in the near future." In every ideological camp, people firmly believe that everyone in another camp from suffers from a "bozone" problem. This creates a "sarchasm" problem, or, "The gulf between the author of sarcastic wit and the person who doesn't get it." Bringing some humour back to the world economy could play a part in its revival.

A little imagination permits a glimpse of the possible outcomes. Start by asking a simple question: "What if it works?" What if this historic effort by the industrialised countries to deal with the debt problem by throwing money at it *actually works*? This will no doubt set the stage for government intervention for many years to come. Consider the way in which governments have been so quick, like football goalies, to jump into the void left by "market failure". It could be that the challenge of the Gordian Knot is simply swept under the carpet of history in the belief that government intervention will enable prosperity, willfully ignoring the fact that the size of the problem continues to compound every day. Remember the person who wanted to be paid one grain of rice for each square on the chessboard and then double that on the next? Remember Einstein's observation that those who don't understand compounding interest will be the ones who pay for it.

The implications are enormous. We may indeed be entering a world where people begin to believe that recessions can never occur again because governments will always step in with interventions, price controls and endless liquidity to protect the public from the downside. What will happen in such a world, where people believe that asset prices and interest rates can be controlled like a temperature dial?

How quickly we forget that central planning and state-imposed price controls do not work. Many believe that the Soviet Union collapsed under the weight of Russian technocrats who got it wrong, yet have great faith that the new breed of policymakers today from America to China are much smarter, more benevolent and better equipped with super-sophisticated tools and algorithms that permit them to arrive at the "right" answer. History tells us that state control does not work.

Some want to believe that somehow the Fed and other central banks can establish "optimal control" over prices and markets, forgetting that price controls destroy the market mechanism altogether and take liberty down with it.[248] Some may dismiss this reference to modern government interventions. After all, you may say, most governments are not seeking to control the price of bread or energy. But this would be wrong. In June 2013 Argentina introduced price controls on 500 food items, including bread.[249] The Morsi government in Egypt tried to control rising bread prices by rationing bread in 2013.[250] Other Middle Eastern countries from Abu Dhabi to Jordan try to control prices by offering government subsidies on a wide array of food and energy items, including bread and milk. India tries to keep a lid on prices by treating "hoarders" and "profiteers" harshly. China arguably uses moral suasion to try and prevent or slow price hikes. The President of Panama made an embarrassing visit in 2014 to grocery stores to show that his price controls were working. They were working alright. The shelves were empty. The shortages that price controls induce had already begun.

Price controls are the new protectionism. In the old days governments sought to protect their economies and populations by restricting imports. Now they prefer to focus on restricting price movements. If the price of food starts to rise, they restrict exports or control food prices directly. Indonesia bans the export of certain raw materials. In Latin America, food producers like Brazil and Argentina have put restrictions on some food exports. When the

---

248 See *The Financial Times*, 7 November 2013: "Fed Wonk Special, Now With QA" by David Keohane

249 See www.bloomberg.com, 16 December 2013: "Argentina to Tighten Food Price Controls as Inflation Quickens" by Charlie Devereux and Camila Russo

250 See www.globalpost.com, 20 March 2013: "Egypt bread protests begin after rationing announced" by David Trifunov and Erin Cunningham

price of the currency moves enough to risk the wellbeing of the population, capital and price controls can be introduced, as they were in India, Cyprus, Brazil, Russia and elsewhere in recent years.

When property prices begin to rise too much, governments find clever ways to cap or restrict their upward movement, as China did and Britain is attempting to do. Property taxes, stamp duties, penalties on mortgage prepayments and the like serve this purpose. When property prices fall too low, governments step in to support them with a variety of measures from generous lending programmes to low interest rates. When the bond market threatens to sell off and push interest rates up, the regulators intervene with words or asset purchases to prevent the price movement.

Immigration restrictions are a form of price control as well. After all, immigrants typically push the price of labour down. This is less welcome in weak economies with high unemployment, so it is not surprising to see governments finding ways to protect the existing price of wages from competition. All these actions are signals that governments want to control price levels.

Price controls and freedom

It is easy to dismiss the idea of outright price controls in the industrialised world. Nobody imagines these governments want to control the price of beef or chocolate, though they may concede such governments have an interest in the price of housing and wages. No, instead, the governments of industrial economies are intervening in the single most important price in any economy: the price of money. In the words of Friedrich von Hayek:

> Any attempt to control prices or quantities of particular commodities deprives competition of its power of bringing about an effective co-ordination of individual efforts, because price changes then cease to register all the relevant changes in circumstances and no longer provide a reliable guide for the individual's actions.[251]

---

251 See *The Road to Serfdom* (1944) by Friedrich von Hayek, page 38

Keynes also felt controlling the price of money was especially noxious because "the importance of money essentially flows from its being a link between the present and the future".[252]

Interest rates are about as low as they have ever been since the Roman Empire.[253] What does the artificially low and subsidised price of money tell us about the future now? It seeks to lure the public into borrowing and making investments, which they would not otherwise do. It seeks to make the public take a bet on asset prices and on the future. In other words, the policy is designed to artificially induce economic activity that a rational person would not otherwise undertake.

No price can be more important than the price of money itself. Government intervention to suppress interest rates perverts the bond market, which has serious consequences. Government bonds are supposed to constitute the risk-free rate of return against which all other investments are measured and judged. If your venture or investment cannot outperform the return on a government bond, then you are taking too much risk for insufficient reward. When governments buy their own bonds and thereby keep interest rates down, they support their own cause. Now government itself can borrow more cheaply and avoid the risk that higher interest payments would bankrupt them. This also erodes, if not removes, the incentive to fix their debt problems.

The return-free rate of risk

This artificial control over the price of money means that far from being a risk-free rate of return, the government bond market can be perverted into a return-free rate of risk.[254] It is return-free because interest rates are so low that holding bonds offers virtually no income to the owner. Should the government's effort fail at

---

252 See *The General Theory of Employment, Interest and Money* (1936), by JM Keynes, chapter 21: "The Theory of Prices"

253 According to Sydney Homer and Richard Sylla's *A History of Interest Rates, 4th Edition* (2005)

254 See the article, The Safety Catch, by Robert Jenkins (formerly on the Financial Policy Committee (FPC) at the Bank of England) in *Financial World*, July 2014.

some point, should interest rates rise, the government would be the first to find it lacks the resources to repay its debt, other than relying on its ability to print its own money.

Some countries have greater freedom than others to choose this path. Perhaps the definition of a superpower is when a nation state, like the United States, can repeatedly default on its debts by printing money and inflating away the debt and yet foreigners are still willing to buy the country's IOUs. At worst, a government can always find ways to compel its citizens to hand over their own hard-earned cash to the government. Through moral and regulatory suasion, governments can direct pension funds and fund managers to hold more and more of their capital in "safe" assets. The definition of "safe" will be "our government's bonds".

I spoke to a group of Chief Risk Officers of the world's largest banks. Their top priority is to create investment vehicles that will allow the government/sovereign debt they hold to be sold – though the actual word they used was "offloaded" – to savers among the general public, whom I pointed out were pensioners and their grandmothers and to which they replied, "whatever".

No brakes

Usually the bond market serves as a kind of brake that signals when borrowing is exceeding the ability of a government or an economy to repay. When government borrowing rises, the bond market usually starts selling the bonds, which pushes the price down and the yield, or interest rate, on the bond up. The market usually automatically forces interest rates up to "check" governments' inclination to spend, spend, spend. But, the bond markets of the US, Britain, Japan and even the Eurozone no longer have any brakes. Even the rise of inflation cannot compel the bond market to sell off because the government itself is the largest buyer of the bonds unless it finds ways to force the public to own them. In this sense, QE has snapped off the antennae of the bond market. Inflation can creep in without the bond market reacting as long as governments keep buying their own pieces of paper or forcing us, the citizens, to buy more.

The models and algorithms may show that this policy can persist, but common sense says that it is a mug's game. Keynes himself warned us about this in his book, *The Economic Consequences of the Peace*, published one year after the end of the First World War: "The presumption of a spurious value for the currency, by the force of law expressed in the regulation of prices, contains in itself, however, the seeds of final economic decay."[255] This is why we see so many states closing the exit doors, preventing people from turning to alternative assets or currencies. The desire to regulate unconventional lending channels, such as crowd-source financing, is one example of this. Any effort to prevent the use of cyber-currencies is another. People might want to escape by placing more capital in precious metals such as gold or platinum or high-grade diamonds and even Bitcoin, but it is easy for government to restrict the legal methods by which an investor can own or transact in such assets. Prohibitions on private ownership or the freedom to transact in such alternative "currencies" can very easily by imposed. All that is required is the stroke of a pen. Suddenly we can see why some prefer to store their wealth in the form of high-grade artwork that can hang in their home or under the security protection of a modern museum. You can see why the price of hard assets from diamonds to buildings to art have been rising.

Controls on the movement of people, goods and capital are also aimed at preserving the interests of the state against the interests of innovation. If you cannot "exit" your country for a better life or "exit" your money in a better currency, then there are only two other options, as Albert O Hirschman explained: voice and loyalty. How ironic that a man whose ideas underpin the notion of state control and collectivism should have so wisely noted that the vice of inflation and debt deflation will create such pain for so many. As Vladimir Ilyich Lenin said, "The way to crush the bourgeoisie is to grind them down between the millstones of taxation and inflation."

---

255 From *The Economic Consequences of the Peace* by JM Keynes (1919), chapter 6: "Europe After the Treaty"

Exit, voice, loyalty

The fact that people feel the need to express themselves through Hirschman's "Exit, Voice and Loyalty", is itself a signal of the formidable pressures building in the world economy. There are those who will use their voice to deliver dissent, alternative views, and demands for change. There will be those who hunker down into loyalty to the system, the policies, the current mathematical models as they stand. States will do almost anything to maintain loyalty to the status quo, including reaching across borders and channelling domestic angst toward foreign interests.

The Chinese pose a different but similar question: Should the United States continue to be the reserve currency of the world when it is making choices that work in the favour of (some) American citizens and against those of everybody else? The Chinese government would like to "exit" a dollar-dominated world. This is why China buys gold faster than anywhere else today and enters into Renminbi-based bilateral deals with various countries. At some point, when it is ready for a fully convertible capital account, China's leaders hope it may well emerge as the only "hard" currency around. As for Chinese higher-income families, there are doubts about whether the Chinese model will succeed, or whether they too will suffer confiscation. As a result, many of them are seeking exit to other nations, diversifying their wealth among several locations.

Markets are obviously far from perfect. Markets can fail. But this does not mean that government control produces better results. The market, assuming it isn't rigged or distorted by the government, is supposed to allow wealth to be distributed based on merits rather than based on entrenched interests. If the market is failing us, we might ask questions about how governments are causing the market to fail and how a failing market can be made to work better. The social contract demands we address this question, as Ludwig Erhard reminds us:

"Whoever is serious in this must be prepared to energetically oppose all attacks on the stability of our currency. The social market economy is unthinkable without a parallel stability of the currency. Only a policy of this kind guarantees that individual sections of the population do not profit at the cost of others."[256]

The problem lies at the heart of the Gordian Knot. Time is of the essence because, as von Hayek noted in 1944, "The one thing modern democracy will not bear without cracking is the necessity of a substantial lowering of the standards of living in peace time or even prolonged stationariness of its economic conditions."[257]

This is why post-crisis witch hunts are typical or maybe even necessary. After every burst of hubris and the ensuing flames of nemesis, we enter something never taught in economics class: the recrimination phase of the economic cycle.[258] A magazine cover from November 2009 still burns in my mind. It was a potent signal of how many people would be spending the next few years: trying to find someone to blame. The atmosphere of blame persists today, some five years after the most recent crisis began. The cover of *W Magazine* that month featured the beautiful model Linda Evangelista (photographed by Pierpaolo Ferrari) standing on Wall Street wearing a demure little black dress, a lot of diamonds and a deeply perplexed expression, her perfectly manicured hands holding the type of

We are grateful to Pierpaolo Ferrari for giving us permission to use this image.

256 *Prosperity Through Competition* (1957) by Ludwig Erhard, page 7
257 *The Road to Serfdom* (1944), by Friedrich von Hayek, page 216
258 I am ever so grateful to Larry Lindsey for this illuminating concept and also for all the time he spent teaching me about the world economy.

cardboard sign favoured by hobos and panhandlers. It read: "It must be somebody's fault".[259]

Witch hunts are one way out of a Gordian Knot. You find someone to blame and hang them from a high post or burn them. But, reaching into the past diverts attention from the future. Politicians love to show that government is protecting the citizens from loss. But the point is that government cannot protect us from loss. Nor do we need them to. Loss is an inherent part of being in the world economy. Losses bring lessons. Sure governments van mitigate losses but they cannot and should not prevent them.

Who has time for such great philosophical issues? Many do, but most need to get on with daily life. As the former Mayors of New York, Fiorello de La Guardia and Rudolph Giuliani, famously said, "There is no Republican or Democratic way to pick up the garbage". One wonders whether there may be a freshwater or saltwater way.[260]

People will be arguing for years about who is right and who is wrong. It would be unreasonable to expect that the debate will be resolved in a timely and smooth way. My father tells great stories about the early 1970s when the US Government veered back and forth from prioritising unemployment as the top policy goal to prioritising the management of rising inflation. The slanging match between the President's advisors reverberated through the entire economy as they wildly flitted from one conflicting policy goal to another. We should look back at this "stop-go" era of the early 1970s. It may presage what is to come. If the "tapering/no tapering" debate was enough to set the markets into a tailspin, then imagine what can happen if policymakers are forced to make a much more difficult set of choices.

We will be arguing for many years to come about whether government prolonged the slow down or protected us from

---

259 See Linda Evangelista photographed by Pierpaolo Ferrari for the cover of *W Magazine*, November 2009 at www.fashiongonerogue.com

260 See *The Economist* blog at www.economist.com/blogs, 6 November 2013: "Why has New York Voted for a Democratic Mayor?" by RW, New York

something worse for many years to come. Vince Reinhart put the issue beautifully in his eloquent article, "The Perfect Financial Storm Fallacy". Was it a perfect storm that blew up from nowhere and to which policymakers have been forced to respond? Or, was the storm caused by policy choices? The irony, Reinhart rightly points out, is that the phrase comes from a non-fiction book by Sebastian Junger and the film with George Clooney that followed, "The Perfect Storm." The true-life story is about fishermen who were killed at sea. "The *Andrea Gail* (the fishing vessel) sailed far from the safe harbour of Gloucester, Massachusetts, in the fall of 1991 toward an evident risk. Why was its crew prepared to take such a risk? Perhaps it matters that the United States was amid a sluggish economic recovery after a painful recession. The crew needed the money, even if it meant sailing into a storm. The men needed to take the risk in order to earn some income. Monetary policy matters in many ways."[261] How many of us are now forced by monetary policy to take more risk, to buy assets whose prices are rising to dizzying levels (from property to food items), to leverage all our efforts just to maintain the standard of living? Monetary policy matters.

Do my choices make sense?

The destiny of the economy lies in the hands of those who are brave enough to ask Peter Drucker's question: "What would make sense now if I weren't already doing things the way I am doing them?" This means there needs to be recognition and support not only for the entrepreneur who spots an opportunity but also for the individual who leaves financial services to join the sewage industry.

This also means we must appreciate that there is a fight raging in the policy world and it matters who wins it. We should be wary when the views of dissenters are ignored, suppressed or maligned and when it becomes common wisdom that the views of the establishment will inevitably be proved right, good and true. I, for

---

261 See *The American*, 31 July 2009: "The Perfect Financial Storm Fallacy" by Vincent R. Reinhart

one, was very struck by the apology issued by Andrew Huszar, a former Federal Reserve staffer who went to Wall Street and was then asked back to the Fed to administer the first round of quantitative easing. In November 2013 he made the following statement:

> I can only say: I'm sorry, America. As a former Federal Reserve official, I was responsible for executing the centrepiece programme of the Fed's first plunge into the bond-buying experiment known as quantitative easing. The central bank continues to spin QE as a tool for helping Main Street. But I've come to recognise the programme for what it really is: the greatest backdoor Wall Street bailout of all time.[262]

What was especially striking was the revelation that the government forged ahead even though it was not at all sure of the efficacy or possible consequences of its choices.[263] This is where policymakers need to ask themselves whether they are suffering from the kind of blind overconfidence in their own views and abilities that renders them evermore vulnerable to preferring "apparent success to real progress".[264]

Today, it is an open question whether the policies being pursued by the Federal Reserve and other central banks, as well as by governments who continue to expand their debt, "prefer apparent success to real progress". Is it real progress if the stock market goes up but the standard of living goes down? Is it real progress if holding down interest rates gives rise to an inflation that the rich can outrun but which traps the poor? Is it progress if the regular person can no longer distinguish how much of their

262 See *The Wall Street Journal*, 11 November 2013: "Andrew Huszar: Confessions of a Quantitative Easer" by Andrew Huszar
263 See cnbc.com, 12 November 2013: "Ex-Fed Official: 'I'm Sorry for QE'" by Bruno J Navarro, interview with Andrew Huszar. "I can only say: I'm sorry, America... The central bank continues to spin QE as a tool for helping Main Street. But I've come to recognise the programme for what it really is: the greatest backdoor Wall Street bailout of all time."
264 *Prosperity Through Competition*, page 6, as above

success belongs to their own efforts and how much belongs to free money that was theirs to begin with?

When Ludwig Erhard reflected on his extraordinary life experience, he wrote:

> The experiences of those winter months gave me much food for thought. They showed me how easy it was to assume that the market economy was permanently secure... how necessary it was that the freedom, even in the economic sphere, should be defended every day anew.[265]

This is why we should view the social protests in emerging markets, from the Arab Spring to street demonstrations in Latin America and Asia, as innovation too. The public everywhere is doing its best to not only build the economy of tomorrow but to establish what the rules of the game will be.

Choosing sides

The argument over what should and should not be included in the social contract is as important an innovation as the actions of individuals building GDP. The critical question is whether the innovations by government work to support the creation of the economy of tomorrow or whether they mitigate against it. This means choosing sides in the freshwater-saltwater debate. We can try to pretend that we don't have a view or that we are not on one side or the other, but the outcome of that fight will set the stage for the life we will or will not be leading in the future.

Others will claim that no matter what we do in terms of policy, the simple fact remains that human beings around the world have insufficient education and skills to build the economy we want and need. No doubt education can be improved, and this would help, but as someone who is armed with many academic credentials but who cannot fix a dripping tap in the bathroom, I feel that Matthew Crawford, whom I cited in chapter four, is right. We made a mistake assuming that the only path to success is one involving university,

---

265 As above, page 254

degrees and training for white-collar jobs. The algorithms pushed us all into believing that test scores define success. But this is not true. Innovation defines success. As a society, we could protect those that education has and will leave behind by putting practical hand craft and domestic science, what we in the US used to call "shop class", back into the school system.

My grandmother made a living as a seamstress and today Tara Ralph hand-makes Beyoncé's tour costumes. Sewing provided them both with a reliable income. If "home economics" does not appeal, then we should also not forget that Einstein spent hours in his uncle's repair shop playing around with broken electrical appliances and vacuum tube radios, which no doubt informed his understanding of the laws of physics. It may be true that the Chinese and Indian students score better in math and engineering tests than Westerners, but there is still more to innovation than test scores. Anybody who wants to get a motorcycle to actually work has a bigger chance of learning physics and engineering than someone learning the mathematics for its own sake.

Is college really necessary? Perhaps it makes sense that companies are starting to return to the old model, where a firm hired someone out of high school and trained them to become proficient in practical skills. More and more firms are building their own talent and skills sets from the inside. Apprenticeships are also coming back. *The New York Times* has written about "Apprenticeship Carolina", a programme that started in 2007 with 777 students at 90 companies and now has 4,500 students at more than 600 companies, with the average age of the apprentice being in their late twenties.[266] BMW in Greer, South Carolina, is actively looking for young people to train because of "a serious shortage of medium-skilled workers who specialise in mechatronics, or repairing robots and metal presses when they break down and operating the computers that dot the paint shop, body shop and assembly shop".

266 See *The New York Times*, 30 November 2013: "Where Factory Apprenticeship is Latest Model from Germany" by Nelson D Schwarz

Mining and Engineering Schools

One of the most encouraging signals is the simple fact that the graduates of mining and engineering schools are now being paid more than the graduates of Harvard. *Forbes* reports, "The median salary of the Rapid City school's graduates (the South Dakota School of Mines and Technology known as SDSM&T) was $56,700. By contrast, the median salary of Harvard graduates – where the tuition (cost) is nearly four times as high as at SDSM&T – was $54,100."[267] People are smart enough to see and follow such a clear signal. If engineering pays more, then the young will go into engineering instead of financial services.

Are these signals important? Yes, but that is not to say that all signals hold the same weight or meaning for all people. Signals can be, indeed *need* to be interpreted differently by different people who have different skills and different goals. Each of us manages our personal balance of hubris and the fear of nemesis differently. Each of us faces different circumstances and challenges, and brings different skills and thoughts to the task. Just because you open a restaurant at the start of an economic bust does not mean you will fail. Just because you join manufacturing in the Midwest just as manufacturing moves back to North America does not mean you will succeed. Nor does the continued globalisation of manufacturing mean that China has failed. The innovative in China and America alike will survive.

What leads us into error?

It also makes no sense to ignore signals, or remain willfully ignorant of them, simply because they don't fit a preconception of reality. This is dangerous. This is why JM Keynes recommended that economists pay attention to the things that don't "fit" the model:

> The object of our analysis is, not to provide a machine, or a method of blind manipulation, which will furnish an

---

267 See www.forbes.com, 19 September 2012: "Dig This: South Dakota Mining Grads Crush Harvard On Pay" by James Marshall Crotty

infallible answer, but to provide ourselves with an organised and orderly method of thinking out particular problems; and, after we have reached a provisional conclusion by isolating the complicating factors one by one, we then have to go back on ourselves and allow, as well as we can, for the probable interactions of the factors amongst themselves. This is the nature of economic thinking. Any other way of applying formal principles of thought (without which, however, we shall be lost in the wood) will lead us into error.

Too large a proportion of recent 'mathematical' economics are merely concoctions, as imprecise as the initial assumptions they rest on, which allow the author to lose sight of the complexities and interdependencies of the real world in a maze of pretentious and unhelpful symbols.[268]

I would like to think that there might be some consideration of the signals that fall outside the mathematical models. These signals might be considered and debated among the class of econometricians and statisticians on whose models the public depend. But the public can join in now. Only by asking such common sense-based questions about the signals we see can we create an economy where we won't be compelled to say, "The algorithm made me do it." My friend James Galbraith suggested that the picture I have painted in this book is of "Impressionist/ Pointillist" economics. Perhaps there is a place for this alongside the standard mathematical blueprint approach? Perhaps this approach would permit many more to see what's going on across the landscape.

I also hope that my own observation of signals, and those made by others, can be met with a robust opponent who can help us discover where our own "intellectual arrogance" may be "causing disabling ignorance and overcome it".[269] This is as

---

268 See JM Keynes, *The General Theory* (Cambridge: Cambridge University Press, 2013 [1936]), pages 297–298
269 As above, page 5

applicable to policymakers as to business people as to someone managing the household's finances.

By raising an awareness of the signals that we see every day, we can be empowered to make our own judgements and thereby better decisions about how to manage our economic life. No one has a monopoly on the truth, nor is there a crystal ball that empowers any one person or school of thought to predict the future with certainty. Instead, the world economy moves forward, or backward, based on a multitude of decisions, whether made by famous policymakers or by anonymous individuals. This requires, as the Queen of Hearts noted in *Alice in Wonderland*, imagination.

Steve Jobs and eccentricity

Steve Jobs also explained this with great clarity when he gave the Stanford University Commencement Address in 2005:

> "You can't connect the dots looking forward; you can only connect them looking backwards. So you have to trust that the dots will somehow connect in your future. You have to trust in something – your gut, destiny, life, karma, whatever. Because believing that the dots will connect down the road will give you the confidence to follow your heart even when it leads you off the well-worn path; and that will make all the difference."[270]

The more lively and robust the debate about signals and what they mean, the better, because each one of us will strike out on various paths and we will be more likely to succeed if we are better armed with knowledge of the forces and risks that may await us. No one should shy away from asking questions or making observations about the world economy, which may indeed take them "off the well-worn path". I recall John Stewart Mill's observation that, "The amount of eccentricity in a society has generally been

---

270 See Steve Jobs address at Stanford University's graduation ceremony on 14 June 2005: "You've Got to Find What You Love"

proportional to the amount of genius, mental vigour, and moral courage which it contained. That so few now dare to be eccentric, marks the chief danger of the time."[271]

Emerson and economics

Some of those who have great expertise in economics will mock the average person who notices the world economy with naïve and fresh eyes and energetically enters the debate. They will probably knock down my simple suggestion that anyone can see signals in the world economy and decide for themselves what they mean. But such backward-looking, data-dependent naysayers would do well to remember Emerson's comment that "an ounce of action is worth a tonne of theory".

There are many who are prepared to devote years of time and effort to figuring out whether what works in practice can be made to work in theory. Happily, there are more who are prepared to engage in the decisions and acts that will have great consequences for the character of our future economy. They do not need a theory to engage in their edgework.

When I flip through women's magazines and see that the fashion industry cannot decide which hemline or silhouette to offer, it encourages me that there are profits and revenues to be made by someone who boldly declares what it ought to be. If you think this cannot happen, look at what Christian Dior did in Paris on the 12th of February 1947 when he unveiled the "New Look" to the world, with its chiselled waistline and "wasteful" round skirt that required reams of fabric simply for the purpose of serving beauty. He changed the way women dressed forever.

When I see nation states competing for ownership or control over territories or even over prices, I think, "Thank goodness there are signals that forewarn!" At least there are opportunities to ward off and address the economic and geopolitical forces that might otherwise come as an unpleasant surprise to many.

When I see people protest at the breakdown of the social contract, I am encouraged that innovation applies in the field of

---

271 John Stuart Mill, *On Liberty* (1869)

politics as well. Social contracts around the world will need to better serve the interests of the citizens who agree to abide by them. Their renegotiation can only be a good thing for the world economy. Of course, there will be missteps and accidents. As an American, I know that it took several efforts to create the institutions and ideals that permit our social contract to bend and change without threatening the collapse of society. Let us not forget that America did not even manage to sort out the right model for a central bank until 1914 – and only after quite a few false starts. Many will argue the current model is still not right. The model may well be in need of review today, but the institution is strong enough to withstand a good hard look.

When I open any journal on the newsagent's shelf, from *Wired* to *Wooden Boat*, all I see is innovation. I see artists taking cast-offs from the Large Hadron Collider at CERN[272] and from Formula One cars and turning them into art, furniture and useful machines. On television, I see one of the world's most widely watched sports, cricket, innovating with the introduction of Twenty 20 Cricket.[273] Frankly, it's hard not to see innovation once you look for it.

The question going forward is this: Can inflation really destroy deflation? In my view, the competition is not so much between inflation and deflation. Instead, there will be an epic battle between these two conflicting forces, these two demons. But, the one thing that can vanquish both is innovation. Great innovations create growth and wealth and will help keep prices where they should be. Great innovation is going to come mainly from the quiet every day acts of calculated risk taking which brave individuals undertake all the time. The only question for them is whether the state will help them or hurt them as they forge the path forward.

When I listen to people's life stories from recent years, full of heartbreak and loss and recovery and reinvention, I hear innovation.

---

272 See the article on Alex Duffner in *Wired* Magazine (UK Edition), December 2013: "Inspired by CERN, these lab instruments double as kitchen appliances" by Madhumita Venkatarmanan

273 This new sport was introduced in 2003 but the momentum behind it has exploded since the Financial crisis.

When I look for signals I see the opportunity to innovate, to adapt, to prepare, to create the life that I hope to have.

Serendipity

Serendipity will play its part. Some will misinterpret the signals. Some will interpret them correctly but balance their own hubris badly and find themselves confronted by failure. Nonetheless, failure brings its own lessons and rewards. Chanel No5, the classic perfume, was an epic mistake. The assistants of perfumer Ernest Beaux apparently misread his formula and added some ten times the required amount of aldehyde. When Coco Chanel chose from the many samples Beaux provided, she chose No 5, the one with the huge mistake. Not only has Chanel No5 been a massive success, but the use of aldehydes is mainstream in most perfumes today.

The stakes may be extremely high. I mentioned racing cars earlier, and I have witnessed terrible car accidents on the F1 circuit over the years. One involved a car driving straight over the top of another. I thought there was no chance the driver of the car underneath could survive. Instead, he jumped out looking hopping mad. Such a moment makes me remember that it was the death of one of Formula One's greatest drivers, Ayrton Senna, that led the F1 authorities to commit to whatever was necessary to protect their drivers.[274] Many safety features and procedures resulted from that decision, including safety belts, fireproof face masks and clothing, chicanes and safety helmets. Some of these innovations were later applied to the general public. Senna paid with his life but left a legacy that has protected the many drivers who followed him. Yes, the edgeworker went over the edge. But, he also opened the door for safer driving. But getting the balance between safety and speed is essential both in race car driving and when it comes to managing the world economy. Too much "safety" (regulation) limits the speed of growth.

Failure is a fact of life that involves losses at every level: loss of confidence, vision, money, time, resources. The cutting edge of

---

274 *The Science of Safety: The Battle Against Unacceptable Risks in Motor Racing* by Sid Watkins, Haynes (Manuals Inc, 2000)

the world economy is a bloody business. So, if permitted, I would write a second letter to the Queen.

Her Majesty The Queen
Buckingham Palace
London SW1A 1AA
United Kingdom

Your Majesty

I was moved by your question at the LSE in November 2008,[275] and though unqualified to answer it myself, I hope that bringing the concept of signals to attention, it will empower people to make better decisions about their economic future. The business of engaging in edgework, in reaching for something beyond our grasp, in building a future without knowing the outcome for sure, is a challenging task. But, as you said in 1952 in your first BBC Christmas Broadcast, human beings are surely capable of adapting to change and building a new future. We would do well to remember your wise words:

> *"Many grave problems and difficulties confront us all, but with a new faith in the old and splendid beliefs given us by our forefathers, and the strength to venture beyond the safeties of the past, I know we shall be worthy of our duty. Above all, we must keep alive that courageous spirit of adventure that is the finest quality of youth; and by youth I do not just mean those who are young in years; I mean too all those who are young in heart, no matter how old they may be...*

> *On this broad foundation let us set out to build a truer knowledge of ourselves and our fellow men, to work for tolerance and understanding among the nations and to use the tremendous forces of science and learning for the betterment of man's lot upon this earth."[276]*

---

275 See *The Daily Telegraph*, 5 November 2008: "The Queen asks why no one saw the credit crunch coming" by Andrew Pierce
276 Read the full transcript in *The Daily Telegraph* online, 25 December 2012

Yes, there has been loss. Yes, everyone should be aware of the effort to pass this loss onto us – the common man and woman. Everyone should be given a chance to prepare for the consequences. But, this loss has also created the foundation for transformation. Perhaps we can all spend the coming years trying to imagine the impossible and the unexpected – a more dynamic economy than before, because that is what is most likely to actually happen. This notion is best explained by your grandmother's former subject, Lewis Carroll, in 'Alice in Wonderland' by The Queen of Hearts.

It is my hope that by introducing the concept of learning to interpret signals, we can all, at the very least, become more flexible, more attuned to the dynamic nature of the world economy. With this knowledge we can then better pursue the best personal vision that hubris and fear of nemesis will permit. In this way, the world economy of tomorrow will progress regardless of the damage it has caused in the past.

I believe the same signal can be interpreted in different ways by different people. That's the essence of a market. It's a place where all views (buyers and sellers) meet. But the really important point is that signals and their interpretation are personal. I may have seen the same signals as say Steve Jobs, but his skills, opportunities and his vision were different from mine. I would never have been able to build Apple even if we had entirely agreed on the signals that led him to believe that Apple could and would come to life. Then again, the signals I've noted, my skills, and the way I have balanced my hubris against the risk of nemesis have brought me to a different place. That's the key: the same signals are subject to different interpretations and different outcomes. The business of matching the external awareness of signals and the internal awareness of one's own skills and ability to manage risk is the key to managing no matter what happens to the world economy.

Sincerely,
Pippa Malmgren

André Malraux, the French novelist, art theorist and Minister for Cultural Affairs, once said, "Often the difference between a successful person and a failure is not that one has better abilities or ideas, but the courage that one has to bet on one's ideas, to take a calculated risk – and to act." This is as true of those who are building the economy as it is of those who are addressing the policy infrastructure and the social contract, but which signals should be acted upon? Deciphering which is which is now the task. We must all decide for ourselves.

In or out?

I have endeavoured to fulfill Henry James' request that we must all "try to be someone on whom nothing is lost", but have I explained what a person should "do" about the signals the economy is sending? Should we be in or out of stocks? In or out of bonds? Buy or sell property? Should we invest in ourselves or in the economy? Should a person take the free money today and put it in risky assets that might pay off or might lose a fortune in the future? The answer is that each one of us must make such decisions for ourselves based on our own skills, appetite for risk, our own level of hubris and fear of nemesis. There are many answers but only a few are right for you.

Hopefully, everyone will make a different decision from everyone else. The diversity of opinion and action is what will reinforce society's ability to withstand the sharp ebbs and flows of the world economy. It is the diversity of opinion about signals that gives strength to the economy. Some will be right, some will be wrong, but without edgework and calculated risk-taking there won't be an economy at all. No one has a crystal ball or a monopoly on the truth – not the Federal Reserve, not the White House or any equivalent and not your neighbor. Instead, there is a range of opinions, which form a "market". A market is a clearing mechanism that efficiently matches buyers and sellers. This is a better approach than relying on the views of a few "smart" people who happen to work at the top of government or at the top of businesses who we presume to "know" the answer. We can read and interpret signals for ourselves based on individual experience, skills and risk taking inclinations.

You, my reader, may or may not agree with my own conclusion – that without sufficient bread at the right price, a country and a family can become... well, toast. The vice of pain is spurring social unrest and innovation alike. Quantitative Easing is creating qualitative squeezing and converting the peace dividend into a conflict premium. Social contracts all over the world are straining under these pressures, but new social contracts are being forged almost everywhere, which are also examples of innovation. It is worth considering the possibility that these new ideas might be right. The new social contracts may be better than the old ones. For what it is worth, I don't think we will fix the ogre of deflation by unleashing the genie of inflation. Instead, we will have to contend with both demons. Redistributing the existing wealth is a circular game that drives down new wealth creation. The only productive way out is innovation. But, everyone must decipher the signals those demons are sending for themselves. Only then can everyone know what kind of edgework and calculated risk-taking each of us can safely undertake.

The thread of the story

I have tried to weave together a picture of the world economy, connecting seemingly unrelated and even contradictory pieces of information that actually come together to form patterns. There are endless, easily observable signals that illuminate these patterns on the landscape of the world economy. One need not be an economist or an expert at algorithms to detect and discuss them. In fact, a little common sense might be a welcome addition to the usual conversation about economics. The thread of the story travels from the central bankers who are potentially "pushing on a string" to textile workers in China and Bangladesh to couturiers and quilters to all those who are ripping up or re-stitching the fabric of social contracts. Loose ends are everywhere no doubt. Some threads of information clash. The news says, as I finish this manuscript, that the price of beef, eggs, cheese and other core staples are reaching all time record high prices and also that global commodity prices in the aggregate are falling to a four year low. Nor is economics the only or even the most important thread in this fabric. Culture, history, politics all play their part. But, I hope to have imbued the thread of economics with some colour. Economics is not grey. If anything it is a shocking colour that flashes warnings all the time. It now demands that history once again considers what sort of social contract is desired and desirable. But, history seems to demand that everyone consider once again what sort of social contract is desired and desirable. What is the right relationship and balance between the government the citizens? What are the rights and responsibilities of the state versus those of the citizens? What social fabric do we want? This is the central political economy question that the world economy is compelling everyone to address.

The liquidity problem continues to wash over the fabric of every day life. It matters that there is such a deep divide between those who think deflation is the biggest risk and those who think inflation is the biggest risk. Those who are quick to declare inflation dead somehow cannot see that they stand in the largest pool of liquidity ever known. An inflationist believes the pool that is filled with accelerant rather than innocuous water. A deflationist believes it is water and will drown out doubt and bring growth to life. There are those who are quick to declare that the accelerant will blow us all sky high and return us to the hyperinflation of earlier eras. But, they underestimate the role of innovation in keeping prices down. Either way, until the liquidity returns to normal levels, we cannot see whether it has enhanced or damaged the fabric of society. Once again, the answer lies in the collective decisions we all make. Much depends on how everyday people and policymakers alike proceed and whether they proceed in a freshwater or saltwater direction.

There is an ironic twist in the tale of geopolitics. Central banks have injected record sums of money into the world economy thus driving down the price of money, volatility and the cost of insuring against risk while driving up the price of assets from food to property to stock and bond markets. As a result, fund managers and business people are disinclined to spend money on insurance of any kind. The investment industry believe that they do not have to pay any attention to such risks because there is assurance that central banks will "fix" any problems by simply adding more liquidity. As a result, many geopolitical events can occur while the level of risk actually falls. Nothing moves the markets (or moves it much) from coups and juntas, to events involving Ukraine and Russia's departure from international dialogue, to the dissolving of long standing borders in Iraq and across the Southern boundary of the United States, to near misses involving China and Russia's military vessels and airplanes.

Meanwhile, central banks have had to engage in this policy, in QE, precisely because governments are so deeply in debt that they are often incapable of sustaining military action or expenditure. This inability or unwillingness to respond, invites other states to test the boundaries of territory and diplomacy thus increasing the risk of geopolitical events.

But an even greater irony lies in the notion I have tried to explain here. Rightly or wrongly, there are also those who believe the efforts by central banks to create inflation should be viewed as a hostile act since the consequences, higher food and energy prices and the attendant social unrest, fully justify reaching for such assets across borders. The logic is this: If you default on us, and inflation is just a form of default, we are justified in protecting ourselves by any means. The end result is a circular problem where the solution to the debt problem actually provokes both greater complacency and greater risk of geopolitical stress at the same time. We find the thread of the story loops back on itself and creates a knotty problem that we will be tangling with for some time.

I can't help but think that the shrinkflation and zigzagging I see at the grocer's correlates to the near-misses between military airplanes and vessels I see reported in the press. How can we expect nations to defend their interests abroad if they are having to default on their citizens at home? How can nations enforce the global "social contract", the "rules of the game" abroad if the local social contract at home is itself fluid and changing?

It would be nice if nations could find ways to get along. But, interests can clash when prices move in one direction or another. If only a high degree of economic interconnectedness was sufficient glue to hold the common interests of nations together. But, we know for a fact that Britain and Germany were among each other's largest trading partners one year before World War One broke out. While I do not condone the military actions that I have written about here, I can see why many nations will use or see economics as an excuse to step into the realm of geopolitics and conflict. On the other hand, Bernard Shaw was surely right when he said, any "nation that lets its duty get onto the opposite side of its interest is lost".[277] Some careful thought has to be put into managing the "common wealth" of the world economy in ways that meet everybody's needs. Price stability is perhaps an even more valuable "common wealth" commodity than we ever thought. It is worth fighting over price stability whether the fight occurs inside the Federal Reserve or between central banks. We should not have to learn the hard way that, for some, it may be worth fighting for militarily as well.

Meanwhile, it is a small miracle that workers in the industrialised world have accepted a lower standard of living so quietly thus far. It is harder to expect emerging market workers to silently accept a reduction in their standard of living. We cannot say "I am very sorry but you are no longer as competitive, so you can't have as much meat in your diet or anything else you aspire to for now. Let us know when you have a new business model". We have to expect a reaction. People will not quietly tolerate the growing pain forever. They may feel that the culprit lies in the growing gap between the rich countries and the poor countries, or between the rich and the poor within nations. But, the real issue is that we need more wealth generation all around. The solution is innovation: in business models, in entrepreneurial ventures, in diplomacy, in governance, in technology and in personal goals. Only innovation can generate a greater alignment of interests between nations and among the people who inhabit them.

No one now needs to fall back on the excuse that "the algorithm made me do it". No one now needs to push all of the

---

277 *The Man and the Mask*, Bernard Shaw and Richard Burton (Henry Holt and Company, 1916), page 87

risks they can't quantify off the table into a box labelled "black swans". Some risks belong in that category no doubt but, armed with an awareness of signals, it will be easier to see the things that can be seen. We can take comfort from the Nobel Prize-winning physicist, Niels Bohr, who reminds us that, "Prediction is very difficult, especially about the future." Nobody should feel bad about being unable to predict or forecast accurately. All that is asked is better preparedness for a range of possibilities. It is heartening when Shakespeare reminds us that, "All things are ready, if our mind be so."[278]

The Gordian Knot will be cut asunder not by unraveling the past, or even by correctly predicting the future, but by acts of creation, by the stitching together of something new, something more robust out of whatever it is we have to work with. What we have are different people with different skills, different talents, different goals, different interpretations of signals. Out of that rich mix will emerge a social fabric that serves better and is more robust than before. It is only through these quiet individual choices that anything can be done to rebalance societies and better the balance between the rich and the poor, the haves and the have-nots, between governments and their citizens.

People can create something out of nothing and often do. They can also make something out of nothing[279] and often do. So, whether you are saltwater or freshwater; an entrepreneur or intrapreneur; a high-flyer, 9 to 5-er or job-seeker; a plumber or a policymaker; a politician; a butcher, a baker, a candlestick maker; tinker, tailor, soldier, spy; someone who only speaks the language of math and algorithms or someone who only knows plain speaking; "hardscrabble or high roller",[280] please join in the ongoing conversation about signals instead of leaving it to the economists and policymakers alone. Your views are the key that unlocks the gift that is the economy of the future. No one

---

278 Spoken by King Henry: Act IV, scene 3, page 3 in *Henry V*
279 In other words, people are inclined to exaggerate
280 I am grateful to Charles Blow for this elegant turn of phrase which he used in a *New York Times* Opinion article of 14 March 2014: "We Can't Grow the Gap Away". But, I would argue, we can innovate the gap away.

can predict what this gift will look like, but its character depends on the nature of the decisions everyone makes today. Think of the world economy as a constant character test that demands an eccentric and edgy response, a calculated risk that can result in hurt (as opposed to injury) or fulfill hope. The edgework we choose to pursue, or not pursue, defines the character of the outcome.

The alternative is clear. If we lack the character to face the signals and we choose to avoid the edgework, we will once again hear people say the cause of the next crisis was "principally a failure of the collective imagination".[281]

Knowing all this, and being better armed with an awareness of signals, we may all be better prepared to balance our hubris and nemesis and thereby take advantage of and better manage the diverse troubles and treasures the world economy inevitably brings.

---

281 From the letter to the Queen of 10 August, 2009 as signed by Geoffrey M Hodgson